# UNIFIED ARCHITECTURAL THEORY

*Nikos Salingaros, Christopher Alexander and Ken Foster, Austin, 1998*

# UNIFIED ARCHITECTURAL THEORY: FORM, LANGUAGE, COMPLEXITY

A Companion to Christopher Alexander's
"The Phenomenon of Life — The Nature of Order, Book 1"

## Nikos A. Salingaros

*With contributions by Christopher Alexander, Zaheer Allam,*
*Michael Carey, Peter Eisenman, Léon Krier, Kenneth G. Masden II,*
*Michael W. Mehaffy, and Edward O. Wilson.*

Vajra Books
www.vajrabooks.com.np

Asian Edition Published & Distributed by:
Vajra Books
Jyatha, Thamel, P.O. Box 21779, Kathmandu, Nepal
Tel.: 977-1-4220562, Fax: 977-1-4246536
e-mail: bidur_la@mos.com.np
www.vajrabooks.com.np

Formatted by Yulia Kryazheva,
Yulia Ink, Amsterdam (The Netherlands)

Printed in Nepal

Wiley, New York, 2008), pages 59-83. © John Wiley & Sons, Inc., 2008. All rights reserved. This material is reproduced with permission of John Wiley & Sons, Inc.

Nikos A. Salingaros & Kenneth G. Masden, "Architecture: Biological Form and Artificial Intelligence", *The Structurist*, No. 45/46 (2006), pages 54-61. Reprinted by permission of The Structurist, University of Saskatchewan, Canada.

Edward O. Wilson, "Integrated Science and the Coming Century of the Environment", *Science*, Volume 279, No. 5359 (27 March 1998), pages 2048-2049. © Science, American Association for the Advancement of Science, 1998. All rights reserved. Reprinted with permission from AAAS, and by permission of the author.

Library of Congress Cataloging-in-Publication Data

*Unified Architectural Theory: Form, Language, Complexity*

By Nikos A. Salingaros


ISBN 978-9937-623-05-6 (Nepal Edition)
ISBN 978-0-9893469-0-0 (USA Edition)

*Christopher Alexander and Nikos Salingaros, Los Angeles, 1985*

# TABLE OF CONTENTS

# 1. Preface

In the Fall Semester of 2012 I taught a course on architectural theory for the Architecture School at the University of Texas at San Antonio. It was organized so that external students could follow much of it online from wherever they were located. They only needed to find and read our two textbooks, supplemented by my lecture notes and external readings (which are collected here). Even those students who had no access to the textbooks could still learn a great deal about the basic concepts from my notes summarizing the reading material. I'm now offering here my lecture notes from this course, together with the extra reading material, which complement but do not substitute for the two textbooks we used:

- Christopher Alexander, *The Nature of Order: An Essay on the Art of Building and the Nature of the Universe*, Book 1 — *The Phenomenon of Life*, Center for Environmental Structure, Berkeley, 2001.

- Nikos A. Salingaros, *A Theory of Architecture*, Umbau-Verlag, Solingen, 2006. (This book is also available in Chinese and in Persian).

Altogether, this material represents a new and ultimately more intelligent approach to understanding architecture. By the end of the semester, students had covered and hopefully absorbed all of Alexander's book and Chapters 1 to 7 & 11 of my book, which are directly relevant to *The Nature of Order*. My *Weekly Lecture Notes* included here summarize and comment on the principal arguments from the reading assignments, which were revised after the class discussed the content in a roundtable manner. (Since neither Alexander's Volume 1 nor my own textbook were written explicitly for the precise course I had in mind to offer, it was necessary to skip around the order of the book chapters somewhat, and this sequence is important.)

The focus was on a Unified Architectural Theory, which includes and describes *all of architecture*, from traditional buildings to the latest design trends currently in fashion. More importantly, this comprehensive theoretical framework is based upon science and not on personal opinion. The theory is testable and has predictive value. Many architects drawn to study Alexander's work have resisted applying his ideas to their own current work because they have been under the mistaken belief that Alexander deals with only a particular ("Eurocentric" or "nostalgic") type of building. Our course dispelled this false impression. The unified theoretical framework is practical, original, entirely general, and applies directly to cutting-edge design.

Students by the end of the course could judge what makes a "good" building, not only for its adaptation to human use, but also from the point of view of being able to learn something from it. Is it functional and emotionally satisfying, and does it contribute to elevating the quality of life of its users? A separate but related criterion is whether a building is a helpful model that teaches us techniques of design which can be used directly in practice. Our analysis provides a tool that reveals design errors in building on many different conceptual levels, or at least things one would do differently with hindsight. A "good" building can teach us tectonic solutions to admire and repeat in our own projects; other buildings teach us what to avoid.

Both Alexander and I have continued to publish relevant research on how architecture interacts with human nature, after our books (used here as the two textbooks) were finished. New articles I wrote with Kenneth Masden and with Michael Mehaffy are included as readings for this course. From outside writings, I included an interview by the distinguished classical architect Léon Krier. Biologist Edward O. Wilson (one of our age's greatest scientists, and founder of Biophilia) kindly gave me permission to use his essay, which is directly pertinent to this course. Finally, as one of the four editors of the online publication *Katarxis 3* (along with Lucien Steil, Brian Hanson, and Michael Mehaffy), I used the 1982 Alexander-Eisenman debate (which I had originally prepared for the web), an additional essay by Alexander, and a portion of one of my own essays from there.

A major component of this course is contained in the two student projects. Both have to do with documenting and using a particular architectural form language. The first project required each student to choose and document a form language, then design a new building using it (only a very rough conceptual sketch). An estimate of its regional adaptation was correlated to a measure of its complexity. This exercise introduces quantitative methods in architectural theory. The second project went much deeper into relating the adaptability and complexity of the form language, using a much more sophisticated model for geometrical complexity and regional adaptation. More precise measures were used to search for possible correlations. The general outline of these projects is included here in the appendices.

The experience obtained from the readings and projects taught students how to distinguish those parts of a building that work well — the places we connect with the most — from parts that are poorly designed for human connection. Successful form and space are based on respecting emotions and not at all on intellectual and formal concerns that can lead to cold or chaotic forms. In this way, current design priorities are reversed. A successful user-specific building happens to appeal to the greatest number of people. That's because it has been adapted to human sensibilities. Correcting an old misunderstanding, we don't need to make a building bland or generic to achieve this universal appeal, but rather the opposite. Adaptation to region and user connects true regionalism to meaning triggered by complex form.

Having a theoretical basis available with objective measurements helped to explain why a building's immediate intuitive appeal actually works. At the same time, our theoretical understanding distinguished between an impression of "liking" something at first glance because it is provocative or flashy, and the deeper connection that reveals it to be a good or poor working and living environment. This second state is more like the perceived serenity of a natural environment, and we found the mathematical and biological reasons why this analogy is correct. Also, many students always felt uneasy about particular buildings but could not pinpoint their flaws — now they could find them through analysis based on objective criteria. All in all, the theory changed one's perspective of how to evaluate structures.

The revolutionary nature of this course becomes apparent only after someone compares the readings with the projects. The students were allowed to choose any architectural form language of their liking, and more than half of them chose from among the buildings and styles of contemporary Starchitects. Most of the rest chose a famous Modernist architect from the early 20th century, which means that only a few students chose traditional form languages. Despite this bias in selection, the students learned of the adaptive advantages of traditional form languages, and declared they would revise their own future designs towards that end. We provided objective criteria for judging the suitability of a particular form language for use today. It was possible to do this, and very successfully indeed, using as a basis a theoretical framework that supports human-oriented architecture.

Architecture schools could eventually adopt this course as a regular requirement, although that requires a faculty member who wishes to teach this material. An instructor is essential to lead the in-class discussions, to direct the two projects, and to evaluate the students' work. Even without an instructor, however, interested students can learn a great deal from the framework of the course by working on their own, as was evidenced by the positive feedback received from students who read the *Weekly Lecture Notes* online. The important thing is the synthesis of ideas represented here.

At the end of the present book, some practical details of how the course was organized are documented. The experience from the course might come in useful to a colleague who is considering presenting this or a similar course in the future. Of course, every instructor will have an individual idea of how to handle the syllabus and reading material, and how to structure any projects that might be included.

# 2. A BIOLOGICAL UNDERSTANDING OF ARCHITECTURE

*Extract from one of my essays in Katarxis No. 3, September 2004. Reprinted by permission.*

Architecture is indeed linked to biology. This observation is intuitively true from a structural perspective, since human beings perceive a kinship between the different processes — natural and artificial — that generate form. Nevertheless, the broadness of the claim might appear surprising, considering that it comes from architects holding radically different ideas about what buildings ought to look like. The idea of a biological connection has been used in turn by traditional architects, modernists, postmodernists, deconstructivists, and naturally, the "organic form" architects. One might say that architecture's proposed link to biology is used to support any architectural style whatsoever. When it is applied so generally, then the biological connection loses its value, or at least becomes so confused as to be meaningless. Is there a way to clear up the resulting contradiction and confusion?

Up until now, architects and those scientists interested in architecture have focused on the morphological imitation of nature. Sometimes explicitly, more often implicitly, natural forms, including biological forms, have inspired the constructions of human beings. Nevertheless, I believe that an understanding of the biological roots of architecture and urbanism requires another component that is independent of structural imitation. This more elusive aspect of the problem is concerned with how we connect and perceive form to begin with. As such, it has more to do with our own internal structure as human beings than with more general biological structures. The answers are to be found in cognitive processes, perception, and neurophysiology.

In order to begin a search for how biology influences architecture and urbanism, we must establish some overall map of the problem. Because this is a vast subject, it is useful to divide it into a series of questions like the following. This is not meant to be a complete set of questions, only a starting point for an investigation.

1. Why do some built forms resemble biological forms?

2. What types of built forms correspond more closely to biological prototypes?

3. Are human beings predisposed to like and feel comfortable with certain types of forms?

4. Are human beings also predisposed to *build* certain types of forms?

5. Is it worthwhile mimicking biological forms in what we build?

6. Do we gain more than just aesthetic pleasure — such as physical and psychological benefits, for example — from an environment that captures the essence of biological structure?

7. Can we damage ourselves by living in and around forms that contradict biological forms?

8. Do we really understand biological structure well enough to mimic anything other than its superficial appearance?

These questions can hopefully provide researchers with an impetus to resolve long-standing problems in how humankind relates to its natural and built environments. I would like to focus here on the connection between architecture and urbanism, on the one hand, and inherited structures in the human brain that influence the function of "mind", on the other. A group of innovative architects and thinkers are beginning to formulate the basis for a new architecture that arises out of human needs, and which is supported by an improved understanding of biological structure. Our cognition makes us human; it is certainly responsible for how we perceive structure. Human neurophysiology is therefore essential for answering at least some of the above questions.

# PART ONE
# THE COURSE LECTURES AND READINGS

*"When we try to pick out anything by itself we find that it is bound fast by a thousand invisible cords that cannot be broken, to everything in the Universe." — John Muir.*

# 3. Introduction to the Course

This course is designed to provide students with the theoretical foundation necessary to succeed in architectural practice. The theoretical motivation behind different styles of buildings is explored in depth. We also analyze the scientific background that defines and justifies architectural development in the experience of architecture and the tectonics of structure. Examining ideas and processes that give shape to built form, we then go further to judge those forms in an objective manner. This approach is totally innovative. A course that explores the theoretical foundation of places and buildings occupies an important place in the curriculum, as no other courses deal with the subject. The format of the class consists of lecture, design and analysis projects, and discussion.

Students need to have an idea of what to expect in this course. At present, architectural theory consists of rather disparate writings by architects, critics, architectural historians, and philosophers. The philosophy behind the present course assumes that the present state of affairs is confusing and not really helpful for design, and that a novel unified theory of architecture is possible using recent, predominantly scientific results. A student should note that the discipline itself is barely emerging, with ongoing contradictions and polemics among the experts. The categories of subjects covered are meant to bring clarity and a coherent form of categorization to this issue.

Firstly, the presentation depends upon a significant broadening of what is currently used as the philosophical underpinning of architecture. There exist several, very distinct, philosophical currents in contemporary society, each of which supposes a particular interpretation of the structure of matter and humankind's place in the universe. The most visible and discussed examples of contemporary architecture are consistent with only one of those philosophical currents. They disagree, often violently, with the other philosophical interpretations. Nevertheless, architecture students are not normally exposed to any philosophy other than that which supports what is currently in fashion. This is a totally subjective state of affairs.

Secondly, this question goes to the core of what is architectural theory. I define it, following scientific practice, as an explanatory framework for architecture and for its interaction with both human beings as users, and with the earth's environment. The discipline of architecture consists of two complementary portions: the buildings themselves, and a theoretical framework for explaining and evaluating those buildings. Theory without explanatory value is useless. Even better is when a theory has predictive value that can be verified by experiment. Contemporary architectural discourse is strangely removed from any tangible connection to buildings, however. Yes, architects offer theoretical explanations for their buildings' form, but often it is difficult to draw the connection. What many people regard as architectural theory today is a very narrow sub-branch of philosophy.

Thirdly, a student might be surprised to hear me dismiss other authors who are now accepted as prominent architectural theorists. Since I happen to write and publish architectural theory, I naturally find myself arguing and disagreeing with other presumed architectural theorists. All of our ideas are competing against each other for legitimacy. If someone's discourse disagrees fundamentally with what I am proposing, then I consider it my right to declare that those writings are at best not useful to understanding architecture, or, at worst, flawed or even meaningless.

This attitude will alarm architectural academics. A teacher in an architecture school is seldom also an architectural theorist. A faculty member might have a practice on the side, but even this is not always true, and it is does not imply that he or she contributes to theory. Furthermore, the academic environment accepts all architectural discourse as valid, especially if it comes from famous names, and so an instructor would normally present writings of well-known authors to students without judgment. The available textbooks for teaching a course in architectural theory consist of collected readings from a variety of authors. The instructor assumes that the editors of those books have validated the content of every essay included, but that assumption is false. The task of an editor is to include authors that are somehow known names, itself no guarantee of the validity of their ideas.

All of this has consequences that might be most disturbing to an architecture student. Setting up of what I believe is a genuine architectural theory leads to predictions and a basis for judgment. If we have been careful enough in laying the groundwork for the theory in an accurate and honest manner, then we have to live with its predictions. If the theory leads me to criticize buildings by famous starchitects, this might shock a student used to accepting those buildings as noteworthy examples of contemporary architecture. The shock is even more severe if other architectural theorists praise the same buildings that we are criticizing. Students are not used to such contradictions. How does one judge who is ultimately right? What are the different criteria for judgment? Here we enter the subjective realm of opinion that is validated by political and media predominance.

It is the purpose of this course to open up the discipline in such a way that these tensions lead to a better understanding of what architecture is.

# 4. Lecture Notes, First Week.
# The Structure of Architectural Theories

## Readings for the First Week:

- Alexander, *The Phenomenon of Life*, Prologue & Chapter 1, "The Phenomenon of Life".
- Salingaros, "Architectural Theory", extracts from *Anti-Architecture and Deconstruction* (Umbau-Verlag, Solingen, 2008), also available in Chinese, French, Italian, and Russian.
- Edward O. Wilson, "Integrated Science and the Coming Century of the Environment", *Science*, Volume 279, No. 5359 (March 27, 1998), pages 2048-2049.

Architecture is a human act that invades and displaces the natural ecosystem. Biological order is destroyed every time we clear native plant growth and erect buildings and infrastructure. The goal of architecture is to create structures to house humans and their activities. Humans are parts of the earth's ecosystem, even though we tend to forget that.

Logically, architecture has to have a theoretical basis that begins with the natural ecosystem. The act of building orders materials in very specific ways, and humans generate an artificial ordering out of materials they have extracted from nature and transformed to various degrees. Some of today's most widely-used materials, such as plate glass and steel, require energy-intensive processes, and thus contain high embodied energy costs. Those cannot be the basis for any sustainable solution, despite all the industry hype.

Resource depletion and a looming ecological catastrophe are consequences of detachment from nature, and a blind faith in technology to solve the problems it creates.

Architectural theory, in the sense understood in this course, is a framework that studies architectural phenomena using scientific logic and methods of experimentation. Many experiments have been done by others, and we are going to apply them to architecture. Theory provides a model that explains investigations and observations about form and structure.

A successful theory will help us interpret what an architect does, even though each architect will likely have his/her own motivation and explanation. Nevertheless, the theory will allow us to compare among different types of buildings, and to evaluate how well those connect to users and with nature. We can understand how a building came about, and how it connects and interacts with its surroundings.

It will also be good if common people, not just architects, can understand architectural theory, and thus it should be formulated with that goal in mind. The advantages are that it is ordinary people who are going to inhabit those buildings, whereas architects can choose to live and work wherever they like. Another crucial point is that the majority of building activity is, and has always been, the erection of self-built informal settlements. People, not architects, build these structures.

Christopher Alexander has pioneered a theory of human-made order. It is based directly upon natural order, so there is neither contradiction nor confusion between the two types.

Alexander made five key assumptions that permitted him to pursue his work.

(1) Natural and artificial order rely upon the same mechanisms for their working.

(2) Natural order is self-organizing and self-correcting. What we observe is there because it works.

(3) Artificial order is not necessarily self-correcting, or maybe it is on a generational timescale so individuals are not going to notice it. As a result, human beings can do things to the natural environment and build buildings and structures that damage the world. It is not easy to diagnose what is good and distinguish it from what is bad.

(4) It is possible to use science to create diagnostic tools for what is good and bad in human creations — in how they affect the natural environment, including us humans.

(5) We can use the human body as a sensing instrument for what is good and bad in architecture. Basic assumption: human feeling is universal, and people share 90% of their responses, even if individuals come from different cultures or backgrounds.

To make good buildings, we need a worldview, a conception of the world that is healthy and that enables us to understand things deeply. A healthy worldview is based upon connectivity to the world: direct connection to the order of the universe and to natural processes as they are continuously occurring.

The opposite — detachment — leads to a dangerous condition where people analyze a situation as a mechanism isolated from the world. This is the model of a building or a city as a machine. Modern science is guilty of contributing to this disconnection from nature, since scientific models are necessarily self-contained and limited in scope — otherwise they would be useless.

Science gives us an excellent model of how something works as a mechanical system. Nevertheless, this is not a complete description even of the cases we do understand well. And there are a vast number of instances where we ignore any mechanical description at all of an observed phenomenon.

What is completely missing from a strictly mechanistic worldview is human consciousness, our personal and emotional connection to the universe. This might not matter when investigating some technical problems, but it's all-important for things that affect us, like architecture. Another significant consequence is the lack of value in a mechanistic worldview. A human connected to the universe knows the distinction between good and bad, true and false, beautiful and ugly. These qualities are not relative, and are not matters of opinion. A consumer disconnected from natural values, by contrast, can be fed toxic products and be made to believe they are good.

The way out of the present, highly restricted view of the universe is to develop an immensely more connected state between humans and their environment. Attention is given to what affects us reciprocally with the world, when we are tightly connected.

Following this reasoning, people have a shared basis for judgment, and can intuitively judge whether something has order or life, and expect their gut reaction to be 90% shared across cultures and distances. In this new worldview, ornament plays a critical role to connect humans with the order of the world. Ornament is thus intimately related to function in the non-mechanistic sense.

We wish to consider architecture and the production of human artifacts also as essential components of natural ecosystems. Order and life are related. Natural things have an intrinsic order, and life as we usually know it and understand it is simply an extension of that order. For this reason, human constructions should not damage or contradict natural order.

The earth's ecosystems (many of which are connected to each other) contain, and are contained by other components that neither metabolize, nor replicate. But every layer of the system is interdependent. This property of life in inanimate objects and situations arises out of their degree of natural order, and the human body has evolved mechanisms to sense that order. Thus, it is not surprising to feel that something is "alive", because of its geometrical properties, even though that object is not biological.

Biological organisms have the additional features of metabolism and replication. A very simple consequence of thinking of a building as a "living" entity is that it requires repair and restoration. This analogy with metabolism takes us away from a central tenet of 20th Century industrial architecture: the quest for absolutely permanent and weather-resisting materials. This search has become very expensive. But worse of all, it denies living qualities. Materials that do weather in fact produce buildings that are more in keeping with biological organisms. For example, the Ise Shrine Complex in Japan is re-built every 20 years.

Buildings also engage in replication: if a form language is adopted by other builders, then the original prototype building is replicated in more copies, not exactly the same, but containing the same "genetic" information.

Since the perception of something as being "alive" is due to a very strong connection with our mind and body, there is a reciprocal effect: that object, place, or configuration makes *us* feel more alive. It is possible to find myriads of artifacts, buildings, urban spaces that feel "alive" and that in turn make us feel "alive". They invariably come from vernacular traditions and hardly ever from design.

The perceived living quality comes from specific geometrical configurations, and it is possible to discover the rules that generate a living quality. Even in non-traditional 20th-century examples of objects and places having perceived "life", the life comes from their geometry. It is not based on concepts, or images, or fashions. By connecting to the thing, we feel that we are connecting directly with its maker, who therefore doesn't hide behind any notions or ideas that contaminate its genuine character.

To get at a genuine understanding of architecture, it is useful to use the approach that scientists employ to discover nature's secrets.

Edward Wilson outlines what science achieves:

(1) Systematic gathering of knowledge about the world, which is organized and condensed into basic principles as far as possible.

(2) Results must pass the test of independent and repeated verification.

(3) It helps to quantify information, for then, principles can use

mathematical models.

(4) Condensation of information via systematization and classification helps in storage.

(5) A safeguard for truth comes from consilience: the horizontal links across diverse disciplines.

Consilience acts as a test for the soundness of a theory. Within itself, a theory might look good even when it contains fundamental flaws. Internal consistency can be misleading, since it could relate several false assumptions, but in a very convincing manner. We normally should be able to transition from one sound theory into another one that acts on a distinct domain. If there is a contradiction, then something is wrong. It could be that there is no barrier but a large gap, in which case that needs to be filled in.

Architectural theory can be formulated and verified by employing two mechanisms: internal hypotheses that are repeatedly verified, and external consilient links to other disciplines that have a verifiable basis. These include the hard sciences.

Good architecture is less of a reductionist discipline and must necessarily be a synthetic discipline. If it is applied in a reductionist manner, then it probably contains serious errors that damage the environment. To be adaptive means to synthesize many distinct responses to human needs and natural order.

Most important is for architecture to be directly linked to human evolution, the physical needs of the organism, and to use information according to evolved culture. Neglecting the biological origins of human needs and behavior detaches architecture from the world and from humanity. The architect should design a building that makes common people feel comfortable, and not to be liked just by architects. It should also adapt to its locality, not designed for somewhere else, or for no place in particular.

# 5. ARCHITECTURAL THEORY

*By Nikos A. Salingaros*

*Extracts from: Anti-Architecture and Deconstruction (AAAD), Third Edition (Umbau-Verlag, Solingen, 2008). Reprinted by permission.*

## Architectural Theory (AAAD, pages 149-150)

In order to discuss any supposed contributions to architectural theory, it is necessary to define what architectural theory is. A theory in any discipline is a general framework that:

(1) explains observed phenomena;

(2) predicts effects that appear under specific circumstances; and

(3) enables one to create new situations that perform in a way predicted by the theory.

In architecture, a theoretical framework ought to explain why buildings affect human beings in certain ways, and why some buildings are more successful than others, both in practical as well as in psychological and aesthetic terms. One important requirement of an architectural theory is to coordinate and make sense of scattered and apparently unrelated observations of how human beings interact with built form. Another is to formalize those observations into an easy-to-apply framework that can be used for design.

Sadly, architecture is only now embarking on a long-overdue formulation of its theoretical basis. It is not an exaggeration to say that up until now, the field has been driven by personal whim and fashion rather than being supported by any theoretical foundation. As a result of a serious misunderstanding (due to scientific ignorance by three generations of architects), a voluminous body of writings has been mistaken for "architectural theory", even though it is nothing of the sort. This material is taught to architecture students, and is studied by practicing architects; nevertheless, it merely serves to promote certain stylistic fashions and dogmas rather than an understanding of architectural form. Enough genuine architectural theory now exists to form a nucleus from which the topic can be built. This nucleus consists of the writings of Christopher Alexander (Alexander, 2001; Alexander *et al.*, 1977), Léon Krier (1998), the present author (Salingaros, 2006), and a few others.

Genuine architectural theory has developed into two parallel strands. The first is the approach based on solutions that work historically. Not surprisingly, this strand turns to traditional architecture, using its typologies in an innovative manner. Architects ignorant of this strand of architectural theory misjudge it, falsely thinking that it merely copies older models, whereas in fact, it is using a well-developed vocabulary to generate novel solutions. The second strand of genuine architectural theory is based on science.

Here, models from biology, physics, and computer science are used to explain how architectonic form emerges, and why human beings react in certain predictable ways to different structures. The scientific approach is in many ways complementary to the traditional approach to design. The main difference in practice is that, since the scientific approach is not tied to any specific typology, it leads to a much broader design vocabulary than does the traditional approach.

Architects have difficulties in appreciating the scientific strand of genuine architectural theory, because of certain misstatements in the body of existing architectural texts. Authors claiming to explain architectural form using scientific theories and their vocabulary are invariably confused, and so confuse the reader. Much of this architectural literature is plainly incorrect, but architects have insufficient scientific knowledge to realize this. Well-respected architectural commentators write misleading statements that are taken as meaningful explanations by architects and students, who then become so bewildered that they cannot appreciate genuine scientific explanations. They confuse spurious explanations for the real thing.

This regrettably happens because in architecture, there is as yet no basis for judging between a true and a false theory. Other fields were able to develop their theoretical basis only after they instituted such a criterion, putting in place a mechanism for distinguishing sense from nonsense. Architects erroneously believe that such a set of criteria can exist only in an experimental subject such as physics, without realizing that architecture is itself an experimental field. The problem is that the observational, experimental side of architecture has been willfully neglected for several decades, to the point where its practitioners have forgotten this fundamental quality of their discipline.

## The Necessity for Theory (*AAAD*, pages 164-166)

I pointed out which contemporary authors have in my opinion actually contributed to creating a theoretical foundation for architecture. I also argued that what is currently accepted by many architects as architectural theory is not theory at all, but rather a clever means to propagate a particular design style. Outsiders (which includes most people) naively assume that contemporary architecture possesses a theoretical basis, like for example chemistry and neuroscience, which explains why buildings ought to look the way they do. However, a mass of writings mislabeled as architectural theory only helps to generate and support certain images; those images are then copied, and used as templates for buildings in an alien style. That is not a theoretical foundation. Those writings fail to satisfy any of the accepted criteria for a theory in any field.

Every discipline has a store of knowledge accumulated over time, which explains a huge range of phenomena. (Architecture has been collecting information for millennia). Some of this knowledge is codified into a compact theoretical framework; other parts are strictly phenomenological but tested by observation and experiment. Facts and ideas combine in a particular manner, common to all proper disciplines.

The crucial characteristic of a valid theoretical framework is a transparent internal complexity coupled with external connectivity. This arises from the way explanatory networks develop in time:

(1) More recent knowledge about a topic builds upon existing knowledge.

(2) Older knowledge is replaced only by a better explanation of the same phenomenon, never because a fashion has changed — this process creates multiple, connected layers of knowledge.

(3) A theory in one discipline must transition sensibly to other disciplines.

This means that there ought to be some interface where one discipline merges into another, all the way around its periphery. Any theory that isolates itself because it is incomprehensible to others is automatically suspect. A tightly-knit internal connectivity, along with a looser external connectivity, provides the foundations for a mechanism of self-correction and maintenance. This holds true for any complex system.

Architecture as a profession has repeatedly disconnected itself both from its knowledge base, and from other disciplines in an effort to remain eternally "contemporary" (the much-publicized recent connections to philosophy, linguistics, and science notwithstanding, since they are now exposed as deceptions). This is, of course, the defining characteristic of a fashion; the opposite of a proper discipline. Again and again, architecture has ignored derived knowledge about buildings and cities, and has embraced nonsensical slogans and influences.

Those who profit from the instability and superficiality of the fashion industry are deathly afraid of facing genuine knowledge about the world. It would put them out of business. Architects and critics periodically change the reigning fashion so as to keep the market stimulated. They have to devote an enormous amount of resources to promoting whatever ephemeral style is in vogue. In order to sell their fashion, they are obliged to suppress any application of accumulated architectural knowledge. This prevents a theoretical basis from ever developing. Ever-changing fashion is parasitic on timeless processes.

Critics dismiss neo-traditional buildings as facile copies of classical prototypes, even though those need not resemble anything built in the previous two millennia. The architectural media declare that "a classical column represents tyranny", and that by confessing to an attraction to classical architecture, we somehow support totalitarianism. At the same time, a liking for non-classical vernacular architecture of any kind is ridiculed. In this instance, we are branded as being ignorant and "sentimental" (which, in contemporary architectural values, is an unforgivable offense). Novel buildings with human qualities, which nevertheless have nothing to do with the classical typology, are also forbidden.

People are now misled to believe that the "architecture of the future" is necessarily broken and twisted, and made out of glass and polished metal. Any doubt is dispelled by awarding their architects the most prestigious prizes. Some of those who participate in disseminating this style act from an almost religious conviction. They fervently believe that they are doing civilization a favor, promoting the future and protecting us from backwardness and retrogression. Architectural schools are steeped in righteousness. Ever since the Bauhaus of the 1920s, many schools' aim has been to restructure society for the betterment of all people; whether those welcome this or not. If ordinary people are sentimental about past methods of design, and crave buildings that appeal to the human scale, that is only an indication of human weakness.

We stand of the threshold of a historic architectural reckoning. A new architecture mixes exuberant curved forms and fractal scaling with the broken forms of deconstruction. Let me suggest that architects who wish to be contemporary ought to drop their deconstructive baggage. They should instead extend a hand to those whom they have formerly disdained and slandered — I mean the traditionalists, and those innovative architects who respect human scale and sensibilities. By mixing novel forms with typologies that have undergone a competitive selection during historical time, we can define a new architecture that is fit for human beings instead of remaining forever alien. Younger practitioners have been duped into identifying novelty with the essential "alien look" of deconstruction. Nevertheless, a new generation of architects is intelligent enough to realize what is going on, and to snap out of an unfortunate deception.

## The Traditional Patrimony (*AAAD*, pages 112-115)

Some traditions are anachronistic and misguided, but as reservoirs of traditional solutions against which to check new proposals they are of immense importance. A new solution may at some point replace a traditional solution, but it must succeed in reestablishing the connections to the rest of knowledge. In the context of social patterns, architecture, and urbanism, new solutions are useful if they connect to traditional social, architectural, and urban patterns (i.e., all those before the 1920s). If there is an obvious gap where nothing in a discipline refers to anything outside, then there could be a serious problem.

Recently, Edward Wilson has introduced the notion of "consilience" as *"the interlocking of causal explanations across disciplines"* (Wilson, 1998a). Consilience claims that all explanations in nature are connected; there are no totally isolated phenomena. Wilson focuses on incomplete pieces of knowledge: the wide region separating the sciences from the humanities. He is happy to see it being slowly filled in by evolutionary biologists, cognitive neuroscientists, and researchers in artificial intelligence. At the same time, he is alarmed by people in the humanities who are erasing parts of the existing body of knowledge. These include deconstructive philosophers. Wilson characterizes their efforts as based on ignorance. On Derrida's work, he writes: *"It ... is the opposite of science, rendered in fragments with the incoherence of a dream, at once banal and fantastical. It is innocent of the science of mind and language developed elsewhere in the civilized world, rather like the pronouncements of a faith healer unaware of the location of the pancreas."* (Wilson, 1998b: p. 41).

Unfortunately, most of the humanities today subscribe to belief systems that damage the web of consilient knowledge. Although never directly expressed, the goal of deconstruction is to erase institutions of knowledge. What Derrida has said is alarming enough: *"Deconstruction goes through certain social and political structures, meeting with resistance and displacing institutions as it does so ... effectively, you have to displace, I would say 'solid' structures, not only in the sense of material structures, but 'solid' in the sense of cultural, pedagogical, political, economic structures."* (Norris, 1989: p. 8).

Many people crave novelty without regard for possible consequences. This craving is often manipulated by unscrupulous individuals. Not everything that is novel is necessarily good. An example of this is a new, artificially-developed virus unleashed into the world. Because of the immense destructive power that humanity now possesses, it is imperative to understand possible consequences.

In a hilarious hoax, Alan Sokal developed a nonsensical deconstructive critique of well known scientific claims in an article submitted for publication to a pretentious, deconstructive academic journal (Sokal, 1996). None of the referees for that journal challenged Sokal's account before accepting the article as worthy of publication. Sokal was so obvious in his deception that he assumed it would have been exposed; but it was not. Subsequently, Sokal and Jean Bricmont (1998) exposed deconstructivist criticism as nonsensical and showed that several respected deconstructive texts are based on nonsensical scientific references. This is only the most famous exposure of nonsensical deconstructive writings; there are many others (Huth, 1998). In a debunking of deconstructivist texts, Andrew Bulhak codified the deconstructivists' literary style into a computer program called *Postmodernism Generator* (1996). It is remarkably successful in generating nonsensical texts that are indistinguishable from those written by revered deconstructivist philosophers.

Putting aside the question of truthful content, a discipline is not valid unless it rests on a solid intellectual edifice. One characteristic of a coherent discipline is hierarchical complexity, in which correlated ideas and results define a unique internal structure. Like a valid bank note, this structure should be extremely difficult to counterfeit. That is not the case with deconstruction. Thus, a phony article in Statistical Mechanics, using all the appropriate words and mathematical symbols in a nice-sounding but scientifically-meaningless jumble, would be detected instantly.

Even a single mistake in such an article could not survive unnoticed. It is the function of referees to check each and every step in the argument of a scientific article submitted for publication in a professional journal. The very survival of the discipline depends on a system of checks that identifies and expels bogus contributions. By contrast, the survival of deconstruction — in which there is nothing to verify — depends upon generating more and more deconstructed texts and buildings.

A well-crafted deconstructive text does make sense, but not in any logical fashion. It is a piece of poetry that abuses the human capacity for pattern recognition to create associations, employing random technical jargon.

As Roger Scruton has pointed out: "*Deconstruction ... should be understood on the model of magic incantation. Incantations are not arguments, and avoid completed thoughts and finished sentences. They depend on crucial terms, which derive their effect from repetition, and from their appearance in long lists of cryptic syllables. Their purpose is not to describe what is there, but to summon what is not there ... Incantations can do their work only if key words and phrases acquire a mystical penumbra."* (Scruton, 2000: pp. 141-142).

The use of words for emotional effect is a common technique of cult indoctrination. This practice reinforces the cult's message. Whether in chants that make little sense yet can raise followers' emotions to fever pitch, or in the speeches of political demagogues that rouse a wild and passionate allegiance, the emotional manipulation *is* the message. Even after the exposure of the deconstructive philosophers' fraudulent character, their work continues to be taken seriously. Deconstructionist books are available in any university bookstore, while respectable academics offer lengthy critical commentary supporting these books' supposed authority. By affording them the trappings of scholarly inquiry, the impression is carefully maintained that they constitute a valid body of work.

Followers of deconstruction apply the classic techniques of cults to seize academic positions; infiltrate the literature; displace competitors; establish a power base by employing propaganda and manipulating the media, etc. They use indoctrination to recruit followers, usually from among disaffected students in the humanities. As David Lehman put it: *"An antitheological theology, [deconstruction] ... shrouds itself in cabalistic mysteries and rituals as elaborate as those of a religious ceremony ... it is determined to show that the ideals and values by which we live are not natural and inevitable but are artificial constructions, arbitrary choices that ought to have no power to command us. Yet, like a religion-substitute, deconstruction employs an arcane vocabulary seemingly designed to keep the laity in a state of permanent mystification. Putatively antidogmatic, it has become a dogma. Founded on extreme skepticism and disbelief, it attracts true believers and demands their total immersion."* (Lehman, 1991: p. 55).

# References

- Christopher Alexander (2001) *The Phenomenon of Life: The Nature of Order*, Book 1, The Center for Environmental Structure, Berkeley, California.
- Christopher Alexander, S. Ishikawa, M. Silverstein, M. Jacobson, I. Fiksdahl-King & S. Angel (1977) *A Pattern Language*, Oxford University Press, New York.

- Andrew Bulhak (1996) "Postmodernism Generator", available online from <http://www.elsewhere.org/cgi-bin/postmodern>.

- John Huth (1998) "Latour's Relativity", in: *A House Built on Sand*, Edited by Noretta Koertge, Oxford University Press, New York, pages 181-192.

- Léon Krier (1998) *Architecture: Choice or Fate*, Andreas Papadakis, Windsor, England. Retitled *The Architecture of Community*, with new material, Island Press, Washington, DC, 2009.

- David Lehman (1991) *Signs of the Times: Deconstruction and the Fall of Paul de Man*, Poseidon Press, New York.

- Christopher Norris (1989) "Interview of Jacques Derrida", *AD — Architectural Design*, 59 No. 1/2, pages 6-11.

- Nikos A. Salingaros (2006) *A Theory of Architecture*, Umbau-Verlag, Solingen, Germany.

- Roger Scruton (2000) "The Devil's Work", Chapter 12 of: *An Intelligent Person's Guide to Modern Culture*, St. Augustine's Press, South Bend, Indiana.

- Alan Sokal (1996), "Transgressing the Boundaries: Toward a Transformative Hermeneutics of Quantum Gravity", *Social Text*, 46/47, pages 217-252.

- Alan Sokal & Jean Bricmont (1998) *Fashionable Nonsense*, Picador, New York. European title: *Intellectual Impostures*.

- Edward O. Wilson (1998a) "Integrating Science and the Coming Century of the Environment", *Science*, 279, pages 2048-2049.

- Edward O. Wilson (1998b) *Consilience: The Unity of Knowledge*, Alfred A. Knopf, New York.

# 6. INTEGRATED SCIENCE AND THE COMING CENTURY OF THE ENVIRONMENT

*By Edward O. Wilson*

*Science, Vol. 279, no. 5359 (27 March 1998), pp. 2048-2049.*
*Reprinted by permission.*

The sesquicentennial of the American Association for the Advancement of Science is a good time to acknowledge that science is no longer the specialized activity of a professional elite. Nor is it a philosophy, or a belief system, or, as some postmodernist thinkers would have it, just one world view out of a vast number of possible views. It is rather a combination of mental operations, a culture of illuminations born during the Enlightenment four centuries ago and enriched at a near-geometric rate to establish science as the most effective way of learning about the material world ever devised. The sword that humanity finally pulled, it has become part of the permanent world culture and available to all.

"Science, to put its warrant as concisely as possible, is the organized systematic enterprise that gathers knowledge about the world and condenses the knowledge into testable laws and principles." (Wilson, 1998: p. 53) Its defining traits are first, the confirmation of discoveries and support of hypotheses through repetition by independent investigators, preferably with different tests and analyses; second, mensuration, the quantitative description of the phenomena on universally accepted scales; third, economy, by which the largest amount of information is abstracted into a simple and precise form, which can be unpacked to re-create detail; fourth, heuristics, the opening of avenues to new discovery and interpretation.

And fifth, and finally, is consilience, the interlocking of causal explanations across disciplines. "This consilience," said William Whewell when he introduced the term in his 1840 synthesis *The Philosophy of the Inductive Sciences*, "is a test of the truth of the theory in which it occurs." (Whewell, 1840: p. 230) And so it has proved within the natural sciences, where the webwork of established cause and effect, while still gossamer frail in many places, is almost continuous from quantum physics to biogeography. This webwork traverses vast scales of space, time, and complexity to unite what in Whewell's time appeared to be radically different classes of phenomena. Thus, chemistry has been rendered consilient with physics, both undergird molecular biology, and molecular biology is solidly connected to cellular, organismic, and evolutionary biology.

The scales of space, time, and complexity in the explanatory webwork have been widened to bracket some 40 orders of magnitude. Consider, for example, the webwork's reach from quantum electrodynamics to the birth of galaxies; or the great breadth it has attained in the biological sciences, which are not only united with physics and chemistry but now touch the borders of the social sciences and humanities.

This last augmentation, while still controversial, deserves special attention because of its implications for the human condition. For most of the last two centuries following the decline of the Enlightenment, scholars have traditionally drawn sharp distinctions between the great branches of learning, and particularly between the natural sciences as opposed to the social sciences and humanities. The latter dividing line, roughly demarcating the scientific and literary cultures, has been considered an epistemological discontinuity, a permanent difference in ways of knowing. But now growing evidence exists that the boundary is not a line at all, but a broad, mostly unexplored domain of causally linked phenomena awaiting cooperative exploration from both sides.

Researchers from four disciplines of the natural sciences have entered the borderland:

- Cognitive neuroscientists, outriders of the once but no longer "quiet" revolution, are using an arsenal of new techniques to map the physical basis of mental events. They have shifted the frame of discourse concerning the mind from semantic and introspective analysis to nerve cells, neurotransmitters, hormones, and recurrent neural networks. Working on a parallel track, students of artificial intelligence, with an eye on the future possibility of artificial emotion, search with neuroscientists for a general theory of cognition.

- Combining molecular genetics with traditional psychological tests, behavioral geneticists have started to characterize and even pinpoint genes that affect mental activity, from drug addiction to mood and cognitive operations. They are also tracing the epigenesis of the activity, the complex molecular and cellular pathways of mental development that lead from prescription to phenotype, in the quest for a fuller and much-needed understanding of the interaction between genes and environment.

- Evolutionary biologists, especially sociobiologists (also known within the social sciences as evolutionary psychologists and evolutionary anthropologists), are reconstructing the origins of human social behavior with special reference to evolution by natural selection.

- Environmental scientists in diverse specialties, including human ecology, are more precisely defining the arena in which our species arose, and those parts that must be sustained for human survival. The very idea of a borderland of causal connections between the great branches of learning is typically dismissed by social theorists and philosophers as reductionistic. This diagnosis is of course quite correct. But consider this: Reduction and the consilience it implies are the key to the success of the natural sciences. Why should the same not be true of other kinds of knowledge? Because mind and culture are material processes, there is every reason to suppose, and none compelling enough to deny, that the social sciences and humanities will be strengthened by assimilation of the borderland disciplines. For however tortuous the unfolding of the causal links among genes, mind, and culture, and however sensitive they are to the caprice of historical circumstance, the links form an unbreakable webwork, and human understanding will be better off to the extent that these links are explored. Francis Bacon, at the dawn of the Enlightenment in 1605, prefigured this principle of integrative science (by which he meant a large part of all the branches of learning) with an image I especially like: "No perfect discovery can be made upon a flat or a level: neither is it possible to discover the more remote or deeper parts of any science, if you stand but upon the level of the same science and ascend not to a higher science." (Bacon, 1605)

The unavoidable complement of reduction is synthesis, the step that completes consilience from one discipline to the next. Synthesis is far more difficult to achieve than reduction, and that is why reductionistic studies dominate the cutting edge of investigation. To reduce an enzyme molecule to its constituent amino acids and describe its three-dimensional structure is far easier, for example, than to predict the structure of an enzyme molecule from the sequence of its amino acids alone. As the century closes, however, the balance between reduction and synthesis appears to be changing. Attention within the natural sciences has begun to shift away from the search for elemental units and fundamental laws and toward highly organized systems. Researchers are devoting proportionately more time to the self-assembly of macromolecules, cells, organisms, planets, universes — and mind and culture.

If this view of universal consilience is correct, the central question of the social sciences is, in my opinion, the nature of the linkage between genetic evolution and cultural evolution. It is also one of the great

36

remaining problems of the natural sciences. This part of the overlap of the two great branches of learning can be summarized as follows. We know that all culture is learned, yet its form and the manner in which it is transmitted are shaped by biology. Conversely, the genes prescribing much of human behavioral biology evolved in a cultural environment, which itself was evolving. A great deal has been learned about these two modes of evolution viewed as separate processes. What we do not understand very well is how they are linked.

The surest entry to the linkage, or gene-culture coevolution as it is usually called, is (again in my opinion) to view human nature in a new and more heuristic manner. Human nature is not the genes, which prescribe it, or the universals of culture, which are its products. It is rather the epigenetic rules of cognition, the inherited regularities of cognitive development that predispose individuals to perceive reality in certain ways and to create and learn some cultural variants in preference to competing variants.

Epigenetic rules have been documented in a diversity of cultural categories, from syntax acquisition and paralinguistic communication to incest avoidance, color vocabularies, cheater detection, and others. The continuing quest for such inborn biasing effects promises to be the most effective means to understand gene-culture coevolution and hence to link biology and the social sciences causally. It also offers a way, I believe, to build a secure theoretical foundation for the humanities, by addressing, for example, the biological origins of ethical precepts and aesthetic properties of the arts.

The naturalistic world view, by encouraging the search for consilience across the great branches of learning, is far more than just another exercise for philosophers and social theorists. To understand the physical basis of human nature, down to its evolutionary roots and genetic biases, is to provide needed tools for the diagnosis and management of some of the worst crises afflicting humanity.

Arguably the foremost of global problems grounded in the idiosyncrasies of human nature is overpopulation and the destruction of the environment. The crisis is not long-term but here and now; it is upon us. Like it or not, we are entering the century of the environment, when science and polities will give the highest priority to settling humanity down before we wreck the planet.

Here in brief is the problem — or better, complex of interlocking problems — as researchers see it. In their consensus, "[t]he global population is precariously large, will grow another third by 2020, and climb still more before peaking sometime after 2050. Humanity is improving per capita production, health, and longevity. But it is doing so by eating up the planet's capital, including irreplaceable natural resources. Humankind is approaching the limit of its food and water supply. As many as a billion people, moreover, remain in absolute poverty, with inadequate food from one day to the next and little or no medical care. Unlike any species that lived before, *Homo sapiens* is also changing the world's atmosphere and climate, lowering and polluting water tables, shrinking forests, and spreading deserts. It is extinguishing a large fraction of plant and animal species, an irreplaceable loss that will be viewed as catastrophic by future generations. Most of the stress originates directly or indirectly from a handful of industrialized countries. Their proven formulas are being eagerly adopted by the rest of the world. The emulation cannot be sustained, not with the same levels of consumption and waste. Even if the industrialization of developing countries is only partly successful, the environmental aftershock will dwarf the population explosion that preceded it." (Wilson, 1998: p. 280) Recent studies indicate that to raise the rest of the world to the level of the United States using present technology would require the natural resources of two more planet Earths.

The time has come to look at ourselves closely as a biological as well as cultural species, using all of the intellectual tools we can muster. We are brilliant catarrhine primates, whose success is eroding the environment to which a billion years of evolutionary history exquisitely adapted us. We are dangerously baffled by the meaning of this existence, remaining instinct-driven, reckless, and conflicted. Wisdom for the long-term eludes us. There is ample practical reason — should no other kind prove persuasive — to aim for an explanatory integration not just of the natural sciences but also of the social sciences and humanities, in order to cope with issues of urgency and complexity that may otherwise be too great to manage.

# References

- Francis Bacon (1605) *Advancement of Learning* (Tomes, London).

- William Whewell (1840) *The Philosophy of Inductive Sciences* (Parker, London).

- Edward O. Wilson (1998) *Consilience: The Unity of Knowledge* (Knopf, New York).

**Edward O. Wilson,** *Pellegrino University Research Professor and Honorary Curator in Entomology at Harvard University, is the author of 18 books, 2 of which have received the Pulitzer Prize; an ardent defender of the liberal arts; and a promoter of global conservation of species and* *natural ecosystems. He is at the Museum of Comparative Zoology, Harvard University, 26 Oxford Street, Cambridge, MA 02138, USA.*

# 7. LECTURE NOTES, SECOND WEEK.
# FORM LANGUAGES AND THEIR VOCABULARY

## Readings for the Second Week:

- Alexander, *The Phenomenon of Life*, Chapter 2, "Degrees of Life".

- Alexander, sampler from "A Pattern Language", available online at http://www.patternlanguage.com/apl/aplsample/aplsample.htm

- Or see the book itself: C. Alexander, S. Ishikawa, M. Silverstein, M. Jacobson, I. Fiksdahl-King, and S. Angel (1977) *A Pattern Language* (Oxford University Press, New York).

- Salingaros, *A Theory of Architecture*, Chapter 11, "Two Languages for Architecture".

The perceived quality of life in buildings and urban spaces comes from the geometry (the form of structures on all scales, and their coherence), and how that geometry connects to the individual. It also catalyzes interactions among people — if it is done successfully.

The easiest way to perceive this quality of "life" is to compare pairs of objects or settings and judge intuitively which one has more "life". After a series of such experiments, it becomes obvious that degree of "life" in architecture arises from geometrical structure.

However, the perceived life has nothing to do with formal geometry. It arises rather from configurations, the complexity and patterns in a situation; often unexpected juxtapositions and shapes that work very well, and that usually evolved over time and were not planned at the start.

A building's geometry is a result of applying a particular form language chosen by the architect. This will determine, to a large extent, the emotional and physiological response of the user. A form language can aim at maximizing the perceived degree of "life" in the building. Otherwise it can have other, entirely distinct objectives, depending on the preference of the architect who employs it or creates it.

A form language includes the basic elements: floors, walls, ceilings, volumes and their subdivision, windows, materials, ornamentation, and the rules for combining them. Architectural composition within the context of a particular form language enables design in that idiom.

Every traditional architecture has its own form language: more accurately, a group of related languages, since languages evolve with variations over time and across locality. The language depends upon climate and local materials. It is also a continuation of traditional arts, social practices, and material culture.

Architecture is adaptive if its form language blends and connects with the Pattern language, and all traditional evolved form languages do so. Nevertheless, a form language could have other goals and not be adaptive.

The 20th century witnessed a new phenomenon: form languages that were detached from Pattern languages. Those form languages were no longer part of an adaptive system of architecture, but became self-sufficient entities. They were validated from artistic, political, and philosophical criteria.

Another related phenomenon that arises when architectural practice is not rooted in a Pattern language is the replacement of an evolved Pattern (which accommodates human life and sensibilities) by its opposite — an Antipattern. An Antipattern could be dysfunctional, and could cause anxiety and physical distress. A form language could attach itself to Anti-patterns, but that of course does not make it adaptive.

Form languages can be studied separately from their link to Pattern languages. Form languages can have different degrees of internal complexity. Just like written and spoken languages, form languages are characterized by their size of vocabulary; richness of combinatoric rules for generating new expressions; adaptability to the situation at hand, which might be novel. Or a form language could be very primitive, with limited vocabulary and combinatoric rules.

A particular form language may have very poor adaptation, but could appeal visually. This feature is sufficient to assure its survival in contemporary society, especially since the communications revolution. It is doubtful whether this would have occurred in a historic traditional society where resources were scarcer.

In contrast to historical times, today's global consumerist culture treats a form language as a commercial product. Thus, its success depends upon both the marketing strategies of its proponents, and profits to be made by those who apply it. Adaptivity does not enter the equation.

A form language lives or dies based on rather commonplace considerations: *(i)* Someone decides to use that form language for a new building, and *(ii)* society values an older form language sufficiently to leave its examples alone. Decisions on new buildings could be based on adaptive value, how comfortable people feel in a building, ease of use, proven environment for human productivity, proven durability of materials, practicality for re-use, etc. Or a client could use totally different motives, such as perceived marketing appeal, re-use of a commercially-successful typology in speculative building, cost cutting, maximization of usable space, etc.

Another crucial factor is the inertia that comes from embedded bureaucratic costs invested by the banking, construction, and insurance industries. These all resist technical changes in their established way of doing business with architecture and construction.

For the second factor, which presents threats to conservation, every generation faces the siren call of giving older buildings and urban spaces a face-lift to follow new fashions. Human societies crave to appear to be up-to-date, and decide what to sacrifice in pursuing this desire.

Putting aside questions of adaptation, it is essential to catalogue and classify disparate form languages. A single building, group of buildings, the work of a single architect, or an entire architectural movement depend upon a form language. The fact of being built provides information on the form language. Another architect can extract the form language by studying built examples.

In rare cases, an architect writes down the rules for the form language, so that it is then easy for someone else to apply it. Most of the time, however, the rules have to be derived from the buildings themselves.

Architects can learn a form language, and then use it to build many buildings, without altering the language in any way. Other architects vary a form language to different degrees, introducing their own changes, which may be adaptive or not. Others still invent their own form language so that their buildings become a "brand". This helps achieve success in an age of corporate branding.

Some architects can go through their careers switching from one form language to another, either traditionally-evolved form languages, or ones that they themselves have invented. For this reason, it is not always possible to identify an architect with a specific form language.

All traditional form languages had to evolve in conjunction with adaptive design, and this presupposes a certain complexity threshold.

Just as all human languages share an underlying complexity that permits a variety of expression. Newer form languages, however, follow no such constraint.

There are many examples of form languages from the 20th century that fall below the complexity threshold. That is true for two related reasons: (1) the language has been invented and has not involved, and (2) it did not have to adapt to a Pattern language.

I will use a biological analogy for architecture and its two languages. We consider the Pattern language as the metabolizing part of organisms, and the form language as the replicating portion of an organism's structure. Architecture is thus directly identified as a living process (more on this later). Humans interact with buildings in order to use them and repair them, an analogous process to metabolism.

The replicating function is taken care of by the form language. A type of architecture survives only by generating copies and variations of itself using a specific form language. Just as with organisms, however, a replicating entity does not need to metabolize.

Viruses are replicating organic complexes that do not metabolize. For this reason, they therefore have a far lower complexity content. As a result, they replicate far more efficiently than more complex metabolizing organisms can.

This course attempts to present a genuine theory of architecture, as the notions we study have predictions that can be verified. Simpler forms propagate more rapidly and can end up displacing more complex entities. Indeed, simplified form languages using industrial forms and materials proliferated in the 20th century, replacing form languages that were adaptive — hence more complex. [I have developed a theory of form language propagation in terms of memes: this is treated in the chapters of our textbook not covered in this course.]

There is another phenomenon that now has some sort of explanation: why Pattern language is not routinely taught in architecture schools. The reason is that, since the form languages of Modernism did not couple with Pattern language, the latter ceased to be of any interest to a profession that focused exclusively on Modernism.

Pattern language determines the human adaptation of buildings, however, and the connection of buildings to nature. In order to create a responsive and sustainable built environment, Pattern language has to once again take its central position in architecture.

The 20th century form languages were, and continue to be, a tremendous marketing success. They have generated enormous sales and profits for the architects and builders who use them, and greater brand recognition. But that does not mean they had the best interests of the user and the environment in mind. In fact, the reasons habitually given for those form languages' success, like new industrial materials that permitted greater spanned spaces and building heights, already occurred at the end of the 19th century. Those factors pre-date and have nothing to do with the characteristic modernist "look".

Today, with the looming ecological collapse, our attitudes are less narrowly profit–oriented for the strict benefit of individuals or small groups. We are more concerned with sustainability in the real sense, not just with gizmos added on, and for society as a whole.

Connection to the deep needs of human beings and the natural order brings us back to reconsidering using Pattern language once again. We would like to be able to distinguish between form languages that connect to nature, from those that are merely fashionable symbols of success. Such symbols are based upon criteria set by others, but they are not expressions of deep human values.

# 8. Lecture Notes, Third Week. Complexity of Form Languages. Ecophobia

## Readings for the Third Week:

- Salingaros, *A Theory of Architecture*, Chapter 1, "The Laws of Architecture From a Physicist's Perspective" (also available in Spanish).
- Salingaros, "Kolmogorov-Chaitin Complexity", *Meandering Through Mathematics*, 23 September 2012.
- Salingaros & Masden, "Against Ecophobia", *Philadelphia Society*, 8 October 2011.

We are going to collect and document different form languages from different locations, times, and cultures. Sometimes a form language has been applied unchanged for centuries before it evolved into something related but sufficiently distinct. Sometimes a form language exists only as an example in a single building.

How do we document a form language? The framework for documentation has to be broad enough to handle and describe *all* examples of form languages. Trying to achieve this is instructive because it raises crucial questions about the basis for architectural form.

A spoken or written language is composed of letters, words, phrases, paragraphs, essays, books, etc. We have basic elements and combinatoric rules that construct higher-order entities. The higher-scale constructs convey meaning, and the meaning is cumulative. That is, everything — all components and their connections, on each subscale — contribute to the meaning of the whole. This communicates a message.

If the student properly and accurately documents a form language, then it could be used to design an entirely new building. The measure of success is if an observer thinks that the new design resembles an original building enough to be considered as arising from the same language. I want to end the common practice of students copying buildings as images directly, which is both unintelligent and uncreative. The proper way to design in a particular language of choice is first to extract and document that form language from one or more examples, then use the form language to design a new building.

Going through the process of documenting a form language is an educational experience. First, it reveals the complexity of the language: how many words (and diagrams) are required to describe it so it can be applied to design something. There exists a very simple measure of complexity that we can employ here. The Kolmogorov-Chaitin complexity measure is the minimum length of a system's descriptor. It's the "length of code" without redundancies. For a form language, it would be the word count of your completed "form language checklist". [Section 38 of this book].

This first measure of the complexity of a form language opens up new dimensions for understanding architecture. Satisfying user needs, adaptations to climate, region, and materials should make a form language more complex — with a longer word count. Actually, both highly-ordered and random systems are complex, but in a different way. We will study that distinction later on (in week nine). Now we note that complexity of form language does not necessarily imply adaptation, and will look for a correlation between Kolmogorov-Chaitin complexity and regional adaptation.

So far this discussion has talked about the intrinsic complexity of some form language. The model also allows us to compare very different form languages in terms of their complexity. Distinct form languages cannot be compared visually, because of the very different images they present, but rather in terms of each language's overall complexity.

Traditional regionalism involves adaptation to local materials, climate, culture, and societal practices. (We will discuss later the possibilities of combining regionalism with 20th-century modernism.) Using the model of measuring the complexity of a form language through a word count of its verbal description, we can investigate how adaptation to local practices and building culture requires a longer or shorter description of the design process. Our intuitive experience would lead us to say that better adaptation to local requirements requires a longer description.

A form language is one prescription for creating structural order, and its products will have their own characteristic appearance. At the heart of every spoken or written language is a set of rules common to all languages. We can look for these general rules in other sciences to understand the commonality among visually distinct architectural styles.

I introduced some rules for structural order to help explain Alexander's theory of adaptive design, which we study later (in week seven). These rules are taken from physics, not architecture, and establish a helpful rubric for analyzing form languages. They represent the means of achieving coherence of forms.

Three laws for architecture are proposed: (1) Smallest-scale order consists of paired contrasting elements. (2) Large-scale order occurs when every element collaborates to reduce randomness. (3) Small is connected to large through a hierarchy of intermediate scales, using a scaling ratio around $e \approx 2.7$.

Let's see the consequences of these rules for creating coherent order. The smallest scale will need to have well-defined components so that they can indeed couple. It cannot be empty altogether. Coupling is achieved through geometric interlock and contrast. It then follows that whenever there is repetition, it is a coupled pair that repeats.

Randomness is reduced by using symmetries of all types: repetition, alignment or translational symmetry, reflectional, rotational, and glide symmetries (which are a translation plus a reflection). The intention is to be able to experience the structure as a whole, rather than to have to account for each individual component separately. Components on the same scale are related using common symmetries, whereas those on different scales are related through scaling symmetries.

These rules, originally given in the context of a specific theory of design, prove useful in writing down form languages. For example, look for repeating and contrasting (paired) components on the small scales. Pay attention to what is happening at many distinct scales. Look for symmetries, or their absence where they would ordinarily be expected.

We are also sensitized by this framework to recognize frames and boundaries in form languages. In traditional building and design, two structural elements rarely come together without some form of trim, intermediate region, or border. This was eliminated in the minimalist form language we are most familiar with, so we should not overlook the boundaries — which appear in all traditional form languages — now.

There exists a volume of writings by architects in the early 20th century, and we can look through them for the form languages of Modernism. Unfortunately, the useful material turns out to be very little, most of it describing not a form language but rather marketing and declarations of a political nature. Moreover, those pieces of very personal form languages are presented as normative theories:

a prescription of what to do and what not to do, with the weight of universal ethics, even though they are based solely on opinion, not empirical observations or systematic study.

Here are some practical lists of rules I have found.

*By the brothers Naum Gabo and Antoine Pevsner, 1920: "Reject closed mass and volume, and model space from within outwards. Reject color, and use only the natural color of the building materials. Reject all ornament."*

*Ludwig Mies van der Rohe, 1923: "Open plan for interiors. Materials are limited to concrete, iron, and glass. Use only curtain walls and reinforced concrete — no load-bearing construction."*

*Le Corbusier, 1927: "Lift the building from sitting with its basement in the earth, to being suspended on posts (pilotis). Only curtain-wall construction is allowed. Roofs have to be flat. Windows can only be horizontal and will extend from one load-bearing pillar to another, which makes them very wide (narrow and long)."*

These three sets of rules for a modernist form language do contrast with traditional form languages, so that of course the product looks markedly different from a traditional building erected prior to the 20th Century. This "new look" was part of the modernist form language's appeal when it was first introduced.

Without discussing the merits of the modernist form language and its variants here, there is an appeal to universality, and thus a rejection of regional adaptation. There is also a strong motivation to reject elements simply because they belong to traditional form languages: turning against one's cultural tradition for the sake of innovation.

Our society adopted the modernist form language for an enormous number of buildings, and so we have forgotten the store of older and traditional form languages. This represents a great loss for the knowledge base of the architectural profession. No rational society should throw out practical information, unless that body of knowledge has been proved wrong, or is no longer useful.

Nothing wrong was ever discovered in older form languages: indeed, they have a great number of adaptive qualities that create pleasant, functional, and comfortable living and working environments. We suggest that an architect can learn from all form languages. Some languages are going to be more relevant to the location than others — a welcome return to valuing regionalism because this leads to sustainability.

When deciding to employ an older form language to design a building today, the architect has an option. He or she may use the form language in its original form. Otherwise, the architect may choose to upgrade it by introducing improvements or savings through more contemporary materials. Architects also have the option to add individual innovative elements of their own, unless commissioned to design in a particular form language.

A form language evolves in time, just as a written and spoken language does, so change is natural. What is not natural is drastic reversal in a form language. The crucial concern here is to modify an architectural form language so that it does not lose its adaptive and expressive power. In order to achieve this, the architect must begin from a deep respect of what evolved traditional form languages represent.

According to the Kolmogorov-Chaitin complexity measure, I point out how a very simple rule (that we don't know) can generate a very complex information string. Thus, there could be a "shortcut" to generating a very complex form language with a large word count. Can we guess such a shortcut for a particular form language? This is a very good question with no easy answer. On the one hand, an adaptive or regional form language is complex, but cannot be generated using a very simple rule, for the reason that it arises from many adaptations. There is nothing to compress here: no shortcut.

On the other hand, non-adaptive form languages could in fact be generated by rather simple rules. For example, "generate a sculptural form with a computer program then build it as a building", or "crumple a piece of paper then build it as a building", or "draw a doodle on a piece of paper then build it as a building". These are descriptions of only a few words. Yet they rely upon some industrial form language, say, for warehouses or aircraft hangars, to get the job done — the sculptural model is not enough to make working drawings for the contractor. Brief rules like these work together with a developed form language. The result is a building having a very complex description.

Another brief rule that can generate a complex form language works by reversing or negating an existing form language. Again, this requires a developed language to act upon. We can imagine prescriptions such as: "reverse the scaling hierarchies", or "eliminate straight lines", or "smash forms to the point just before they become uninhabitable", or "slash walls to cut diagonal strip windows". These simple rules change an existing form language radically, and create complex buildings with novelty appeal. Otherwise, an architect can drastically simplify an existing form language with the rule "strip everything off except supporting structure", which reduces its complexity.

Architects are not in the habit of writing down their form languages. Either they feel they own a design secret that they don't wish to see copied by others, or they are simply not used to documenting design in this manner. It could also be the case that they are generating their form language by a "shortcut", such as one of the above. Other architects and researchers usually study buildings afterwards, and these are the people who delve into a form language. But even those don't usually document the form language. One exception is Henry Glassie's "Folk Housing in Middle Virginia", 1975.

# 9. KOLMOGOROV-CHAITIN COMPLEXITY

*By Nikos A. Salingaros*

*Meandering Through Mathematics, 23 September 2012. Reprinted by permission.*

Trying to measure the complexity of a system is not straightforward. The simplest measure of a system's complexity reflects not so much its intrinsic complexity, or the complexity of the process that generated it, but the complexity of the system's description. As such, this approach is not without its limitations.

We can measure the complexity of a one-dimensional system by using a very simple notion: the length of its description in some programming language. This measure is known as the Kolmogorov-Chaitin Complexity. Analyzing a string of letters or numbers might reveal a pattern that repeats, and in that case, its description becomes shorter. I'm going to use binary entries of **0** and **1** in 70-character strings, yet the discussion is valid for any letters or digits. For example, it is obvious that this information string is not complex at all:

1111111111111111111111111111111111111111111111111111111111
1111111111111

Its generative algorithm is: repeat the digit **1** 70 times, or "**1** x 70". On the other hand, the more complex string

1010101010101010101010101010101010101010101010101010101010
0101010101010

still has only minimal complexity, since its algorithm is a short one: "**10** x 35". But it has slightly more complexity than the first trivial string. The next orderly sequence is very different, yet it also possesses low complexity:

11111111111111111111111111111111111110000000000000000000000000
0000000000000

It has the generating algorithm "**1** x 35, **0** x 35". Something non-trivial occurs only at the 36th position. For genuinely complex strings of digits, we face two distinct types of complexity. First, there is organized or coherent complexity, such as the following binary sequence:

10001101011000110101100011010110001101011000110101100011010110001 10
1011000110101

Analyzing this information string for patterns, we discover hidden symmetries, and those allow us to reduce its generating code to alternating **10001** with **10101** 7 times, or "**10001** alternate **10101** x 7". We do have a complex string, yet internal patterns reduce the coding length of its generating algorithm.

The second type of complexity represents random, or disorganized complexity, as for example the following random sequence:

0010001110101011000010111001011111101011111110100111000
1101000100101

It has maximal complexity, because its shortest description is exactly as long as the string itself. There is no possible compression, such as hidden patterns in its descriptive rule. We can be sure of that, since we generated this string by using a random-number generator.

Probability arguments produce one complication, however: it is quite possible to obtain internal patterns in a randomly-generated string. But you cannot count on it, and might have to try an astronomical number of times before you come up with a regular pattern.

The key mechanism revealed by these examples is the presence or not of patterns, which then permit compression of the informational string. Total compression is equivalent to informational collapse, and this occurs in cases of extremely low complexity. In examples of strings with non-trivial complexity, the ability to compress them reduces their complexity measure, but never to near zero.

I will now compute the length of the description of each algorithm for the informational strings presented as examples. This is a simple character count of the description in English, and I obtain the following values for all the strings:

1 x 70 → 4 characters

10 x 35 → 5 characters

1 x 35, 0 x 35 → 9 characters

10001 alternate 10101 x 7 → 21 characters

[Random] → 70 characters

Since we partially depend upon the English language for our descriptions, these algorithms are not expressed in the most efficient way; hence their length is not unique. The shortest description length obviously varies with the programming language used. But that doesn't matter here, as the model serves to illustrate one-dimensional complexity in a very simple manner. For example, the above complex string with internal patterns could be generated equally by the description "**1000110101** x 7", which has a character count of only 12. This number is different from 21, yet still falls between 9 and 70; that is, between a trivially-simple string and a random string, which is the key point.

Another issue is that human perception plays an important role in describing complexity, even though this has nothing to do with the actual algorithm. Informationally-minimal strings do indeed look trivially simple to us. They are of no interest, as they do not communicate a message. Thus, extreme simplicity is not useful, and we require complexity above some threshold to transmit a message. Humans pay attention to ordered information, but too much information overwhelms our cognitive system. And complex strings of very different complexity may at first appear to be equally complex. It is only after we "see" a pattern that we can recognize the relative complexity of an informational string.

The Kolmogorov-Chaitin complexity has obvious limitations because it ignores the degree of internal symmetries, such as repetition and nesting, yet those directly affect our cognition. For example, the string referred to above is generated by the two "words" **10001** and **10101**, each one of which is internally symmetric. This important feature is not measured by the character count. In fact, the algorithm in terms of the symmetric words gives us a higher character count (21) than the simpler repetition that takes no symmetry into account (12), which is counter-intuitive. We are most interested in, and wish to investigate, systems of information with complex ordered patterns.

Another important phenomenon not described by this model is when a very simple algorithm generates complexity iteratively throughout the entire system. Here, a simple rule such as a cellular automaton computes configurations in which every entry is constantly changing. With very few exceptions, there is no final state for a cellular automaton: the generated pattern continues to grow and transform. Any one of these states could be irreducibly complex, i.e. not compressible. When we try to find a description of such a system in terms of an algorithm that generates the information string sequentially (not in the way it was actually generated), it appears highly complex.

My interest in this topic arises from the description of design in general, and architectural styles, or "form languages", in particular. Each form language is a description of how a building looks like and also how it is constructed, and I wish to measure the relative complexity of different form languages. Traditional form languages adapt to climate, local materials, human needs and uses, and culture, and are therefore irreducibly complex. They have many forces and constraints to adapt to, and have evolved step-by-step over time. Even though the buildings that distinct form languages generate obviously look very different, all of them (languages and resulting designs) have an equivalent measure of complexity.

A word count of a form language's verbal description is a very rough measure of its Kolmogorov-Chaitin complexity. I ask my architecture students to fill out a rather standard checklist for a form language, and use their word processor to obtain a word count. Then students are able to compare their assigned form languages by comparing these numbers. This exercise separates minimalist from more complex buildings. Nevertheless, I don't know how to solve the problem of distinguishing evolved form languages with high complexity, from randomly-generated and thus non-adaptive form languages.

Some architects introduce deliberate randomness for the sake of an innovative "look". Nothing has evolved here, since no adaptation is involved. The design method is performed as an instantaneous artistic act. Those architects often use a "shortcut" to design their building, which, while not generating any adaptations, could be very complex indeed. This case is analogous to a simple rule (that we don't know) generating a random string. It would be useful to understand when a form language is simple, and to distinguish the two cases when it is complex due to adaptation, or complex because it is generated randomly.

Perhaps a future essay could discuss these matters.

# References

- "Kolmogorov complexity", entry from Wikipedia. http://en.wikipedia.org/wiki/Kolmogorov_complexity

- A. Klinger & N. A. Salingaros (2000) "A Pattern Measure", *Environment and Planning B: Planning and Design*, volume 27, pages 537-547. Republished by the *Cornell University Library Arxiv*, 28 August 2011, http://arxiv.org/html/1108.5508v1

# 10. AGAINST ECOPHOBIA: TOWARDS A HUMAN HABITAT

By Nikos A. Salingaros & Kenneth G. Masden II

*Archnet-IJAR: International Journal of Architectural Research,*
*Volume 2, Issue 1 (March 2008), pages 129-188. Reprinted for*
*the Philadelphia Society Regional Meeting, Cincinnati, 8 October*
*2011. Reprinted by permission.*

Most building and planning today follow unwritten rules that have no empirical foundation, being based strictly upon visual/ideological constructs from the early twentieth century. Contemporary design avoids any criterion of quality that draws upon evolved precedent and tradition from a prior era, and thinks that this refusal is a great virtue. In this way, architects and urbanists end up obeying simplistic criteria for design, rejecting any sense of beauty that links human beings with their land, tradition, and culture.

## Introduction

The term "ecophobia" refers to an unreasonable but deeply conditioned reaction against natural forms. It has also been used in clinical psychology to denote a phobia against one's dwelling, but that specific use now appears to be antiquated. The philosopher Roger Scruton coined the related term "oikophobia" to denote an unreasonable hatred of one's native culture. We believe that these two terms "ecophobia" and "oikophobia" may in many cases be used interchangeably. (Linguistically, the common Greek root for "house" can be written either as *ecos* or *oikos*).

Regarding the social domain, our age is experiencing deep philosophical and social tensions. These are as serious as the concerns with our detachment from nature. The 21st century has begun with a continuation, and perhaps intensification, of the worst prejudices seen in the twentieth. Those prejudices include a disdain of traditional cultures, and all that links a human being to his/her local history.

Scruton reminds us that: "the oikophobe repudiates national loyalties and defines his goals and ideals *against* the nation, promoting transnational institutions over national governments ... defining his political vision in terms of universal values that have been purified of all reference to the particular attachments of a real historical community." Here we have the "modern man", who embraces all forms of technological toys while he rejects evolved solutions that have held society together for millennia.

## Ideology and publicity

As Scruton points out, there is a deep political component in ecophobia, since many political parties promote themselves by promising liberation from society's problems through embracing universal (yet abstract) utopias. Governments of radically distinct political orientations nevertheless fall prey to an infatuation with foreign goods and ideas, and this dependence is manipulated for the benefit of multinational corporations. It is easy to be helped along by advertising, now reaching into even the most remote places on this planet, which promotes foreign products loudly in the local market.

At the same time, local traditions are erased, along with what held that society together. The underlying phenomenon is a disregard or even loathing of one's own culture, and its artifacts and practices. This hatred drives people to reject what is traditionally theirs, and to embrace new foreign symbols of capital progress as somehow better.

Architecture as image, operating in the service of global capital, is now present in everyone's backyard. To sacrifice identity for globalization corrupts the values and beliefs that people of traditional cultures have sustained for millennia.

Today's fashionable architecture instead serves a culture of "capital and consumption". That culture's values and beliefs underlie and structure architectural practice in the U.S.A. and increasingly throughout the world.

Fueled by billions of dollars in capital, this process of promoting new foreign symbols is sustained by influencing the rest of the world to buy what the West is selling. As universities and cultural institutions from the West seek greater access to the untapped resources of other industrializing countries, they present, under the guise of Western prosperity, a set of circumstances that serve only to destroy culture. Those values effectively destabilize traditional civilization. Strong commercial interests are aligned with economic exploitation via the imposition of hyped-up contemporary architects on the rest of the world. Governments mistakenly believe that they are doing good for their people by erecting "showcase" buildings such as museums by internationally famous architects. Instead, they are letting in agents of intolerance, paving the way for an extinction of the local architectural heritage.

## Us, masters of the absurd

Young persons are exposed to promotional images of design in schools and the media, and are told that this is what they must value from now on. They are indoctrinated to hate and destroy traditional architectural expressions, as something noble to pursue.

Many people correctly blame the West and powerful local interests for turning the country's young against their own culture. For the wealthy Western nations, teaching nihilism is just another silliness of contemporary society, along with pseudo-art that intentionally profanes God. But developing countries stand to risk all they have — their traditional art and architecture — in imitating the West on this point.

Our proposal is for education reform that would immediately stop teaching hatred of one's own architectural heritage and culture. No crime is more unpardonable than parricide: killing one's own parents. But how do we judge an architecture school that teaches students to despise their own heritage, and instills in them an eagerness to destroy it?

The target is the society that brought forth those individuals, in a shared responsibility with their biological parents. We read with alarm about Bauhaus images and practices introduced into the architectural education of developing countries. The press announces these as "progressive" moves, little realizing what danger that poses to that country's tradition.

A great deal is gained from utilizing scientifically-based knowledge as a new paradigm of how to teach architecture. The way to re-establish architecture as a knowledge-based discipline is simply to rebuild its knowledge base. Without a knowledge base grounded in the reality of human perception and science, architecture remains open to corruption and is prey to the whims of ideology, fashion, and the cult of the individual. Making allowances for the inherent differences between architecture and science as disciplines, there are many lessons to be learned through the immediate juxtaposition of their intellectual structures. Science and scientific enquiry operate through the application of an accumulated knowledge base. Scientists undertake research desiring to extend their discipline's corpus of knowledge. They meticulously document successful results of their investigations for inclusion into the greater body of knowledge. To this end, scientific disciplines develop languages for this explicit purpose over time, to enable transcribing and saving discovered knowledge for posterity. Knowledge itself rests upon having efficient information storage systems.

## The incentive of science

This process of documentation allows scientists to build upon previous discoveries. It saves having to reinvent the wheel every time one needs to perform a basic application. Science also has a mechanism that allows one to sift useless or outdated information from the working corpus of knowledge. A theory that is superseded or proven wrong is immediately discarded or consigned to having strictly historical interest. This replacement occurs because a better method than the old one is found THAT EXPLAINS THE PHENOMENA. Science is therefore constantly expanding its information base, while maintaining its order and relevance in a compact corpus of knowledge. This process exists through an ordering and compacting of scientific information, much as libraries develop a coherent ordering system to handle enormous and steadily increasing amounts of information. Knowledge can only be useful if it is easily retrievable, and that depends upon having an efficient systematization.

By contrast, architecture has yet to develop an effective system of ordering its inherited information. In fact, what happened in architecture is unthinkable in the sciences: sometime in the 1920s, in their quest for design innovation, a group of ideologues arbitrarily threw out architecture's informational basis. The excuse for this elimination was to help the discipline to venture off into new territories. Those wanting to do this in the name of innovation felt no obligation to conserve the knowledge previously developed or discovered. Obviously, since those individuals felt no need to document inherited information, they also considered it unnecessary to develop an ordering system for current knowledge. Ever since, architectural innovation has been judged to be successful strictly by how completely it disregards previous knowledge.

## Aesthetic taste

Paradoxically, this devastating practice has led to the accumulation of both rigid dogma and a plethora of mutually contradictory styles. Architects failed to develop or implement an ordering system even for architectural styles that they deal with and refer to daily. Champions of each distinct style fight against the other styles, declaring them to be useless, outdated, or morally indefensible. This irresolvable dispute is the source of tremendous systemic conflict and instability (which hinders instead of encouraging development). Styles are validated only if approved by the discipline's self-appointed "taste makers", a defensive gesture to make architecture more mysterious and unavailable to those who are not tutored in its multifarious "theories".

Scientific debate, on the other hand, while it can become quite contentious, has strict guidelines for resolution. The scientific criterion for validity is whether any knowledge works to explain phenomena adequately, and whether in the process it creates or establishes something of value to humanity. Scientists abandon an old belief even though it may be supported by a large number of followers, if it fails to explain observed structures. Conflicts can be intense, but are usually brief. Eventually, scientists reach a consensus on an experimental basis.

## The loss of information

If we adopt the scientific approach, we drop nothing arbitrarily from a discipline's informational store. Most architects don't yet treat architecture as a scientist would, since they refrain from looking for its evidence base. The catastrophic loss of urban and architectural information that occurred following World War II, implemented by modernist-trained teachers taking over architectural schools, would never have been allowed to occur if we had followed a scientific model in determining our architecture.

Derived knowledge is far too valuable to throw away capriciously. Older knowledge can be superseded only by an updated explanatory framework, not by unproven ideas or opinions. Again and again, we return to the need for a set of evidence-based criteria for judging what is valuable in architecture.

In typical courses of architectural theory, a collection of mutually contradictory and oftentimes obscure readings leave a student bewildered about what is relevant or irrelevant. Yet, all are presented as being equally valid, since they are included in some authoritative anthology. Students are not given any criteria for judgment: indeed, neither their professor, nor the author of the anthology would dare adopt any measure that makes such a judgment possible. Doing so would be perceived as preferring one point of view over another, hence undemocratic.

## The cult of useless ugliness

Nevertheless, this flawed notion of plurality unravels what any intellectually-developed discipline has found necessary to evolve.

Outdated or discredited notions that keep reappearing in architectural readings should finally be allowed to fade into obscurity. Without a criterion of what is valid or not, architects cannot really allow anything to drop if it is associated with a reigning ideology. This means that they endlessly perpetuate useless intellectual bric-a-brac.

Diverse styles can indeed be tied together by the commonality among positive solutions that each has to offer. Introducing a theoretical classification of architectural typologies is an essential part of the needed new curriculum. Such an explanation ties together diverse styles from among competing contemporary movements, and from those developed in the past. Some of these styles are judged inadequate because they do not serve human needs, and the faculty of existing architectural programs must be prepared for this. If one looks carefully, one discovers that many of the unstated principles in use today are not founded on anything architectural, but rest strictly on ideological arguments. Architecture can never go forward if it continues to blindly support design dogmas.

*(\*Note: This essay is a section from the longer paper "Intelligence-Based Design: A Sustainable Foundation For Worldwide Architectural Education", Archnet-IJAR: International Journal of Architectural Research, Volume 2, Issue 1 (March 2008), pages 129-188. This extract was published in Greekarchitects (20 September 2008). Italian version of the present extract published in Il Domenicale, Number 14 (5 April 2008), pages 6-8, then included as Chapter 6 in the book NO ALLE ARCHISTAR: IL MANIFESTO CONTRO LE AVANGUARDIE, Libreria Editrice Fiorentina, 2009. Original paper is available from <http://zeta.math.utsa.edu/~yxk833/Intelligence-Based-IJAR.pdf>.)*

**Kenneth G. Masden II**, *AIA, is an NCARB certified architect with a B.Arch from the University of Kentucky and an M.Arch from Yale University — where he studied with Léon Krier, Vincent Scully, Fred Koetter, and Andrés Duany. He has extensive experience with large scale planning projects, including base relocation and land reclamation projects for the U.S. Government totaling over $4 billion, on which he has worked as project architect, environmental engineer, planner, and program manager in Japan, Germany, Spain, Italy, and the United States. From 2001-2010 he was an Assistant/Associate Professor of Architecture and Urban Design at the University of Texas at San Antonio. Before beginning his academic career he worked with Peter Eisenman on the Memorial to the Murdered Jews of Europe, in Berlin and the Cidade da Cultura de Galicia in Santiago de Campostela, Spain. Currently the Director of Planning and Development for* *the Hawaii Department of Education, he manages a capital improvement budget of $250 million/year for the 9th largest public school system in the nation. His architecture and practice are influenced by his international travels and his research in biological form, neuroscience, and Intelligence-Based Design.*

# 11. Lecture Notes, Fourth Week. Degree of complexity Measures a Form Language's Adaptivity

## Readings for the Fourth Week:

- Alexander, *The Phenomenon of Life*, Chapter 7, "The Personal Nature of Order".
- Léon Krier, "Building Civil Cities", *Traditional Building*, 2005.
- Salingaros & Masden, "Politics, Philosophy, Critical Theory", *Philadelphia Society*, 2011.

Suppose that we have successfully documented and catalogued all form languages, including those from vernacular traditions, past times, and contemporary practice. A scientific approach requires the next step, which comprises both analysis and classification. A catalogue is a useful store of information, but it is only the beginning of a systematic study.

We need several more things: one is a method of evaluating distinct characteristics of form languages that they have in common, or in which they contrast. The goal is to turn this mass of information into a group of related knowledge: namely, a classification.

What do some form languages have in common, and on what qualities do some of them differ? One measure is their degree of complexity, as documented by the length of description of the form language. Another is adaptation to locality. How far does a form language justify itself as being regional? Here, regional is the opposite of universal.

It is therefore useful to classify form languages by how much they adapt to a certain locality. If it does adapt, each language will, of course, adapt to its own specific locality: what we measure is how good that adaptation is. Success of adaptation is measured if buildings are energy efficient in the low-tech sense, so that the majority population can profit from them. By contrast, high-tech energy efficiency may be very useful, but it usually relies upon imported technology and materials, and is thus global, not regional. Our "Quantitative Measures for Regionalism and Complexity" description for the second project [Section 41 of this book] lists helpful guidelines on evaluating the regional adaptation of a form language.

Let's try to derive a theoretical result: "*is the complexity of a form language related to its degree of regionalism?*"

Regionalism measures to what degree local materials are used, how local culture is respected in the geometry of the building, how evolved adaptations to climate become part of the design, etc. Conversely, we measure to what degree these factors are ignored for the purposes of imposing a top-down stylistic conception.

In the past, transport was difficult, so people were forced to use locally-available materials. There is a related philosophy of regionalism that respects the landscape and nature. Are trees, rivers, hills, and lakes respected, or are they just cleared indiscriminately to make room for a building? Also, if a building uses good local materials it is long-lived with the necessary repair and maintenance. There is a sense that it belongs to the place and the culture. But buildings that do not respond to the local environment often decay relatively quickly. If they don't, they can become hated intruders.

There is another, vast topic of further investigation, and it has to do with how a person reacts emotionally to a building. This has more to do with the form language, while only a little of the response is specific to a building.

This question makes sense only after we accept Christopher Alexander's claim that 90% of our emotional response to a building is shared across cultures. It is not a matter of opinion, like whether we "like" something or not. That depends upon education and conditioning, and is less fundamental.

Something feels connected to our person, to our deepest self, and we identify with it. As Alexander says, it becomes "personal". This connective effect is due to geometrical properties, a few of which we know (and are going to study here).

Geometrical coherence in a structure, when it achieves an optimal value, induces an intensely positive feeling in us. This could paradoxically be coming from a structure that, for other reasons, we don't particularly like, or we judge it to be not of great artistic or architectural significance. The contradiction between what our body is experiencing, and what our rational mind is telling us, could induce cognitive dissonance.

An intense degree of connectivity with an artifact or structure establishes a personal relationship with the physical object or space. We experience a healing process, a sense of happiness, unless of course we are instead experiencing cognitive dissonance. (That creates a state of stress.)

This discussion has important philosophical implications. It proposes a post-Cartesian view of the universe. Recall that Descartes viewed natural things as machines detached from each other. By contrast, we view a person and the object he/she is interacting with as two component parts of a larger system. The act of experiencing an artifact or building ties the observer with the observed.

Modern physics is in fact based precisely on this concept of close interaction between the observer and what is observed. The experiments demonstrating this phenomenon work on the quantum level. What we are discussing here occurs on the macroscopic level, however. Thus we have to rely upon our perception rather than any physical measurements.

And yet, during the past several decades, philosophical Cartesianism has triumphed, becoming ever more extreme. The universe and its highly-complex mechanisms were all assumed to be like simplistic machines, which is false. Our perception of the world has become reductionistic in many fields, including design, ignoring science as it did so. Nowadays, architectural discourse never considers the complex binding of the observer with the observed.

Tracing the origins of this development leads us to an old political philosophy. A group of philosophers known as the "Frankfurt School" proposed a set of radically new rules for society to follow. This occurred in the 1930s as part of a Marxist drive for a new society. Their writings, labeled as "Critical Theory", ignore human nature, and hope rather naively to mold a new human being to inhabit a proposed utopian world. But any philosophy that is detached from science is bound to be misleading and even dangerous, and this is certainly true of the "Frankfurt School".

A central tenet of Marxist ideology is that the past and all traditions stand in the way of human progress. The only way forward, it claims, is to first reject the past, and to destroy it so it no longer contaminates our newly-constructed Utopia. This thinking has profound consequences for the design of the environment. Traditional notions of connecting to architecture are deemed to be politically incorrect and are strongly condemned.

The problem for architects is that a body of writings labeled "Critical Theory" is mistaken for architectural theory. They are nothing of the sort; in fact, they are not a theory of anything. "Critical Theory" is simply a roadmap for a revolution based on Marxist and technocratic principles. Traditional societies are to be disbanded, and people treated as cogs in a vast industrial machine.

A core of resentment arises here against traditional notions of beauty, and that applies to architecture as well. Traditional form languages are declared to be undesirable, fit only for extinction. They are to be replaced by one universal language that expresses technology, industrialization, and collectivization.

"Critical Regionalism" is a movement to adapt design to local climatic and site conditions, and to some degree, locally-available materials. It represents a healthy reaction to the non-adaptiveness of the International Style of Modernism. Unfortunately, the inclusion of the word "critical" creates a contradiction, since it is tied to an anti-regional and anti-traditional philosophical and political movement. In practice, critical regionalism willfully perpetuates the form languages of Modernism. Our understanding, however, is that regionalism has to protect and re-use traditional form languages. True regionalism has to free itself from any global form language imposed from above, and from any forces of uniformization and conformity.

This raises the issue of form languages being linked to particular philosophies. That may very well be true. But I disagree with almost all other authors, and I insist that philosophy cannot be considered a substitute for architectural theory. Regardless of how a form language arises, theoretical tools from architecture and human biology can be used to explain how effective it is in providing useful buildings. This is the true objective of architectural theory.

By putting the cart before the horse, i.e. when labeling philosophical or political discourse attached to a form language as "theory", totally confuses what theory really is. Unfortunately, most books on "architectural theory" are simply historical accounts of thinking that is used to justify a particular form language using criteria other than human use.

Similar form languages have evolved in different cultures that, however, share local materials, climate, and topography. This is an example of parallel convergent evolution, much like the dorsal fins of sharks and dolphins in biology. By leveling cultural and geographical differences, however, one ends up destroying the evolved sustainability and energy efficiency encoded in traditional form languages.

For about a century, we have experienced project-driven theory, which, again, is not theory at all. An architect designs a building intuitively, using a usually unarticulated form language, and subsequently creates some explanation after-the-fact. This is pure marketing. Architectural critics play the game and elaborate on this *ad hoc* explanation, discussing it as if it were theory, but that makes it neither scientific, nor an honest description of the actual design process.

Very often, the architect invents a "look" that has no rational basis, being only a visceral inspiration of how to express certain favored images. At other times, the architect may be driven by conscious or subconscious forces of destruction, and this motivation is reflected in the built project having a "transgressive" look. The proffered "theoretical" explanation of such a form is never honest about its source of inspiration.

I do not believe that after-the-fact justifications of contemporary buildings can be useful tools for architecture students. They only confuse the basic issue. Students instead need to learn how to distinguish between genuine theory and marketing.

# 12. BUILDING CIVIL CITIES

### Michael Carey talks with Léon Krier

### Traditional Building Magazine, 2005. Reprinted from the Léon Krier website by permission.

**Michael Carey:** *What, in your opinion, is a city and what makes a good city?*

**Léon Krier:** A city is a network of interrelated public spaces and buildings, of individuals and groups. A good city is one where beyond its functional, social, securitarian and economic aspects, the interrelatedness is aesthetic. The meaningful and commonly readable structure of urban plan and silhouette, the quality of buildings, spaces, materials, colors and activities, and the successful relation of all this with the geographic conditions of climate and ecology, mean that the good city is not an idealized abstraction, a utopia, but a crucible for a tangible reality, for desirable forms of human intercourse.

**MC:** *It seems to me that there are two types of characterization going on here: the city as an embodiment of social and cultural ideals and the city as a functioning organism. While we may be able to agree on how best to keep an organism functioning, I wonder if we can agree on what makes a city, as an embodiment of ideals, work. I agree with Tom Rajkovich's insistence on the importance of beauty and on its intentionality, but I also wonder if we can include beauty as an embodiment of ideals. Some very beautiful things have been built in the name of less-than-beautiful ideals. Can cities of the past still serve as useful models today?*

**LK:** Any object of desire, be it natural or artificial, anything that is pleasing, useful or meaningful to us, whatever its age and origin, can and does serve us as a model today. Nature works fundamentally through reproduction/imitation and so do all human activities. For those who don't get it, I propose that they range architecture and urbanism with technology rather than with art history. If they still don't get it and go on repeating that "one can't go back", I propose that they tattoo their forehead with "not *one*, but *I* can't" and then stop all activity related to art or architecture. Those who can't shouldn't stop those who can.

**MC:** *A criticism of New Urbanism is that it takes the village as its model, rather than the city. How does a city differ fundamentally from a village or a series of villages?*

**LK:** The practice of New Urbanism is largely related to commissions coming from the free market sector. The locations, briefs and densities are mostly predetermined and only partially shaped by New Urbanist thinking. As a theory, it is not a set and sealed doctrine, but it evolves like scientific theory, through trial and error. Anyway, it is not a theological or transcendental system, but 90% a technology for how to settle the planet in an intelligent, ecological, aesthetic and socially attractive way.

**MC:** *Is there a limit to the size of a city, if it is to be civil, and how should a city relate to its surroundings?*

**LK:** Anything useful, pleasing and desirable has a limited size, form, weight. Maturity is the end goal of all processes of healthy growth. Cities cannot grow otherwise, without becoming parasites, natural and human disasters. Geography, climate and ecology will eventually define again the location and size of cities and villages. The sooner the better, but New Urbanism is a relatively young discipline.

We know yet very little about the long-term carrying capacity of the planet nor even of given geographic areas. We however assume that gigantism in the form of utilitarian skyscrapers (giant vertical cul-de-sacs), single-use landscrapers or single-use zones (giant horizontal cul-de-sacs) are in every case oversized functional and social isolators, parasites, excluders; they are also network congestors and depressors, if not killers.

In that sense, they are ultimately anti-urban, anti-social and anti-ecological. They are not expressions of vitality and health but of pathological hyperactivity. It should already be possible to define scientifically the carrying capacity (maxima and minima) for existing street networks, as they exist in consolidated urban centers, and describe the necessary network modifications that are imperative if skyscrapers and other "network busters" are implanted into them. Short of radical measures, such giants ought simply be considered unaffordable dinosaurs of a pre-ecological past.

**MC:** *If suburban sprawl is, to use the currently fashionable phrase, "a fact on the ground", how can it be urbanized?*

**LK:** Residential suburbs or single-use zones can be urbanized by canceling the single-use ordinances, allowing higher plot ratios, taking measures for enriching the network of streets, alleys and avenues, creating central urban squares, prohibiting one-way streets, connecting cul-de-sacs, etc. Increased property values will be the motor of such urbanization.

**MC:** *There are many examples of the revitalization of urban areas that are in some sense spontaneous. The revitalization of Williamsburg in New York City, for instance, was not planned and, in some cases, involved violating zoning regulations and codes. Given that these kinds of spontaneous shifts are crucial to the vitality of cities, how is planning and regulation to be balanced with spontaneity?*

**LK:** The NIMBY mentality and fear of property devaluation are now important supporters of single-use zoning ordinances. Only the multiplication of New Urbanist models can eventually turn the tide of sprawl.

**MC:** *A word of clarification: by "spontaneity", I was simply referring to unplanned, unregulated and self-generating changes in the urban fabric. It was not used as a psychological category and there was no intended "therapeutic" meaning. In Tom Rajkovich's opinion a return to traditional building principles is aesthetically desirable, and in Jim Kunstler's opinion this will be an economic necessity. This shows, I think, a central lack of sustainability — ecologically, economically and aesthetically — in many contemporary building technologies and the designs that are derived from them. The organizational principles of city building are often seen as independent of any architectural language, working only at the level of the plan. If the fabric of cities is the result of both planning and architecture, how should these two interact?*

**LK:** Even though traditional cities allow in plan and silhouette an infinite variety of composition and articulation, there are certain rules and principles about networking, building hierarchy, density, location, siting of private and public uses and above all the number of floors, which cannot be ignored without paying a terrible price in quality of environment, space, light, meaning, circulation of people and hardware and foremost in the loss of architectural language. It was the nonsensical and hysterical architectural exaggerations of 19th-century historicism that provoked, as a backlash, the wastelands of Modernism. These cycles of generational hysteria will eventually calm down by exhaustion and rivaling exacerbation. Historicist/Modernist education has produced human bombs that will only vanish when all traditional architectural cultures will have been raped and exploded by two centuries of terrorist attacks.

A city that is functionally and socially mixed, typologically and volumetrically well composed, in plan and silhouette and built along a geographically sensitive network, needs remarkably little architecture to become a beautiful and interesting place.

The marriage of organic geometry and vernacular architecture produces endearing aesthetic effects. However, the natural formal

70

minimalism of vernacular building is ill suited for highly regular and Euclidean geometry, parallel street frontages and uniform cornice heights! I live in a hill town that is essentially made up of naked walls, openings, tiled roofs and tile cornices; only a few doorways and the inside of the church display some architectural elaboration, and yet it is a blessed place. In my opinion, Classical (Euclidean) urban plans need an elaborate display of (Classical) architectural rhetoric in order to reach an acceptable degree of character, sense and life.

For larger cities and groups of cities, the full display of vernacular and Classical geometries, and their artful architectural dosage, is necessary. Overkill or poverty of expression, aesthetic exhaustion or boredom set the upper and lower limits. If they forego their means of control and articulation, cities go into a spin of gigantism; of horizontal or vertical scale breakages and even catastrophes. The hysterical visual violence of most metropolitan centers and deadly anemia of their surrounding sub-urban sprawl, don't seem to be understood yet for what they are, namely, outpourings of deranged human energies; voracious, violent, suicidal, unpredictable and uncontrollable. The vulgar priapism of these centers of activity is but an illusory escape from the suffocating embrace of the suburban matriarchy.

The daily global mobilization between unbearable extremes cultivates the need for ever more virtual forms of sociability, of escape and consolation, namely religion, drugs, etc.

**MC:** *Many cities are now host to diverse communities, diverse in terms of race, religion, economy and, perhaps most importantly, expectation. How important is the role of maintaining cultural continuity in the development of cities and how is this to be balanced with diversity?*

**LK:** Jared Diamond in "Guns, Germs and Steel: The Fates of Human Societies" explains why certain peoples and civilizations expand and conquer whilst other don't. The development of agriculture, language, architecture and cities are intimately linked. And yet it is as if the Christians and Muslims were the only conquerors or settlers to export their architecture to other continents. The Japanese didn't export their architecture to China, nor do the Chinese or Jewish quarters around the world display other than trivial detail of their own original architecture. German towns in Russia, Portuguese towns in Brazil or English towns in Virginia, Dutch towns in Java or South Africa were literal export products. Why the migrations of the Indian, Chinese or Africans around the world, whether voluntary or enforced, were not accompanied with a migration of their architectural and settlement patterns is still not satisfactorily explained.

I am struck by the fact that topography, local materials and climate, more than geographical proximity seem to characterize building and cities. Buildings in the Nepalese, Swiss or Basque mountains have more similarities amongst each other than they have to their neighboring lowlands architecture. Hill towns in the Atlas Mountains or those in Afghanistan have extraordinary similarities more due to geographic and climatological similarities than to those of religion. The development of modern concrete, of the lift and of air conditioning, more than any other inventions have temporarily confused the regional characteristics of traditional architecture and urbanism. I do not think that this development is a historically irreversible fatality. The historicization of traditional tectonics and urbanism was ideologically motivated. It is erroneous because of the fact that nature of traditional building and urbanism are technological and therefore universal. The expansion of the ecological imperatives and conscience will lead to an inevitable resurgence of traditional techniques and their dominance over Historicist/Modernist ideologies.

There is absolutely no reason why some Modernist ideas could not be integrated into the body of traditional architecture. The flat roof and the inclined roof, the curtain wall and the load-bearing wall, the vertical and the horizontal window, are not, as Modernists pretend, ideological opponents or contradictions, but different techniques of roofing, constructing, sealing and lighting buildings.

The nightmare scenarios for the future are ethnic sectarianism at one extreme, and leveling of cultural and geographical differences, on the other. The only certainty is that there will not be a single global architectural style. It is contrary to reason and ecology. Espousing traditional architecture and urbanism should not be an ideological but an intellectual decision, not an emotional but a rational intent. Polyglotism in architecture should be valued in the same way as polyglotism in speech. Rather than marking cities like animals mark their territories, traditional architects spearhead the revival of ecological conscience, of cultivating the spirit of place and leaving the spirit of the age where it belongs.

**MC:** *If the most concrete manifestation of cultural continuity is architecture, to what degree should architects use a traditional architectural language in city building?*

**LK:** Any form of non-Hermetic language, be it written, spoken, sculpted, danced or hand-gestured, is by nature traditional. Unlike spoken languages, traditional architecture and building are universally comprehensive and do not need translation to be understood. Even the forms and elements of artistically elaborate traditional architecture are of a tectonic, technical, fabricated, commonsensical nature. The philosophic error of Modernism was to oppose the idea of the "new" with the idea of the "traditional", to posit the flat and the sloped roof as irreconcilable contradictions; to want to replace the load-bearing wall with the curtain wall, to fight the column with the *piloti*, the vertical with the horizontal window, the multifariousness of regionally and climatically differentiated styles and materials with a unique international style of glass, concrete and steel exclusively. A de-ideologized building technology, be it high, medium or low tech, encompasses all building materials, natural or artificial, according to their specificity and in the long term it is their ecological price that will decide whether a building material, technique, language or type is traditional and therefore modern or obsolete and therefore "historical" and dated.

**MC:** *The Charter of the New Urbanism states: "Civic buildings and public gathering places require important sites to reinforce community identity and the culture of democracy. They deserve distinctive form, because their role is different from that of other buildings and places that constitute the fabric of the city." If cities derive much of their character from their public buildings and these buildings express a communal identity, how should architecture articulate this identity? What does the current fashion for the "stunt" architecture of Gehry, Hadid et al. in public architecture say about the contemporary role of public buildings?*

**LK:** Traditional architectures imitate traditional typologies of construction and organization. They are human artifices and inventions. "Stunt" architectures in general try to escape those patterns, but they are nevertheless and without exception of an imitative nature; their sources being often extra-architectural, rock formations, clouds, trees, road intersections, train collisions, innards, hills, factories, rocket-launch structures — you name it. There is no reason why the designs of Gehry, Hadid, Le Corbusier, Eisenman, could not become grammatical, urban, traditional, typological, tectonic; given the experience and will. So far their intentions are often more guided by a need for recognition than by credible technical, artistic or social visions. Meaningful architectural works, however, gain their value not merely within an art-historical chain of isolated artistic achievements, but as integral parts of a social, urban and architectural context. Modernism has so far merely achieved to replace, at an enormous ecological cost, established traditional languages with incomplete inventories of raw spare parts, assembled into ill-fitting and temporary geographic arrangements.

"Wow-buildings" and "stunt architectures" only make sense for "wow" and "stunt" occasions and building programs. Architectural acrobatics that can make sense for conceiving concert halls or cathedrals became meaningless when applied to residential, industrial or business architecture; this should be as evident as the use of tempi (lentissimo to prestissimo) or dynamics (pianissimo to fortissimo) in music. Architecture as a vehicle for transmitting a commonly understood meaning cannot play havoc with structure or space without defeating its own purpose.

Every organized society needs spaces for large groups of people and spaces for single persons; buildings for assembling or for isolating individuals, families, societies. Those form the basis for a meaningful architectural language, for the collective and the individual, the monumental and the domestic, the serious and the trivial, the joyful and the tragic. Traditional architectures of all cultures and climes have at their disposition a complete grammar and syntax. We can only ignore them at our own expense. We then roam punch drunk from architectural minimalism to architectural maximalism; are permanently torn between anorexia and bulimia; and condemn the environment to ever faster cycles of suicidal resource consumption.

*(*Note: this was originally a round-table discussion conducted by Traditional Building Magazine. Editor-in-Chief Michael Carey moderated a panel that included Andrés Duany, William H. Hudnut III, James Howard Kunstler, and Thomas Norman Rajkovich. The present condensation and edit makes it look like an interview, which is not the original format — Ed.)*

**Léon Krier** *is recognized today as one of the world's outstanding traditional architects and urbanists. He is the architect behind the Prince of Wales's new town of Poundbury in Dorset, England, and is acknowledged as the intellectual Godfather of the New Urbanism movement. Krier has received the Berlin Prize for Architecture, 1977, the Jefferson Memorial Gold Medal, 1985, the Chicago American Institute of Architects Award, 1987, the European Culture Prize, 1995, the Silver Medal of the Académie Française, 1997, the Driehaus Prize for Classical and Traditional Architecture, 2003, and the Athena Medal of the Congress for the New Urbanism, 2006.*

**Michael Carey** *is Editorial Director of Traditional Building Magazine.*

# 13. POLITICS, PHILOSOPHY, CRITICAL THEORY, AND HUMAN PERCEPTION

By Nikos A. Salingaros & Kenneth G. Masden II

*ArchNet-IJAR: International Journal of Architectural Research, Volume 2, Issue 1 (March 2008), pages 129-188. Reprinted for the Philadelphia Society Regional Meeting, Cincinnati, 8 October 2011. Reprinted by permission.*

As the architects of tomorrow, today's students must come to understand the role and responsibility of their profession as something intrinsically tied to human existence and the lived experience. A new suggested educational system provides a direct means to design adaptive environments, in response to growing needs of the marketplace (client demand). Nevertheless, most architectural institutions continue to propagate a curricular model that has sustained an image-based method and its peculiar ideology for decades. We can trace this support to early twentieth-century anti-traditional movements. Reform is impossible without addressing the system's long-forgotten ideological roots.

## Introduction

Evolutionary compulsion forces human beings to establish a system of relationships between the physical body and the human mind's mental perceptions, which enable us to experience the world and our existence. These relationships provide us with our sense of wellbeing, our sense of belonging, and our deeper sense of who we are. Through the physical and the visual aspects of human perception, the body managed humankind's earliest interactions with the world.

Evolution developed a neurological structure in humans by which they could negotiate the immediate conditions of their lives. Through the surrounding informational fields — physical and visual information embedded in the natural structure of the world — humans successfully evolved to construct artifacts for living. These creations range from jewelry, to furniture, to buildings, and ultimately to cities.

As the human mind continued to develop through the impulse of emotion, there came a point where humans were able to manufacture abstract ideas and thoughts, outside the physical reality that confronted them on a daily basis. The schism between the subject/object natures of perception permits the manufacture of an alternative reality. This mental capacity has been the protagonist of human thought and enquiry for millennia — leading to some of the greatest achievements of the human mind — at other times it led humankind towards the greatest atrocities imaginable. During the last century, architecture — as the formation of a world outside our bodies — has been consigned by contemporary doctrine to the intellectual creations of a purely subjective mind.

The informational fields that surround us are more important today than ever, given the dependency of students on image-based learning. Supplanting natural information by intellectual abstraction effectively removes the essential informational content needed for human engagement with the outside world, replacing it with blank walls.

Throughout the twentieth century, one of the important situational constructs that enabled architects to substitute images for what is real was their ability to use the written word to subsidize their informationally-poor structures. So began a long history of political and polemical texts operating as the philosophical surrogate for embedded knowledge, which was henceforth lost from the built world.

## "Critical Theory" and image-based learning

Architecture schools now rely heavily, if not exclusively, on loosely-construed philosophical postulates for educating their students. Schools proffer philosophical doctrines (we cannot call them theories) in the absence of intelligence-based design and direct human experience. The way philosophy is currently taught to architects tends to mix political ideology with idiosyncratic and subjective insights into society, and this muddled mess is presented as a theoretical basis for architectural and urban design. This practice is a terribly dangerous mix, as it gives students a perverted and erroneous, if not fraudulent basis for their profession. Students are normally unable to separate what is useful analysis from what is political rhetoric and so learn little or nothing about buildings and cities.

Certain authors on the political left provide a picture of what is wrong with aspects of contemporary society, offering useful critiques from outside the capitalist economic system. Nevertheless, their proposed solutions are the same unworkable utopian dreams that have in the past led to totalitarian states. One stream of philosophy running throughout contemporary architectural education goes back to the Frankfurt School, which introduced "Critical Theory" into philosophy. The essence of this 1930's movement was to apply extreme anti-traditional prejudices to the new industrial society of the post World-War-I era. The original Marxist authors proposed radical social change through revolution, technology, and the subjection of the individual to collective class structure. They declared tradition to be the enemy of progress, a position that of course included all architectural traditions. Historical notions of beauty were condemned, while art was to be produced henceforth though the negation of universal truths, inspired instead by contradiction, despair, and the shock of human suffering. Schools inherited this prejudiced approach to analyzing built form, in many writings that bear the epithet "critical". Such texts are not helpful in designing buildings but only in the formation of ideological tenets.

Independent of the written legacy of Critical Theory and the Frankfurt school, the post-war tradition in architecture and the arts has inherited the misdirected anger and desperation of 1930's European intellectuals. Those individuals were reacting against earlier class oppression while being threatened by the rise of Nazism. After the Second World War, those same intellectuals reacted to the horrors that had just been perpetrated by casting the blame onto traditional society and its humanistic architecture. These extremely powerful emotions survive in a visceral hatred of traditional architectural forms — an indignation that is transmitted to architecture students today through Pavlovian conditioning.

Even though the majority of architecture professors are not overtly political, and even less declared Marxists, architecture schools have been dominated by a philosophy that arose from the radical political left. Critical theory and its architectural derivatives (which represent ideology rather than theory) continue to dictate architectural texts. Students lack sufficient knowledge to recognize when fourth-generation derivative authors talk about architecture using hidden agendas about the supremacy of technology, class struggle, and abolishing traditional society. While this ideological objective is never made explicit, it colors supposedly theoretical expositions and situates itself in the values of students. After all these years, few people have caught onto the original deceit: while pretending to censure the aristocracy, this rhetoric in fact reviled all of popular vernacular architecture, to boost the personal careers of the Bauhaus members. Now the very same system is used to prop up an architectural elite.

## "Critical Regionalism" and intellectual submission

Critical Theory has had its most insidious effect on architecture with the spread of the doctrine known as "Critical Regionalism". Proponents of this self-contradictory ideology assert that vernacular tradition and culture are dead, and that henceforth, regional architecture must adapt to modernist uniformization. They proclaim that the patterns and practices from which a region's identity is derived are mere "nostalgia", and instead recommend the abstract aesthetics of international modernism. Any architectural expression, other than those possible within the restricted modernist aesthetic, is rejected.

Those writers' avowed intention is to create forms that do not belong to the vernacular form language. What results from this schizophrenic approach is not regional architecture in any sense, but a set of self-referential objects detached from their cultural roots, created and manipulated without regard to their regional context. (One occasionally sees an attempt at site-specific climatic adaptation, but nothing more).

Teachers thus use purely ideological arguments to validate a narrow set of design styles for students. That is as wrong as it is unsupported. It is only a means to further sustain a cult ideology that has dominated architectural education for the past several decades. The point is that good architecture and urbanism have nothing to do with political beliefs. Worst of all, teachers apply techniques learned from political ideologues to coerce students and other academics into intellectual submission. Such forms of censorship are typical of a system that considers itself above all others. It gives itself the authority to re-frame every member's worldview. Whenever evidence is ignored, and is substituted by the irrational, that creates dogma. This erroneous style of teaching has become solidly established in today's system.

One way to maintain the mystique of "architecture as an art" was to embrace ever more abstruse and incomprehensible texts, so as to shield the discipline's shaky intellectual core from outside scrutiny. This obsession (or defensive tactic) has led architecture to embrace the nihilistic and deconstructive philosophers. Having architecture students read Derridean and Deleuzean philosophical texts disorients them, breaking down their critical faculties. Such disorientation could in fact be deliberate: a necessary psychological preparation for imprinting stylistic preferences in their minds (This topic has been treated at length in our book *Anti-Architecture and Deconstruction*, 2008). Throwing the burden of teaching architects onto obscure philosophical texts enables architecture schools to endorse a very narrow set of design styles, embracing those currently in fashion.

## Philosophy informs architecture

The common justification given for studying philosophy is that architecture and urbanism are intimately tied to social phenomena, so that philosophy prepares a student to confront architectural problems.

This explanation is a subterfuge, however, operating more as a means to avoid teaching architecture to students directly. The modernist teaching method, wherein all useful derived knowledge is thrown out in the *tabula rasa* approach, cannot openly admit that architectural and urban knowledge ever existed. If it did, then someone would have to explain how over 2,000 years of knowledge was lost, discarded, or ignored during the modernists' 70-year reign. By diverting architecture students towards carefully selected philosophical authors, this action conveniently covers up the deliberate avoidance of any genuine, newly-derived or historically-relevant architectural theory.

So much of what now passes for "architectural theory" is therefore little more than doctrine. It conditions students to have absolute faith in a body of beliefs established in the absence of real-world criteria. Those beliefs set up the student's worldview as shaped by the dynamics of in-group affiliation: a cognitive filter that bends information to fit, and rejects information that does not fit.

Architectural education must in the future clearly separate architecture from politics, and also separate architecture from self-referential philosophy. Only teachers can train their students to do this. Both teachers and students can achieve this clarity of thought only after they understand the genuine theoretical basis of architecture, expressed in strictly architectural terms. Schools have a responsibility to teach a genuinely architectural basis for design.

Architecture students should ultimately study philosophy, but that is productive once they have formed a basis of what is really going on in architecture. And the philosophy they study has to be positive and humanistic. Many philosophers throughout history emphasize the necessity for human beings to connect to the universe, but architects hardly ever study those authors.

What we propose as *Intelligence-Based Design* has deep philosophical foundations. Humanly-adaptive architecture and urbanism arise out of a respect for humanity's higher meaning in an infinite universe. There exists a vast body of philosophical work connecting humanity both with nature and with the sublime. In his four-volume treatise *The Nature of Order* (2001-2005), Christopher Alexander establishes a genuine philosophical foundation for an adaptive architecture.

## A humanistic basis

Philosophers whose writings are essential for the sustainability of humankind try to understand otherwise puzzling human actions outside a strictly scientific framework. They help us to delineate good from bad in human activities. This historical notion of "morality" recurs throughout the traditional treatises on philosophy of the entire world. Numerous contemporary philosophers celebrate life and the sacredness of humanity.

Traditional religious texts are founded upon morality stories that help humanity to see beyond the limitations of human beings existing as animals or purely subjective beings. But none of this is ever incorporated into architectural teaching today — which still turns to the same peculiar handful of (Western) philosophers, relying upon them to justify "architecture for architecture's sake". Judging by how inhuman its forms are, the driving ideology is purely nihilistic, even as it serves global capital.

The separation between nihilism and humanism is total and uncompromising, however. We have to choose very carefully which philosophers, and which texts to offer students for their reading assignments. A school cannot abrogate its responsibility by teaching architecture as a set of self-serving beliefs.

In the twentieth century, architecture became a mass movement under the influence of leading architects who exploited specific philosophical texts to support their ideals and to promote themselves. Architecture detached itself from any higher order in human existence, turning away from both nature and from the sacred. It was the first time in human history that humans began to intentionally create unnatural structures that are uncomfortable to inhabit and to experience.

## Reference

• Nikos A. Salingaros (2008) *Anti-Architecture and Deconstruction*, 3rd Edition (Umbau-Verlag, Solingen).

*(\*Note: This essay is a section of the longer paper entitled "Intelligence-Based Design: A Sustainable Foundation for Worldwide Architectural Education", ArchNet-IJAR: International Journal of Architectural Research, Volume 2, Issue 1 (March 2008), pages 129-188. The same extract was reprinted in two parts with comments in Archiwatch (February 2009). Original paper is available from <http://zeta.math.utsa.edu/~yxk833/Intelligence-Based-IJAR.pdf>.)*

# 14. Lecture Notes, Fifth Week. Human Physiology and Evidence-Based Design

## Readings for the Fifth Week:

- Alexander, *The Phenomenon of Life*, Chapter 8, "The Mirror of the Self" & Chapter 9, "Beyond Descartes: A New Form of Scientific Observation".

- Mehaffy & Salingaros, "Evidence-Based Design", *Metropolis*, 14 November 2011.

Approaching architecture from the entirely new perspective of organized coherence — what Alexander calls wholeness — unifies many phenomena. The traditional distinctions between ornament and function, between buildings and ecology, between beauty and utilitarian structure are blurred. We can look for the "life" in artifacts and structures, which explains our experience of them.

Later in this course we are going to count features, and measure parameters that contribute to our impression of "life" in an object. These measures will show that the phenomenon of life is not idiosyncratic, but is, to a very large degree, shared among all people.

There is a problem with saying that we "like" something. This is not the same as the perceived degree of life. After all, even the most monstrous, most inhuman building was liked sufficiently by both its architect and the client who commissioned it. We also know that the trillion-dollar advertising industry exists principally to manipulate our opinion of what we like.

The perception of "life" in objects comes instead from a deep connection established between the observer or user, and the object. It comes from a physiological, intuitive interdependence, which we can choose to ignore but probably cannot change.

Alexander lists some characteristics of this emotional connection to artifacts and structures:

(1) We feel a sense of nourishment from them.

(2) If we participate in actually making them, we also feel this sense of nourishment.

(3) When we can identify this connection and distinguish it from media-influenced liking, then we find that we agree with many other people.

(4) This is not merely an aesthetic judgment, but something that overlaps with deeper aspects of culture and life.

(5) The connection can be checked empirically, and is not a simple matter of opinion.

Judging the relative degree of positive connection we experience personally between ourselves and either of two objects is easy. It relies upon a psychological trick to give us the result. The trick forces our brain to compute the organized complexity of the two objects in a comparative, though not absolute, manner.

Alexander's "mirror of the self" test asks which of two objects that I experience provides a better picture of myself. We have to imagine all of our personality, our strengths and weaknesses, our humanity, our emotions, our potential, and our life experiences as somehow encoded in the structure of these two objects. Then, which of the two objects is a more faithful representation of my self?

Alexander found that more than 80% of persons choose the one object from the pair presented that also has the higher degree of life, as computed by other objective measures. Therefore, we could dispense with any of those calculations and just ask this single question about mirroring our self. The correlation is high enough to make it a very useful — though not infallible — test.

This test succeeds in drawing us away from preferences and opinions that we have learned from the outside, but which do not necessarily correspond to what arises deeply from the inside of our being. It cuts through idiosyncratic and possibly biased ideas about beauty to draw from us what we honestly connect to.

It is regrettably true that our taste has been manipulated, so as to manufacture out of us a perfect consumer of fashion and industrial goods. Using the "mirror of the self" test repeatedly not only makes us more proficient in its application, but also helps to liberate us from opinion, images, and ideology. It makes us more astute in perceiving living structure.

Let us turn the topic around and inquire how, in a world that is already in touch with living structure through culture and education, people could be disconnected from their feelings. How does one deny an intuitive talent for recognizing "life" and make humans first ignore it, then forget it entirely? The method is to distract our attention, and use false authority to keep us from re-building the vital connections and cognitive maps.

There exist two totally distinct conceptions of a shared experience of the world. The first occurs as we use our perceptual systems to form an honest and direct worldview. Since our biology is shared with other humans, our experiences are also shared to a large extent. The second scenario is when an entire population buys into a false worldview. In that case, what is shared is not truthful, but exists only as an image.

If we are indeed caught inside an unreal world, reinforced because it is shared with others, these tools can help us to break out. A different way of describing the "mirror of the self" test is to feel how an object or specific environment affects out humanity. Ask yourself: "is my own sense of humanity increasing or decreasing by being exposed to this particular structure?" Here we can forget our mechanical civilization and use only our intuition about our inner emotional states.

The "mirror of the self" test picks out what reminds us of nature, such as natural scaling hierarchies, the organized complexity of natural materials, and other geometrical features that make an object feel more "alive". When we connect to an environment because we feel part of it, and comfortable in it, we can perform our lives and functions with more pleasure and less stress. This sense of wellbeing does not register consciously.

Often, we experience a high degree of life from objects and buildings with imperfections — semi-ruined buildings, antique artifacts with damaged parts, etc. That does not diminish their appeal. Tourists travel a long way to see and experience ruins, and collectors buy antique carpets with holes in them.

Using the "mirror of the self" test gives us a key tool for implementing evidence-based design. There are two aspects to this methodology. The first one was derived in a medical setting, and measures the effects of built structures and environments upon human health. It is not difficult to compare alternative design choices according to their healing potential — hard data of patients healing faster in specific environments. Beginning with hospital design, evidence-based design is now applied to other, more general settings.

Evidence-based design is now fast becoming a standard tool used in school design. See Peter C. Lippman: *"Evidence-Based Design of Elementary and Secondary Schools"*, 2010. And yet, its current application, while laudable, is missing the other key components necessary for adaptive design. Those are: Biophilia, Intelligence in the environment (two topics discussed in this book), and Pattern Language. All of these have to work together to give optimal design results.

Evidence-based design permits an architect to evaluate a design, and variations of that design, to see if they contribute to human wellbeing. This makes possible informed choices that push and guide a design towards a more adaptive final form. We know the result is going to be more adaptive since we check each intermediate stage of an evolving design.

The second aspect of evidence-based design is the use of feedback. In practical terms, adaptive design proceeds by iterations, where each step is checked against the evidence of increasing or decreasing wellbeing. The process does not use a formula, nor does it conform to any abstract rules or images. A design adapts through recursions, with physiological indicators checking every step in the process.

Clearly, this method works best when we make the design process an evolutionary one, with many adjustable steps. It doesn't work at all in cases where the architect or designer reaches a solution in one step. Where is the adaptation there? There is none.

Neither can evidence-based design work in an architectural practice where designs conform to untested prototypes. Why are some, now standard, building typologies copied over and over, but are never tested for evidence of their adaptation? It doesn't occur to those architects to undertake medical response experiments just to make sure that what they are doing is not making people ill. Those untested environments may in fact be stressful or otherwise harmful to their users. The problem is that architects are not at present trained to measure physiological indicators.

Unhealthy designs have something in common: they conform to some *a priori* image or abstract conception of what a building ought to look like. Someone provided the image initially, and everyone else happily copies that image without reflective thought. This visual iconic model is so authoritative as to be placed above the need for evidence. Indeed, if the evidence comes in negative, the original model is supported with religious zeal, while the evidence itself is dismissed. Architects cannot accept failures, being too proud to admit they made a mistake.

The "mirror of the self" test can help reverse this unfortunate practice. Any architecture student or common person can be trained to use it. There is thus no need to be wired up to physiological indicators that would measure body stress levels. Those detect a failed design unambiguously. Anybody can use the test to distinguish between two environments, one of which is more or less healing.

Had people consistently applied the "mirror of the self" test, we would probably have avoided some of the inhuman environments built over the past several decades. One such typology is the extremely long apartment block, which houses thousands of people in a box of about eight stories. From the prototype built by the Nazis on the island of Rügen, Germany, to the Pruitt-Igoe housing complex in St. Louis, to the Corviale complex in Rome, all have been failures.

Such examples of typologies based on low design complexity cannot adapt to human use and sensibilities. Their architects forgot about people, or were well-meaning but didn't know what they were doing. Design became an intellectual exercise in pure form — unfortunately, builders adopted this typology because it is cheap to build. The typology becomes money-driven.

Simplistic forms may ignore people's humanity, yet are loved by today's architects who value them on aesthetic grounds. But formal purity and simplicity have no meaning for the users. Ordinary people are not caught up in architects' intellectual games. By contrast, we see an incredible degree of organized complexity when people build for themselves, as in informal settlements, which are perhaps less than optimally organized. Those represent the opposite of formal design.

The problem boils down to critics judging buildings from their image, and not from direct personal experience. Critics on the whole don't care if things work, or if they really fit. Critics also depend upon famous architects, and on the major engineering firms those work with, and thus never dare to criticize their work. Architects designing strictly for the admiration of other architects, and critics being dishonest in their duty results in a profession that is unlikely to break out of a vicious circle of irresponsible self-validation.

So far during the 20th and now the 21st centuries, the seductive power of iconic images has overridden all other considerations. Rigid geometrical typologies are applied unthinkingly. Even worse, bad typologies are used as the basis for architectural innovation, but the new shapes unfortunately carry over all the worst characteristics of the parent. Evidence-based design and the "mirror of the self" test can help us to get free from this unproductive practice.

# 15. Frontiers of Design Science: "Evidence-Based Design"

*By Michael W. Mehaffy and Nikos A. Salingaros*

*Metropolis, 14 November 2011. Reprinted by permission.*

There's a quiet, but important, revolution going on in environmental design today. It started in hospitals, of all places.

Medical science has long used an "evidence-based" methodology. It's a trial-and-error process that goes through an evolutionary cycle: the doctor tries something, evaluates it, then goes on to use what works. In this way medicine has developed after millennia of experimentation with cures, interventions, herbal remedies, etc.; even today, its application is heuristic. Your doctor might give you a small dose of something, and then if you feel better, will give you more. If you feel worse, stop taking it! Doctors study many patients and their reactions to treatments, and use the collective evidence to modify medicines and procedures, and improve them. Based on this accrued knowledge we can successfully treat diseases today that were once thought to be inevitable afflictions.

Over the years, the medical profession has taken an increasing interest in the design of hospitals, because it has become evident that the patients' health had a lot to do with the design of the spaces. Did infectious diseases spread more rapidly when patients shared rooms? (Yes, they did.) Were certain kinds of surfaces better or worse at preventing the spread of germs? (Yes.) Did patients do better when their rooms had particular kinds of designs that reduced stress? (Yes again.) These observations and many others have become the subject of "evidence-based design" — design that uses the evidentiary methods of medicine.

Gradually doctors as well as environmental designers began asking the same kinds of questions about the larger urban environment. After all, it did no good to treat a patient at the hospital if they went right back out and got sick again. So epidemiologists like Dr. Howard Frumkin and Dr. Richard Jackson began to look at evidence of, for example, how urban environments could promote walking and exercise, and how nature influences health and wellbeing.

*Figure One. Researchers are documenting evidence of the consequences of urban design choices on human health, resource depletion and other worrisome factors — a particularly urgent need as these models proliferate around the world. Photo: David Evers.*

Others, like Dr. Roger Ulrich, investigated how environments of all kinds affected wellbeing in other ways, including the (habitually dismissed) health implications of aesthetic qualities. They made an extraordinary discovery: the characteristics of nature, as observed in plants, trees, water, as well as pleasant views, had measurably positive effects on patients' recovery, stress levels, and physiological wellbeing. (We will have more to say about this extraordinary topic of Biophilia in another paper.)

These discoveries have fed the growth of a new, "evidence-based", approach to design, which anchors human needs within the built environment. Yet many designers still don't appreciate it. One key point to understand is that evidence-based design is not a simple formulaic kind of process — here is Fact X, and it allows me to pop out Design Y. It isn't like that at all, any more than medicine could be that simplistic. Rather, the act of design is more like a process of *adaptive computation.*

Design computations employ a sequence of steps: trial-and-error observations of how a human being interacts with his/her specific environment, each time enhancing that interaction to benefit the specific task to be performed and situating that person optimally in the immediate built environment, like an urban plaza, a building's entrance, a computer screen, to something as small as a cabinet handle.

Technically speaking, the type of environmental computation we use for design is not at all like computation using a formula, but more like approximation by recursion: keep computing and checking until the desired result emerges. (This kind of recursive process is known as an *algorithm*, a sequence of mathematical steps that lead towards the solution.) Using a formula could give a result in only one step — but that's not a solution that is likely to achieve a successfully adaptive design.

*Figure Two. Steve Jobs shows off the MacBook Air, a product of relentless evolutionary iterations. Photo: Matthew Yohe.*

A design has to start with some initial conditions, and then adapt to the boundary conditions — the conditions it encounters as it evolves. This can only happen through recursion, which is how our design achieves adaptive evolution and a much better "fit" with the problem. We might have a very good intuition of what the design has to embody — Steve Jobs, for instance, was famous for his intuition of the final qualities a design needed — but then large teams of people had to refine that initial vision and bring iterations to him to evaluate. He was setting the initial conditions (what he wanted the devices to be able to do for people), as they were adapting to the boundary conditions.

Design computations increase the adaptation of the system towards human wellbeing, as checked by documented evidence. The goal is not to design something rigidly specific (i.e. as laid down in a blueprint prepared in someone's office); the project brief and specifications are merely constraints. For this reason, the exact final product is incompletely known at the beginning of the computation; only certain of its important *qualities* are decided beforehand, and attaining them drives the design to completion. If the product is completely known at the beginning, there can be no adaptation. It is likely to fail on human terms.

This, in a nutshell, is the subject of evidence-based design. We want evidence for all these things — information about whether we are on track, or have strayed, and how to get back. We want evidence of the approaches that are most likely to work. And we want evidence of the design configurations that have been used in the past, that have perhaps resulted from the work of other people collaborating to solve similar problems. In this way, we can build up more useful knowledge about the most likely solutions that will work again — so-called "collective intelligence".

Unfortunately, our world is full of designs that try to reduce this process to a formula, or a template — and they are, quite simply, bad designs. However much glittery imagery or high art is layered over them, they fail at the essential job they are supposed to do for human beings. From the point of view of the "fitness" to the problems they are supposed to solve, we say they are "maladapted". Those simplistic designs may try to hide these flaws with eye-catching imagery or camouflage them with striking (yet superficial) ideas — but they are still failures. And often these failures can be catastrophic.

In fact, bad designs often have something in common — they proceed from a grand theory or an ideology about what the design should be. This is extremely dangerous, because the process becomes immune to evidence. If you are working solely from the text of an idea, you can always add a new bit of text to fit whatever happens. Thus, if Pruitt-Igoe (an infamous social housing "project" in St. Louis) failed as a model of Le Corbusier's "Towers in the Park", it must have been because it was not faithful enough to the "master's vision". Next time it's guaranteed to work, if only our heart is pure enough!

*Figure Three. Pruitt-Igoe social housing complex, St. Louis, Missouri was built 1953-1956, by architect Minoru Yamasaki, demolished 1972-1976. Image courtesy Finnbar5000.*

It is often useful to define an idea by also mentioning its opposite. Here, evidence-based design contrasts sharply to the application of a ready-made template that has not been adaptively computed. Why are such templates adopted by society, and then stubbornly hung onto against all the evidence? Going back to historical medicine, treatments that consistently killed patients sometimes survived a very long time before they were abandoned. Eventually, however, the evidence caught up. But this has been slow to happen with architecture.

*Figure Four. The Prora building on the island of Rügen, Germany was built, 1936-1939, by Clemens Klotz, one of Adolf Hitler's architects. Now largely abandoned. Image courtesy of Giorgio Muratore, Archiwatch.*

For example, five days after the government dynamited Pruitt-Igoe because it proved to be a colossal failure, the authorities in Rome decided to build the very similar "Corviale" social housing complex. Why did they not take a cautionary lesson from such a conspicuous disaster? Arguably, the iconic power of the prototype "Colossus of Prora", built by the Nazis on the island of Rügen, Germany was too seductive. Even now, when schemes for demolishing the Corviale and replacing it with human-scale buildings were presented, Roman architectural academics frantically tried to preserve the Corviale as a classified architectural "monument". The power of iconic images overwhelmed even the *consideration* of evidence of what actually worked for human beings.

*Figure Five. A sad example of ideological, not evidence-based, design is the Corviale social housing complex in Rome, built 1975-1982 by architect Mario Fiorentino with others. In the face of massive evidence of its damage to human lives, defenders insisted the project was sound, but "just wasn't implemented correctly". Image: G. Parise, courtesy of Ateneo Federato Spazio e Società.*

To get past this domination of superficial, image-based design, our trial-and-error design method requires one crucial feature — a testable hypothesis that can be disproven. This is the essence of the "scientific method", and it's fundamentally different from the *ex cathedra* dogmatism that self-justifies much architectural design. For Steve Jobs, the testable hypothesis was something like "this design will be delightfully easy to use, and it will be beautiful in this and other ways." He was famous for telling his designers: It's not just the look and feel. It's how it works. "In most people's vocabularies, design means veneer", he told *Fortune* Magazine. "But to me, nothing could be further from the meaning of design. Design is the fundamental soul of a man-made creation that ends up expressing itself in successive outer layers of the product or service." All of those layers must be seamlessly integrated into one elegantly adaptive expression — the result of relentless evolutionary refinements.

A helpful lesson of evidence-based design here — one that most computer folks have not yet come to terms with — is that we are not finished with our computations just because the "product" has been delivered. The environment continues to be transformed, in ways that we could not have possibly foreseen. The boundary conditions continue to change. So, for example, a few cars might seem like a good idea, but a wholly auto-dependent city turns out to be a very bad idea. We need new adaptations to transform the whole into something more adaptive. This is what the evidence shows us how to do — if we will let it.

But if we don't, we will have no way to arrest a surging tide of maladapted, failing design today, design that hides behind distracting razzle-dazzle decorations, papering over an unsustainable, failing civilization.

**Michael Mehaffy** *is an urbanist and critical thinker in complexity and the built environment. He is a practicing planner and builder, and is known for his many projects as well as his writings. He has been a close associate of the architect and software pioneer Christopher Alexander. Currently he is a Sir David Anderson Fellow at the University of Strathclyde in Glasgow, a Visiting Faculty Associate at Arizona State University; a Research Associate with the Center for Environmental Structure, Chris Alexander's research center founded in 1967; and a strategic consultant on international projects, currently in Europe, North America and South America. He was Director of Education, The Prince's Foundation, London, from 2003-2005.*

# 16. Lecture Notes, Sixth Week. Biophilia: Our Evolved Kinship to Biological Forms

## Readings for the Sixth Week:

- Alexander, *The Phenomenon of Life*, Chapter 10, "The Impact of Living Structure on Human Life".

- Mehaffy & Salingaros, "Biophilia", *Metropolis*, 29 November 2011.

- Salingaros & Masden, extract from "Neuroscience, the Natural Environment, and Building Design", which is Chapter 5 of *Biophilic Design: The Theory, Science and Practice of Bringing Buildings to Life*, edited by Stephen R. Kellert, Judith Heerwagen & Martin Mador (John Wiley, New York, 2008).

The organized complexity in artifacts and buildings, as we have described it, leads to a positive response from users. This is the perception of "life" from certain structures and places in the built environment. The physical structure of the world has a massive effect on human beings. A crucial task of architectural theory is to explain and predict the impact that living structure — or its absence — has on us.

It all resides in the geometry. A certain class of configurations generate stress in the user. Another class of configurations, those we perceive as possessing life, do not generate stress, and moreover, release us to feel positive feelings. In the second instance, we are freer to experience a multitude of healing effects, precisely because we are not dragged down by environmental stress.

Our goal, therefore, is to discover the precise qualities that a healthy environment possesses, and which make you feel free. This is an environment in which no energy is automatically spent in conflict with stress-producing configurations. Alexander's "pattern language" is such a system: each Pattern is the solution to resolving some conflict in the environment.

As long as a configuration is wrong, it continues to generate stress. No amount of superficial "dressing up" will resolve the basic conflicts. This is why my group of friends in Italy and I argue that any money spent on "cleaning up" the Corviale housing complex is wasted. Painting its walls, or creating a "contemporary sculpture garden" on its grounds will not fix it. Only by changing its monolithic geometry could the problems experienced by its residents be solved, but that is precisely what the modernist Italian architectural establishment is fixated on protecting.

What are the precise geometrical qualities of an environment that endow it with healing qualities, so that in such an environment we feel liberated to live our lives to their full potential? We already have the "mirror of the self" test, which is very useful in comparing alternatives, but does not answer this question.

The first step to discovering the geometric qualities we are looking for is to examine natural environments. This brings us to the effect of Biophilia: the kinship we human beings feel with other biological entities. The biophilic effect promotes mental wellbeing and also helps in physiological healing and recovery. The positive effects of biophilia are clinically documented.

A view from a hospital bed onto a natural scene is found to decrease recovery time and to decrease the level of painkillers required. This example of Biophilia at work elevates the traditional valuation of natural environments from "pleasant places to be in" to the more important "healing places". Indeed, traditional cultures do associate natural environments with healing far more than we do in the contemporary West. And yet, using biophilia in healthcare drastically improves the economics of healing patients, which is what our system supposedly prioritizes.

It makes sense that we feel most comfortable in environments similar to those in which we evolved, and, reciprocally, feel stressed in environments with alien qualities. Our neuro-physiological system was developed precisely to deal with those ancestral natural environments: natural light, fresh air, savannah, open plains, bushes and trees, visual access to water, etc. Our body has an extremely sophisticated ability to detect environments that are good for us.

Alexander, myself, and our students have gone further, to argue that the biophilic effect is not some mysterious vitalistic property of biologically living organisms, but rather an effect due to their geometry. Therefore, it follows that we can approximate the biophilic effect from the right inanimate structures. Much of traditional art and architecture embodies biophilic qualities, intuitively sought after by their makers.

The biophilia hypothesis thus turns traditional architecture on its head: we did not build only for utilitarian purposes, but to give ourselves a form of continual nourishment from the result. In brief, we built structures that made us feel good and that healed us. This tradition stopped sometime in the 20th century. We chose not to receive nourishing feedback from the environment such as all of our ancestors had enjoyed.

Direct biophilic nourishment comes from close contact with plants, animals, natural light, and the texture of natural materials. In artificial environments, human beings use a variety of design tools to gain a similar effect. We shape our living spaces according to very specific geometries, and use colors, ornamentation, and patterns to obtain similar environmental nourishment. This process is not a surface imitation of nature, but rather the generation of natural geometry.

Scientists are beginning to document how environmental factors, including information coming from the environment, affect our physiological wellbeing. It appears that geometrical features found in traditional architectures, such as ornamentation, colors, and fractal structures elicit a positive reaction from our neurophysiology. And this reaction is built into our organism.

My former student Yannick Joye is discovering that fractals and complex organized patterns responsible for the biophilic affect are somehow built into our cognitive system. Our reaction is emotional and visceral rather than intellectual. Architects can offer all the intellectual arguments they want, favoring minimalist or high-tech design, but those are not going to affect the way we react physically to forms and environments.

Applying biophilia to design implies the intimate merging of natural with artificial structures. In practical terms, this means building with meandering complex boundaries that interweave the buildings and natural growth. Plants incorporated into environments will be part of complex, not monofunctional green ecosystems. It also implies emphasizing the intimate human scales rather than only the large scale.

Biophilia also requires the partial replacement of industrial materials with natural materials, and the re-introduction of ornament using industrial materials. This latter practice was very widespread in the late 19th – early 20th centuries, but soon stopped. From a certain point onwards, industrial materials were used exclusively in a fetishistic manner, to communicate a severe industrial "look".

Architecture since the early modernism of the beginning of the 20th century has been focused on abstract, formal notions about space, forms, and materials. Human physiological and psychological responses played no part in this thinking, and the same approach continues today. While some architects have recently re-discovered the need for plants and nature, the biophilic connection uniting structures with humans and with nature is still not obvious to the profession as a whole.

As a world based upon impersonal images substituted for the real world of emotions, two distinct but related visions shaped our built environment. First came the mental association of industrial polished metal, porcelain, plate glass, and plastic surfaces with an antiseptic environment. This occurred despite the fact that the "hospital look" is not necessarily cleaner or more germ-free than a more "messy" old-fashioned environment built using natural materials.

Second, architects for some reason latched onto the slogan "honest tectonic expression" to imply moral superiority, when this is only another fetish with industrial materials. There is no "morality" in a physical structure. As a result, however, we are now surrounded with so-called "honest" surfaces that are not merely unconcerned with biophilia, but which deliberately strive to prevent any biophilic effect. Brutalist concrete surfaces are unnatural and hostile. If there is a moral judgment to be drawn here, it is that those architects are acting against human nature. One would think that, by letting go of personal ego and focusing on the mental and physical wellbeing of the user, an architect stops defending alien forms and becomes a better person ethically.

The empirical evidence gathered around biophilia helps to explain the "mirror of the self" test, which uses our body as a sensor of stresses in the environment. Now we understand the source of those stresses as due to departures from a very specific geometry that is akin to the complex geometry of natural structures. 20th and 21st century architects have deliberately celebrated forms and surfaces that look industrial because they contrast with natural forms, so the built environment generates stress.

More specifically, the minimalist environments often favored in styles with an industrial appearance are linked to signals of alarm in our body. Colorless, drab, and featureless surfaces and spaces reproduce clinical symptoms of diseases and pathologies of the eye-brain system (more on that in Week 12). Naturally, when the environment gives us those same signals, our body believes it is breaking down, and reacts with stress.

The interesting research of Judith Heerwagen revealed that zoo animals kept in minimalist environments exhibited neurotic, aberrant, and antisocial behaviors. Returning them to a more stimulating and naturalistic environment resulted in more normal and healthier behavior patterns. Some of the award-winning zoos built in a modernist style in the 20th century proved to be terrible for their residents, and finally, zookeepers were allowed to shape the animals' environments by introducing complexity.

Like zoo animals, children are also affected by their habitat, but cannot articulate the reasons why. The suppression of biophilic nourishment during our children's development has dramatically negative effects. The necessity of informational stimulation during a child's growth can no longer be questioned. We can use laboratory animal studies to draw conclusions by extension. Young animals showed up to a 20% increase in brain size and intelligence when raised in information-rich environments (we delve into this in Week 12). If we are interested in continuing the human race and optimizing our children's intelligence, we need to pay careful attention to these effects.

One final point questions the value of tests where subjects were asked for their preferences of minimalist versus organized complex environments. Many such surveys were conducted with only a moderate preference for the latter, or with widely divergent results that made the study inconclusive. Nevertheless, more recent laboratory experiments using body monitors showed dramatic preferences for organized complexity. The subjects did not express any marked preference when asked; yet their body did. Physiological responses to our environment are thus shown to be innate, and, moreover, to be largely decoupled from personal preferences. What we "like" has nothing to do with what is good for us.

As argued earlier, our likes and dislikes are conditioned by learning, media influence, preconceptions, and crowd psychology (where we are forced to agree with the majority in order to avoid cognitive dissonance). What we think with our mind is not what we physically feel. A building can look interesting but not agree with what is felt while experiencing it. People will not listen to their own body, if that prevents them from "fitting in" a social position.

Another complicating factor is human nature itself, which seeks thrills from experiences that are close to damaging. We human beings have always been fascinated by things that scare us, precisely because those generate distress — the ensuing adrenalin rush creates an emotional "high". The experience has to be carefully balanced so we feel in danger and safe at the same time. For this reason, people watch horror films, go on dizzying amusement-park rides, visit the "Haunted House", practice extreme sports, race cars, and go skydiving. Japanese businessmen eat Sushi made from the almost poisonous flesh of the blowfish, and so on. Architecture that stresses our body does attract us for exactly the same reason. But obviously, such transgressive excitement is not healing.

# 17. BIOPHILIA

*By Michael W. Mehaffy and Nikos A. Salingaros*

*Metropolis, 29 November 2011. Reprinted by permission.*

In 1984, the environmental psychologist Roger Ulrich made a startling discovery. In studying hospital patients recovering from surgery, he found that one factor alone accounted for significant differences in post-operative complications, recovery times, and need for painkillers. It was the view from their windows!

Half the patients had a view out to beautiful nature scenes. The other half saw a blank wall. This was an astonishing result — the mere quality of aesthetic experience had a measurable impact on the patients' health and wellbeing. Moreover — and this certainly caught the attention of hard-nosed economists — because the patients stayed less time, used fewer drugs and had fewer complications, their stay in the hospital actually *cost* less.

*Figure 1. Experiments by Roger Ulrich showed that a simple view out to a natural scene conveyed a range of measurable health benefits to recovering patients.*

Ulrich's study began a wave of research into an area known as *biophilia* — the apparent instinctive preference we have for certain natural geometries, forms, and characteristics within our environments. Over time, many more studies have been done showing that when the characteristics of natural environments are present, human beings tend to feel calmer, more at ease, more comfortable, less stressed — and, most astounding, their health can actually improve.

Most of us know the feeling of oppression that comes from a windowless room with ugly blank walls. We all know the delight of entering a sun-filled space, perhaps with green plants and water. We surely have experienced special places that rejuvenated us, made us feel that we were healing just by being there. Yet what these studies showed was that such experiences are not merely more or less pleasurable, as had been thought. They play a fundamental role in our wellbeing, even if it's below the level of our conscious awareness. They can actually improve our health — or their negative counterpart can damage our health.

The implications are potentially earth-shattering: aesthetic design choices are not just a matter of the designer's artistic expression, for users to enjoy or not enjoy — together with other factors, *they can improve, or damage, the health of users*. If this is true, it means that designers have a level of responsibility for the health of users that is much greater than is commonly realized.

What mechanism could explain such an effect? One of the main proponents of the term biophilia, the noted biologist Edward O. Wilson, hypothesizes that we human beings have spent most of our evolutionary history in natural environments, and we have evolved to find good (i.e. healthy) environments pleasurable. Aesthetics, in this view that is increasingly accepted by scientists, is not some arbitrary experience, but our sophisticated biological ability to detect what is likely to be good for us. There's a sound reason why the ripe tomato, glistening with dewdrops, looks beautiful to us, and the rotten meat looks ugly and disgusting.

We are drawn biologically to certain environments: the aesthetic characteristics of those places tend to reinforce our health, by reducing our stress, and in the case of outdoor spaces, by encouraging us to be more active. A number of studies have shown that biophilic characteristics tend to encourage more walking and other outdoor activity. The health benefits of a walk in the countryside are part of almost every human culture, so there must be something to it.

There are other surprising benefits. For example, researcher Koen Steemers and colleagues at Cambridge University found that the presence of vegetation increases thermal comfort. In principle, that means that simply by adding plants, it could be possible to raise or lower the thermostat and still maintain perceived comfort, while significantly reducing energy loads. This could be a big boost for sustainable building design.

Another way of understanding the importance of biophilia is as a transfer of comprehensible environmental information through a neurological process. Our neural system evolved in response to external stimuli such as the information fields present in the natural environment. We instinctively crave physical and biological connection to the world, and we do so through the mental processes that have evolved over hundreds of thousands of years of life within nature.

*Figure 2. Christopher Alexander's Fresno Market, California — a place of people, foods, vegetation, and natural tile and wood frameworks.*

As organisms, we need to make sense of our environment and its beneficial qualities, and so we are equipped with neurological systems that are extraordinarily good at doing precisely that. These systems are capable of detecting extremely subtle symmetries, variations in color, and states of order or decay. When we perceive this complex order, we often find it intensely pleasurable. But when we encounter disorder, monotony, or confusion, we can actually become queasy and very ill at ease. For example, when we are unable to detect the horizon in a way that agrees with the balance systems in our inner ears, we get motion sickness, and we can become physically ill.

Leaders of the field have begun to identify and classify the various biophilic factors, spanning a comprehensive range. Stephen Kellert has worked with Wilson to lay out a detailed range of the varied biophilic influences in design. The book *Biophilic Design* edited by Kellert, J. Heerwagen, and M. Mador (2008) collects various results coming from different directions, all of which support the Biophilia hypothesis in the specific context of designing buildings and environments. In our own chapter of that book (written with Kenneth Masden) we argue for a biophilic basis for traditional art, architecture, and urbanism. We postulate that humankind has built throughout the ages just as much to give ourselves — the users — nourishment from the built geometry, as for any other more practical reason (such as shelter or a place to accomplish some specific task).

*Figure 3. The British Museum with its fractal hierarchies and sculptured pediment is just as biophilic as the garden in front. The two elements — built structure and natural structure — reinforce each other to create a coherent, complex, and healing environment.*

The Biophilia hypothesis, then, turns architecture and urban design on its head — construction is not fundamentally driven by utilitarianism but is instead a contributing factor for our continued health. We must continue to receive the positive, nourishing feedback from the natural environment that our distant ancestors enjoyed, now using materials to build an artificial environment. Yet this is possible only if the structures themselves have an essential complex geometry that provides positive biophilic nourishment.

Note that this "nourishment" is not simply a drape of green aesthetics, or, say, fake windows made of photographs. Research shows that those tricks quickly cease to have any biophilic effect. Rather, it seems we crave a deep and *genuine* aesthetic/biological connection to the natural context of our world. To be effective, the structures of our designs have to elucidate this *real* structure — not put on a kind of aesthetic costume.

*Figure 4. Many of the best-loved and well-used public spaces, like this one in Oslo, contain splendid examples of biophilia, including vegetation, water, and natural forms and materials.*

People's instinctive craving for environmental nourishment coming from information drives them to shape their living spaces, paint their walls in lively colors and cover them with visual patterns and representational scenes, and ornament their utensils. These artificial structures complement, and do not replace, the biophilic nourishment derived from close contact with plants, animals, sunlight, and the texture of natural materials.

But when we conduct research into the evidence for biophilic properties in our environment, we find something striking: much of post World-War II design is of two types — either (*i*) explicitly anti-biophilic (e.g. brutalist concrete surfaces with the grayness of death and devoid of fractal structure, glass curtain walls, shiny metal surfaces, etc.); or (*ii*) it has a weakly biophilic aesthetic veneer, merely draped over mechanical production buildings (think of fake wood grain, "cultured" stone, etc.). Where the aesthetics tries to be more genuine, expressing its true mechanical roots, it typically becomes anti-biophilic. In fact, disturbing evidence is now emerging that many designs are subtly degrading the quality of life of their users at best, and actually making them ill at worst. What is going on?

Those designs often emphasize the conscious experience of dramatic, attention-getting characteristics, at the expense of the intense and geometrically complex "background" characteristics that shape the important daily experiences of residents and users. The attention-getting features are those of industrial technology and tectonics, which up until recently has been geometrically primitive: simple lines, planes, cubes, and cylinders, structured into dramatic, attention-getting compositions. These geometries are generally very different from the complex organic forms of nature, and of biophilia.

In fact, many iconic buildings misuse biophilic surfaces such as marble and travertine limestone to compensate for their lack of spatial coherence, scaling hierarchy, and enclosure. But biophilia doesn't seem to work that way — while the photos may look attractive, the emotional experience is at best mixed, or negative. A truly biophilic building, on the other hand, can employ modest, inexpensive materials in a way so as to create beneficial ordered complexity, as we consistently find throughout vernacular buildings worldwide.

Biophilic environments succeed only to the extent that they contain a sense of intimacy and communion. "It's nice to see but even better to touch" — as lovers well know. For this reason, the vast monotonous lawns of suburbia are only minimally effective: better than concrete, yes, but again, only pieces of inaccessible visual green at a distance. They may just as well be outdoor green carpets.

Let us not underestimate the radical but unnoticed societal shift, from experiencing our environment intimately yet subconsciously, to requiring a constant conscious effort to navigate it while keeping an intellectual and physical distance. It now appears this is carrying a tremendous if unrecognized cost to the quality of life. Almost everything we built and used in traditional societies and in our own past just "felt good". And it made us wish to touch it.

*Figure 5. Monotonous repetition is anti-biophilic. Nature never produces empty repeating modules on a macroscopic scale. Boston City Hall. Image: Kjetil Ree.*

Nature almost never repeats identical modules that have a mechanical geometry. Although monotonous repetition is a basic typology of post World-War II design (Salingaros, 2011), it is anti-biophilic. We instantly recognize this feature as defining an unnatural, hence anti-biophilic environment. Is that why it is used so extensively?

More recently, architects have sought to integrate biophilic character into urban design again. This is surely welcome. But are the new designs truly seamless integrations of the most instinctive human geometries with natural ones? Or is this one more attempt at a kind of "green cloaking" over the same failed urban models of the modernist era — just another "branding" by artists, of another dubious vision of the sustainable future? These debates go on, and in our minds, they are much-needed ones. We cannot stumble onward on the same unsustainable industrial path.

One thing is certain. Biophilia reminds us that, whatever our acts of culture and humanity, we are in the end living creatures too, and an evolutionary part of the biosphere — and we had better start acting like it.

# References

- Stephen R. Kellert, Judith Heerwagen, & Martin Mador, editors (2008) *Biophilic Design: The Theory, Science and Practice of Bringing Buildings to Life* (John Wiley, New York), Chapter 5: pages 59-83.

- Nikos A. Salingaros (2011) "Why Monotonous Repetition is Unsatisfying", *Meandering Through Mathematics*, 2 September 2011<http://meandering-through-mathematics.blogspot.com/2011/09/why-monotonous-repetition-is.html>.

# 18. NEUROSCIENCE, THE NATURAL ENVIRONMENT, AND BUILDING DESIGN

## By Nikos A. Salingaros and Kenneth G. Masden II

*This is an extract containing pages 61-70, or about 1/3 of Chapter 5 (which covers pages 59-83) of the book Biophilic Design: The Theory, Science and Practice of Bringing Buildings to Life, edited by Stephen R. Kellert, Judith Heerwagen, and Martin Mador, John Wiley, New York, 2008. This material is reproduced with permission of John Wiley & Sons, Inc.*

A new effort has to be made to reconnect human beings to the buildings and places they inhabit. Biophilic design, as one of the most recent and viable reconnection theories, incorporates organic life into the built environment in an essential manner. Extending this logic, the building forms, articulations, and textures could themselves follow the same geometry found in all living forms. Empirical evidence confirms that designs which connect humans to the lived experience enhance our overall sense of wellbeing, with positive and therapeutic consequences on physiology. We offer a theory to help understand and explain these effects.

## Biologically Based Design

The positive effects of biophilic design must be understood in architectural terms: as form and form-making principles, and structural systems. Biologically-based design utilizes observed effects, and tries to document them into an empirical and tested body of knowledge. At the same time, an extensive research program is beginning to uncover the deeper causes for these effects: i.e., a possible innate reaction to the specific geometry of natural forms, detail, hierarchical subdivisions, color, etc. Since this project is far broader than the traditional study of architecture, designers must actively solicit help from other disciplines whose knowledge can help to explain human response to design. It is essential not to be partial in any way, since, in addition to known factors, there are clearly unknown factors playing a role yet to be discovered.

Recent investigations lead us inescapably to the fact that we engage emotionally with the built environment through architectural forms and surfaces. We experience our surroundings no differently than we experience natural environments, other living creatures, and other human beings. We relate to details, surfaces, and architectural spaces in much the same way as we relate to domestic animals such as our pets. The mechanism through which we engage with subjects outside ourselves relies on a connection established via information exchange. Our neurological mechanism reacts to the information field (the transmission component), while inducing a reaction in the state of our body (the physiological component). Some of the highest levels of sensory connection to the built environment have been evidenced in the great buildings and urban spaces of the past (Alexander, 2002-2005; Salingaros, 2005; 2006). Both natural and built environments possess intrinsic qualities that enable such a strong connection, and which in turn can be healing. This works through the sense of wellbeing established and maintained in the life of those who engage with such a structure. Great architects in the past were better able to discern those qualities, and to reproduce them in their buildings, because they were more engaged with their immediate surroundings.

What we are depends on the natural environment that shaped our bodies and senses (Kellert, 2005; Kellert & Wilson, 1993; Orians & Heerwagen, 1992). Far from being able to liberate our modern selves from our historical development, we inherit our biological origin in the structure of our mind and body. Nature has built on top of this over successive millennia, in increasing layers of sophistication. Evolution works by using what is already there, extending and recombining existing pieces to make something new. We thus depend on the presence of certain determinant qualities in the environment not only for our existence, but equally for our sense of belonging and wellbeing. Denying this genetic dependence is akin to denying our necessity for food and air. The typologies of traditional and vernacular architectures are predicated on biological necessity. They are not romantic expressions (as some would have us believe), but in fact a primal source of neurological nourishment.

A new chapter in scientific investigation is beginning to document environmental factors that affect our physiological wellbeing. Going beyond the century-old debates on aesthetics, a neurological basis for aesthetic response is now being established (Ramachandran & Rogers-Ramachandran, 2006). The mechanism for neurological nourishment was recently discovered in studies using Functional Magnetic Resonance Imaging. Humans have an innate hunger for certain types of information: the circuits for this have been associated with the brain's pleasure centers, which also control the reduction of pain (Biederman & Vessel, 2006). It is easy to hypothesize that this neurophysiologic mechanism is the result of an advantageous evolutionary adaptation.

A growing amount of research finds that fractal qualities in our environment (i.e., ordered details arranged in a nested scaling hierarchy) contribute positively to human wellbeing (Hagerhall, Purcell & Taylor, 2004; Taylor, 2006; Taylor et. al., 2005). Gothic architecture is intrinsically fractal, and has been conjectured to be an externalization of the fractal patterns of our brain's neural organization (Goldberger, 1996). The parallel between built fractal patterns and possible cerebral organization is too strong to be a coincidence (Salingaros, 2006). This idea is supported independently by the way we perceive and find meaning in patterns in our environment (Kellert, 2005; Salingaros, 2006). It is no surprise then that humans build those patterns into their creations. Investigations of all traditional architectural and urban forms and ornamentation confirm their essentially fractal qualities (Crompton, 2002; Salingaros, 2005; 2006).

Another direction of research has uncovered undisputed clinical advantages (faster hospital healing) of natural environments, including artificial environments mimicking geometrical qualities of natural environments (Frumkin, 2001; Ulrich, 1984; 2000). Pain relief in hospital settings is significantly improved by viewing natural (or videos of natural) environments (Tse et. al., 2002), thus confirming the link between specific types of informational input and pain reduction. These developments have sparked the interest of organizations concerned with improving the positive human qualities of their spaces. Much of this research has started to be applied in the field of interior design rather than architecture (Augustin & Wise, 2000; Wise & Leigh-Hazzard, 2002). There are principally two reasons for this: first, interiors are much easier to manipulate than entire buildings; and second, environments for work, leisure, or health care can make a more immediate and substantive difference in human wellbeing and performance.

Reviewing the positive effect that fractals and natural complexity have on humans, Yannick Joye (2006; 2007a; 2007b) reinforces our own conclusions on the essential "hard-wired" nature of the process. This is not the result of a conscious response to recognizing fractal or complex patterns in the environment: it is built into our neural system. Reaction to a neurologically-nourishing environment is physiological (i.e. emotional) rather than intellectual. There is mounting evidence of an innate information-processing system that has evolved along with the rest of our physiology (Joye, 2006; 2007a; 2007b). This system is acutely tuned to the visual complexity of the natural environment, specifically to respond positively to the highest levels of organized complexity (Salingaros, 2006).

Some researchers concentrate on human response to fractal qualities, whereas others measure the benefits of the complex geometry found in natural forms. Fractals are an important component of this effect, but by no means represent the full gamut of connective qualities. Additional geometrical properties of natural/biological forms clearly contribute to a positive physiological response in humans (Alexander, 2002-2005; Enquist & Arak, 1994; Kellert, 2005; Klinger & Salingaros, 2000; Salingaros, 2005; 2006). Symmetry — more precisely, a hierarchy of subsymmetries on many distinct scales — plays a crucial role. The overall perceived complexity is better understood using a multi-dimensional model rather than the simplistic one-dimensional model of plainness versus complication. Not only the presence of information, but especially how that information is organized, produces a positive or negative effect on our perceptive system (Klinger & Salingaros, 2000; Salingaros, 2006).

We assume an underlying genetic factor as the basis for why the ordered geometry of biological forms connects with and leads to healing effects on human beings. Many scientists now believe that evolution has a direction: the increasing complexity from emergent life forms in a primordial soup to human beings is not random (Conway-Morris, 2003). While not speaking of "purpose", we may discern a flow of organization towards a very specific type of organized complexity (Carroll, 2001; Valentine, Collins & Meyer, 1994). As such, evolution becomes understandable in informational terms, where adaptive forces act in a fairly restricted direction (though without an end result in sight). Some species do reach a complexity plateau, and individual organismic components may simplify as a result of adaptation, yet the strand of human evolution has moved towards increasing complexity. A corollary to this conclusion is that all life forms share an informational kinship based on very special geometrical complexity, which builds up in a cumulative process. The built environment, considered as an externalization of intrinsic human complexity fits better in the larger scheme of things whenever it follows the same informational template. The design of our buildings and cities should therefore try and adapt to the evolutionary direction of biological life in the universe.

## Biophilic Architecture and Neurological Nourishment

Human beings connect physiologically and psychologically to structures embodying organized complexity more strongly than to environments that are either too plain, or which present disorganized complexity (Salingaros, 2006). It follows that the built environment performs a crucial function — in some instances to the same degree — as does the natural environment. The connection process (outlined in the following sections) plays a key role in our lives, because it influences our health and mental wellbeing. Studying the geometrical characteristics of the type of visual complexity responsible for positive effects reveals its commonality with biological structures. Applying such concepts to architecture leads to two distinct conclusions. First, that we should bring as much of nature as we can into our everyday environments so as to experience it first-hand; and second, that we need to shape our built environment to incorporate those same geometrical qualities found in nature.

Human beings are biologically predisposed to require contact with natural forms. Following the arguments of Edward Wilson (1984), people are not capable of living a complete and healthy life detached from nature. By this, Wilson means that we benefit from direct contact with living biological forms, and not the poor substitute we see in so many urban and architectural settings today. Wilson's *Biophilia Hypothesis* asserts that we need contact with nature, and with the complex geometry of natural forms, just as much as we require nutrients and air for our metabolism (Kellert, 2005; Kellert & Wilson, 1993).

One aspect of biophilic architecture, therefore, is the intimate merging of artificial structures with natural structures. This could involve bringing nature into a building, using natural materials and surfaces, allowing natural light, and incorporating plants into the structure. It also means setting a building within a natural environment instead of simply erasing nature to erect the building (Kellert, 2005). While many architects may indeed claim to practice in this way, they more frequently replace nature by a very poor image of nature: an artificial representation or substitute that lacks the requisite complexity. That is in keeping with the abstract conception of architecture that has been applied throughout the twentieth century, and which continues today. Strips of lawn and a few interior potted plants do not represent anything but an abstraction of nature; not the real thing. This is a minimalist image lacking complexity and hierarchy. Biophilia demands a vastly more intense connection with plant and animal life, leading to the support of ecosystems and native plant species whenever possible.

Some good solutions incorporate small ecosystems consisting of a rich combination of plants within a building, or in a building's garden or courtyard. A flat lawn, by contrast, while better than a rectangular concrete slab, represents the same visual purity (emptiness) as the plain slab. Our senses perceive it as a single scale and are unable to connect to it fractally. Moreover, lawn is an ecological monoculture irrelevant to local ecology, because it exists on a single ecological scale. Nature exhibits ecological complexity: interacting plants that in turn provide visual complexity, which is a source of neurological nourishment. Not

110

surprisingly, this way of thinking leads to buildings that are more sustainable, and which incorporate natural processes that help in energy efficiency. Sustainability goes hand-in-hand with a new respect for nature coming from biophilia (Kellert, 2005).

For all its benefits of helping users to connect with nature in their everyday interior work environment, this first approach is only a partial solution. The biophilic element here is plant life brought next to and into a building, but the building itself could still be made in an alien or artificial form and built using artificial materials. Human connection is then possible only with the plant forms, but never with the building itself. This problem is particularly acute in an age where the majority of architects use industrial materials and modernist typologies without question. This practice only serves to undermine the requisite natural connections that humans need. The natural aspect of an industrial building-plus-garden is simply a biological component grafted onto an armature that is fundamentally hostile to human sensibilities. There is always a sharp contrast between the building and the natural elements that it encloses. It still triggers an underlying neurological disconnection on a basic level.

A second, and much deeper aspect of biophilic architecture requires us to incorporate the essential geometrical qualities of nature into the building and urban structure. This implies a more complex built geometry, following the same complexity as natural forms themselves. Once again, there is a danger of misunderstanding this geometry and superficially copying shapes that are irrelevant to a particular building or city. Architectural magazines are full of images of organic-looking (and unrealizable) buildings; whereas we actually mean ordinary-looking buildings that are more adapted to human sensibilities. For example, making a giant copy of an organism out of industrial materials becomes an iconic statement that fails to provide any level of connectivity. The shape of a giant mollusk, crab, amoeba, or centipede is still an abstract concept imposed on a building; little better in quality of abstraction from a giant box or rectangular slab. That belies a fundamental misconception about living structure, which connects on the human levels of scale through organized details and hierarchical connections (Alexander, 2002-2005; Salingaros, 2005; 2006).

Neurological nourishment depends upon an engagement with information and its organization. This connective mechanism acts on all geometrical levels, from the microscopic, through increasing physical scales up to the size of the city. The correct connective rules were rediscovered repeatedly by traditional societies, and are applied throughout historic and vernacular architectures. Traditional ornamentation, color, articulated surfaces, and the shape of interior space helped to achieve informational connectivity. Long misinterpreted as a copy of natural forms, ornamentation in its deepest expressions is far more than that: it is a distillation of geometrical connective rules that trigger our neurophysiology directly. These qualities are emphatically not present in the dominant architectural ideology of the twentieth century.

Some biophilic architects consider that neurological nourishment comes strictly from living biological forms. In their view, ornamented forms and surfaces are derivative of natural forms, and thus provide only a second-hand (i.e. vicarious) experience. We, on the other hand, believe that the underlying geometrical complexity of living structure is what nourishes humans. This geometry could be equally expressed in biological organisms as in artifacts and buildings: the difference is merely one of degree (Alexander, 2002-2005). If implemented correctly, it is not neurologically discernable, only more or less intense. Every living being incorporates this essential geometry to an astonishing degree (in its physical form), whereas only the greatest of human creations even come close. In this view, the distinction between the living and the artificial is left intentionally vague, and life itself is drawn closer to geometry. At the same time, this approach helps to explain the intense connection people feel with certain inanimate objects, i.e. the artifacts and creations of our human past.

Traditional techniques for creating neurologically-nourishing structures are wedded to spiritual explanations, which are often unacceptable to contemporary architects (and to business clients). Not surprisingly, the most intense connection is achieved in historic sacred sites, buildings, and artifacts. It is only in recent times that a scientific explanation has been given for what were originally religious/mystical practices of architecture and design (Alexander, 2002-2005; Salingaros, 2006). Today, it is finally possible to build an intensely connective building and justify it scientifically, by extending the geometrical logic of the natural world into the built world.

To summarize, two branches of contemporary biophilic architecture are beginning to be practiced today (Kellert, 2005). One basically continues to use industrial typologies but incorporates plants and natural features in a nontrivial manner; while the other alters the building materials, surfaces, and geometry themselves so that they connect neurologically to the user. This second type ties in more deeply to older, traditional, sacred, and vernacular architectures. So far, the first (high-tech) method has an advantage over the second (mathematical/sacred) method, because it is already in line with the industrial building/economic engine of our global society. Visually and philosophically very distinct, nevertheless, these two movements are contributing to a rediscovery of our immediate connection to the environment.

Perhaps the greatest impact of the biophilic movement is to establish a value system for a particular group of essential geometric qualities. Living forms and the geometrical characteristics they embody must be protected from destruction, because they provide us with neurological nourishment (Wilson, 1984). This is the seed for conservation, both of biological species, as well as for historic and traditional architectures.

## An Architecture That Arises From Human Nature

The desire to overcome nature, to separate man from the universe by placing him above natural constraints, led to the ultimate architectural assertion of the twentieth century, one expressing total autonomy. Adaptive processes were replaced by a formalized, self-referential, autonomous architectural order. The degree of separation that architecture placed between itself and nature was celebrated as a great accomplishment. This architectural movement culminated in the 1970s with the declaration made about an exhibition of current design work: "*This spectacularly beautiful work, elegant, formal, and totally detached from the world around it, represents a kind of counterrevolution in today's educational thought and practice.*" (Huxtable, 1999). Indeed, the value of twentieth-century architecture was now solely predicated on its degree of separation from the world around it: the world in which humans seek comfort and shelter (Masden, 2006).

To consider the service of architecture as something other than human seems contradictory to its very inception, for it was human nature that first gave it form by compelling humans to build. If we are to consider whom architecture should serve, and re-establish the relationship between architecture and humanity, then we must consider the essence of human nature, and grasp how human beings came to create particular kinds of structures. We must account for the neurological processes that operate as our interface with the physical world, and ask why, if these processes are intrinsically human, were we ever able to stray so far away from this human dimension.

Edward Wilson's seminal book *On Human Nature* (Wilson, 1978) laid the groundwork for understanding our biological nature, explaining how our actions are determined to a large part by genetic structure and evolution. Wilson thus places human actions on a sound biological foundation. Even so, people often contradict their biological nature by acting against it without any apparent logic, as when they join a mass movement (Hoffer, 1951). People are sometimes manipulated into adopting an ideology, which then controls their actions in violation of their biological nature (Salingaros, 2004).

These ideas are relevant to architecture in a positive sense. The early stages of the artistic process are a result of a vast number of unconscious forces and impulses. To initiate this process towards a healthier architecture, we need to ask: what are the tactile, perceptual, and mental processes necessary for a human sense of wellbeing? We are not going to describe how to incorporate biological elements into the built environment — the principal component of biophilic design — since that is dealt with by other authors (Kellert, 2005). Rather, we have developed techniques for design and construction that use materials to create a source of neurological nourishment. We draw from comprehensive architectural design methods developed only recently (Alexander, 2002-2005; Salingaros, 2005; 2006; Salingaros & Masden, 2007).

Several suggestions can help to implement this program. Appendix I to this Chapter [*not included in this extract*] summarizes some of the underlying principles that we and others are utilizing to design and build new enriching and engaging environments. Although built today with the latest technological materials, these environments reproduce with great effect the best that older built environments were able to offer. We, working today, and historical architects working in centuries past, strived for the same neurological nourishment from what we build. In the past, techniques for achieving this goal were learned intuitively. Modern science is revealing the mechanisms whereby neurological nourishment acts, so that we can learn to use it in a more controlled manner. Today, we are once again aware of the physical properties and natural geometries that architects working in centuries past called upon to create the great human places we now wish to emulate.

Biophilic design's principal contribution makes use of plants and complex natural settings as much — and as intimately — as possible in the built environment (Kellert, 2005). While our design approach does not focus specifically on the biophilic component, it supports it in a fundamental manner. By re-orienting design away from formal or ideological statements, and towards a process of optimizing neurological engagement, we are setting up the conditions for accepting biophilia. Otherwise, the conceptual distance between non-responsive architecture and the natural environment is so vast that most people simply cannot bridge the gap. We are presently living in an alternative mental universe where human creations are forever distanced from natural forms. This gap is spreading daily, as the progressive development of new technologies rewards us with useful gadgets that are increasingly "unnatural".

To implement biophilic design, we need to create a conceptual framework based upon informational connection. This program goes against the current trends of academic specialization, since it requires the cooperation of many different disciplines. Present ways of thinking about architecture are inadequate: the representation of architectural problems has to change from an abstract domain to the natural domain dominated by human physiology and positive emotions. The forces pushing for a re-orientation necessarily come from outside architecture, and may even be resisted by architectural academia. If we are successful in this, then future architects will conceive architecture in a fundamentally different manner.

## Three Different Conceptions Of Being Human

Biophilic design techniques depend upon the mental processes and physical mechanisms that people have evolved in response to the natural environment (Kellert, 2005). It is now necessary to consider the nature of human beings, which underpins biophilic design as a necessity and not an option. Many readers could misinterpret the biophilic focus on nature as diverting attention away from human beings themselves, even though its goal is to enhance human life on earth. This discussion is needed to prevent our work (and our colleagues' work) from being branded as just another architectural "style" that can be applied or ignored depending on the prevailing fashion.

We classify three fundamentally different conceptions of human nature, summarizing each of these levels in turn. In the first level, a human being is regarded as a component placed into an abstract, mechanical world. Here, human beings interact only minimally (superficially) with the natural world, a condition of being disconnected. This is an abstract conception of humanity, yet is representative of much of contemporary thinking. It is the world of the contemporary architect, in which humans participate only as sketches, intentionally blurry photos, or indistinct shadows on a computer screen. The imageability of the design is primary, with the occupant either absent or represented only symbolically. A human here is not even biological: he/she exists as an inert passenger in a fundamentally sterile and non-interactive world.

In the second level, a human being is an organism made of sensors that interact with its environment. Here, humans are biological entities: animals that possess a sensory apparatus enabling them to receive and use measurable input. This is a condition of biological connectedness to the world, i.e. *situatedness* (Salingaros & Masden, 2006a). In this richly biological view, a human being represents a biological system that has

115

evolved to perceive and react with inanimate matter and especially with other organisms. Humans are considered as animals (not meant in any negative way), sharing all the evolved neural apparatus necessary to make sense of the natural world. Human modes of interaction are those we understand through nerves and sensors.

In the third level, a human being is something much more than a biological neural system. The third conception corresponds to the much older metaphysical picture of humans as spiritual beings, connected to the universe in ways that other animals are not. This is a condition of transcendental engagement with the world. The definition of human essence extends into realms more properly covered by humanistic philosophy and religion. Much of what it means to "be human" lies in this domain, and these additional qualities distinguish us from other animals. To dismiss all of this as "unscientific" would be to miss the point of humanity. In the pre-scientific ages — as for example, the Middle Ages in Europe — our conception of what we were as human beings was almost exclusively based upon insight that came from internal development. Transcendental engagement anchored our sense of *self*, and continues to do so for the majority of people in the developing world today. Mystical and religious, this intuitive understanding serves to tie human beings to their world in a manner independent of science. The connection, moreover, is believed to have been much stronger than the later development of a strictly scientific framework linking human beings to the rational dimension of the physical universe.

Curiously, the three levels of being human, going from detachment (disconnected), to a biological connection (situatedness), and finally to a more profound transcendental engagement, correspond to going backwards in historical time as it pertains to human existence. This seems counter-intuitive at best. If one were to reword this observation, it could be said that humankind has regressed in the depth of its connection to its surroundings (i.e. the universe) over the past decades and centuries. Just because we increased our scientific knowledge of the world, this does not guarantee that we maintain our connection to it in the human dimension. Indeed, the Cartesian method required us to detach ourselves from our world in the name of scientific enquiry, in order to be able to perform unbiased experiments. This may be fine for scientific experimentation, but it is certainly no way to maintain our human nature and to effectively operate within the world as human beings.

## Level One: The Abstract Human Being

The "modern" human being inhabits an industrialized, technological world. Since this world has become an ever vaster and encompassing machine, so too its human inhabitant has become but an ever smaller (and, by implication, less significant) component of that machine. The biological constitution of these contemporary human beings has little relevance to their situatedness in the universe: such a person could just as well be made out of metal, wires, and a minimal number of electronic sensors — a robot. The biological (not to mention the transcendental) nature of humanity is herein denied. A human being is simply a neutral cog in the machinery of the universe. It doesn't help that contemporary physics paints precisely such a hopeless picture of cosmic irrelevance for human nature and the human spirit.

In contemporary architecture, reluctant acknowledgment is sometimes made to the genetic structure of a human being, but it is far less than would at first appear. Too often, even the most rudimentary neural capacity of humans does not enter into play when designing buildings and urban environments. Human physiological and psychological response seldom figures in design discussions today. Architects pretend to have surpassed human nature. Instead, certain formal and abstract notions about space, materials, and form are of primary concern. Those do not arise, however, from a full understanding of the processes at work that give human beings their existential foothold on earth.

A movement to mold human beings into manipulable consumers of industrial products has been taking place for many decades. Much broader in scope than architecture and urbanism, these two disciplines have nevertheless played a significant role in an era of massive social engineering. In the drive to transform human beings into controllable objects, people's connection to nature are suppressed. Modern individuals — at least in the more developed countries — live in a physical world defined by machines and industrial materials, and whose information fields come from media images and messages. Nature is either eliminated from the human environment, or has been relegated to a purely decorative role. Evolutionary developed sensibilities have been numbed. The world's remaining population is no better off, because it aspires to emulate this unnatural state as a sign of progress. An automated, disconnected population is insensitive to the healing effects of natural environments.

A more benign, but nevertheless equally effective transformation led to the abstraction/mechanization of the human environment. Early 20th-Century advances in microbiology and sanitary practices coincided with the introduction of industrial materials. A "healthy" environment became associated with a visually sterile, industrial "look" of polished metal or porcelain surfaces. For example, kitchens changed from being geometrically messy to looking like sterile factory environments; and from being made from soft and natural materials to being built using hard industrial materials (Salingaros, 2006). Plants (not to mention domestic animals) had no place there. People's preoccupation with improved health made them suspicious of all life, not just the harmful microbes and fungi that cause disease. This was a great misunderstanding, since microbes can thrive on any surface, even ones that look sterile to the naked eye. But the clean, industrial "look" became part of our worldview, and we are still threatened by signs of life that violate it.

This contemporary condition demonstrates that human beings can be psychologically conditioned to act against their biological nature (Hoffer, 1951; Salingaros, 2004). We are now facing a population whose sensibilities have been detached from most other life forms, and oriented principally towards an artificial world of images and machines. Explaining the benefits of biophilic design to such individuals — who no longer see relevance in real trees, animals, and ecosystems — presents a serious challenge.

## Level Two: The Biological Human Being

We are biological creatures made of sensors that enable us to interact with our surroundings. Intelligence and consciousness are evolutionary products of our sensory systems. Up to a certain point (more than we care to admit), we share this neurological basis with other creatures of the earth (Wilson, 1978; 1984). In the past, an innate understanding of how forms, spaces, and surfaces affect us was used to design the built environment, aiming to maximize its positive effect on us. That changed when formal criteria and abstractions were introduced, replacing those of an older, humanistic architecture. By coincidence, societal discontinuities leading into the twentieth century made this replacement possible, a change which could not have taken place before then (Salingaros, 2006).

However, this does not mean that our sensory apparatus has changed in any way. We still have the same genetic structure, and our physical and psychological needs have remained the same over many millennia (Wilson, 1978; 1984). Our neurophysiologic requirements have been tempered to some extent by fashionable ideas, images, and ideologies, yet our response mechanisms still operate automatically. Therefore, we will instinctively react in a negative manner to a built environment that is neurologically non-nourishing, or which might actually cause physical anxiety and distress. It is very easy to understand the type of environment that is healthy for us — or, conversely, is unhealthy — based upon our sensory apparatus. We need only to pay heed to the signals from our own body, unencumbered by psychological conditioning.

Empirical evidence continues to accumulate towards a greater understanding of how humans operate physiologically in the built environment (Frumkin, 2001). In hospital design, the geometry of the environment plays a significant role in how long it takes for a patient to be cured. Roger Ulrich has done pioneering work in this topic (Ulrich, 1984; 2000). Surprisingly, schools do not show a strong enough interest in human physiological and psychological response to the built environment, despite decades of experimental findings on this topic. Architects instead seek greater distance and obscurity in the ethereal terrain of contemporary philosophies (Salingaros, 2004). Departments of Architecture around the world still train students in Hospital Design based on formal, stylistic ideas of spaces and materials, not paying attention to Ulrich's work.

Our eye/brain system has evolved to perceive fine detail, contrast, symmetries, color, and connections. Symmetry, visual connections, ornament, and fine detail are necessary on buildings; not for any stylistic reason, but because our perception is built to engage with those features (Enquist & Arak, 1994; Salingaros, 2003; 2006). The physiological basis for sensory experience is the ultimate source of our being, which thus relies strongly on certain geometric elements to which we connect. Creating an environment that deliberately eschews these elements (visual elements which are found in nature and in all traditional architectures) has negative consequences for our physiology, and thus for our mental health and sense of wellbeing (Joye, 2006; 2007a; 2007b; Kellert, 2005).

Environments devoid of neurologically-nourishing information mimic signs of human pathology. For example, colorless, drab, minimalist surfaces and spaces reproduce clinical symptoms of macular degeneration, stroke, cerebral achromatopsia, and visual agnosia (Salingaros, 2003; 2006). We feel anxious in such environments, because they provoke in us a similar sensation as sensory deprivation and neurophysiologic breakdown. It is curious that architectural design in the past several decades incorporated more and more such alarming elements and devices as part of its stylistic vocabulary. Some architectural critics attempt to portray those in a positive light using seductive images, and defend them by employing specious references to technological progress (Salingaros, 2004).

The discipline of Environmental Psychology actually began in faculties of architecture, as a natural investigation of how built environments were affecting people. As soon as the first results (several decades ago) indicated that some of the most fashionable contemporary architectural and urban typologies, spaces, and surfaces might in fact be generating physiological and psychological anxiety in their users, fellow architects lost interest. Environmental Psychologists moved (or were systematically relocated) outside architectural academia, into Departments of Psychology, which is where they can be found today.

Ironically, to understand the environmental aspect better, we turn to studies on higher mammals. Judith Heerwagen has studied zoo animal behavior in naturalistic versus more artificial environments (Heerwagen, 2005). Starting from substantial observations of zoo animals, she reports the results of implementing a transformation towards more naturalistic habitats. As a consequence, the animals' psychological and social well-being has been drastically improved. Zoo animals kept in drab, monotonous, and minimalist environments (i.e. those that we humans also perceive as boring and depressing) exhibited neurotic, aberrant, and antisocial behavior never observed in the wild. Moved to more naturalistic and stimulating habitats, the animals returned to more normal, healthier behavior patterns.

This body of results has dramatic implication for our children. Evidence has been accumulating since the 1960s that complexity and stimulation in the environment can lead to increased intelligence of a developing animal. Incontrovertible results are obtained with young rats raised in information-rich environments, whose brains increase in size, and can improve their neural connectivity by up to 20% (Squire & Kandel, 1999: page 200). This represents much more than just an anatomical change in the brain, because it optimizes the cortical physiology responsible for intelligence. Those rats raised in enriched environments are then observed to do much better in intelligence tests (such as solving complex maze problems) and training. We interpret this result as the fulfillment of a necessary external component in the brain's development. It also raises questions of collective culpability for neglecting or minimizing neurological connective structure.

We need to point out the importance of relying on clinical studies rather than on surveys. Many studies recording user preferences have been done over decades, some of them uncovering the advantages of natural environments, and of environments mimicking those geometrical qualities (Joye, 2006; 2007a; 2007b; Kellert, 2005; Kellert & Wilson, 1993). Nevertheless, a large number of those studies showed only moderate preferences, or were inconclusive. A recent experiment raises the possibility that those earlier results may in fact reflect conditioned response. In a clinical comparison of two distinct environments, one a plain room, and the other with wooden beams added to create hierarchical scaling, the subjects did not express any preference. Yet the physiological monitors recorded a marked response in favor of the room with hierarchical subdivisions and natural detail (Tsunetsugu, Miyazaki & Sato, 2005). We (and the study's authors) conclude that physiological effects of the environment cannot always be consciously recognized.

# References

- Alexander, C. (2002-2005) *The Nature of Order*, Books 1 to 4 (Berkeley, California: Center for Environmental Structure).

- Alexander, C., Ishikawa, S., Silverstein, M., Jacobson, M., Fiksdahl-King, I. & Angel, S. (1977) *A Pattern Language* (New York: Oxford University Press).

- Augustin, S. & Wise, J. A. (2000) "From Savannah to Silicon Valley", *IIDA Perspective*, Winter/Spring: 67-72. Available from <http://www.haworth.com/haworth/assets/From%20Savannah%20to%20Silicon%20Valley.pdf>

- Barker, S. B. (1999) "Therapeutic Aspects of the Human-Companion Animal Interaction", *Psychiatric Times*, 16, Issue 2. Available from <http://www.psychiatrictimes.com/p990243.html>

- Biederman, I. & Vessel, E. A. (2006) "Perceptual Pleasure and the Brain", *American Scientist*, 94, May-June: 247-253.

- Brooks, R. A. (2002) *Flesh and Machines* (New York, NY: Pantheon Books).

- Carroll, S. B. (2001) "Chance and Necessity: the Evolution of Morphological Complexity and Diversity", *Nature*, 409: 1102-1109.

- Conway-Morris, S. (2003) *Life's Solution: Inevitable Humans in a Lonely Universe* (Cambridge: Cambridge University Press).

- Crompton, A. (2002) "Fractals and Picturesque Composition", *Environment and Planning* B, 29: 451-459.

- Enquist, M. & Arak, A. (1994) "Symmetry, Beauty and Evolution", *Nature*, 372: 169-172.

- Fathy, H. (1973) *Architecture for the Poor* (Chicago: Chicago University Press).

- Frumkin, H. (2001) "Beyond Toxicity: Human Health and the Natural Environment", *American Journal of Preventive Medicine*, 20: 234-240.

- Goldberger, A. L. (1996) "Fractals and the Birth of Gothic: Reflections on the Biologic Basis of Creativity", *Molecular Psychiatry*, 1: 99-104.

- Hagerhall, C. M., Purcell, T. & Taylor, R. (2004) "Fractal Dimension of Landscape Silhouette Outlines as a Predictor of Landscape Preference", *Journal of Environmental Psychology*, 24: 247-255.

- Heerwagen, J. H. (2005) "Psychosocial Value of Space", *Whole Building Design Guide* <www.wbdg.org/design/psychspace_value.php>, online.

- Hoffer, E. (1951) *The True Believer: Thoughts on the Nature of Mass Movements* (New York, NY: Harper/Collins).

- Huxtable, A. L. (1999) "New York Times review of the Museum of Modern Art exhibition and foreword to *Education of an Architect:a Point of View — The Cooper Union School of Art & Architecture 1964-1971*" (New York, NY: Monacelli Press).

- Joye, J. (2006) "An Interdisciplinary Argument for Natural Morphologies in Architectural Design", *Environment and Planning B*, 33: 239-252.

- Joye, J. (2007a) "Architectural Lessons from Environmental Psychology: The Case of Biophilic Architecture", *Review of General Psychology*, 11: 305-328.

- Joye, J. (2007b) "Fractal Architecture Could be Good for You", *Nexus Network Journal*, 9, No. 2: 311-320.

- Kellert, S. R. (2005) *Building for Life: Designing and Understanding the Human-Nature Connection* (Washington, DC: Island Press).

- Kellert, S. R. & Wilson, E. O., Editors (1993) *The Biophilia Hypothesis* (Washington, DC: Island Press).

- Klein, G. (1998) *Sources of Power: How People Make Decisions* (Cambridge, Massachusetts: MIT Press).

- Klinger, A. & Salingaros, N. A. (2000) "A Pattern Measure", *Environment and Planning B: Planning and Design*, 27: 537-547.

- Kulikauskas, A. (2006) "How Might We Create a Really Human Environment?", *Global Villages* (March 10, 2006), http://groups.yahoo.com/group/globalvillages/message/1015.

- Masden, K. G. II (2005) "Being There", in Allison O'Neill, Editor, *The Catholic University of America Summer Institute for Architecture Journal*, 2: 51-56.

- Masden, K. G. II (2006) "The Education of an Urbanist: a Real Point of View", in José Baganha, Editor, *The Teaching of Architecture and Urbanism in the Age of Globalization* (Casal de Cambra, Portugal: Caleidoscopio Ediçao e Artes Graficas): 173-179.

- McGrath, A. (2005) *Dawkins' God: Genes, Memes, and the Meaning of Life* (Oxford: Blackwell Publishing).

- Orians, G. H. & Heerwagen, J. H. (1992) "Evolved Responses to Landscapes", in J. H. Barkow, L. Cosmides & J. Tooby, *The Adapted Mind* (New York: Oxford University Press): 555-579.

- Pyla, P. I. (2007) "Hassan Fathy Revisited", *Journal of Architectural Education*, 60: 28-39.

- Ramachandran, V. S. & Rogers-Ramachandran, D. (2006) "The Neurology of Aesthetics", *Scientific American Mind*, 17, Issue 5: 16-18.

- Roth, J. (2000) "Pet Therapy Uses with Geriatric Adults", *International Journal of Psychosocial Rehabilitation*, 4: 27-39

- Salingaros, N. A. (2003) "The Sensory Value of Ornament", *Communication & Cognition*, 36, No. 3-4: 331-351. Revised version is Chapter 4 of *A Theory of Architecture* (2006).

- Salingaros, N. A. (2004) *Anti-Architecture and Deconstruction* (Solingen, Germany: Umbau-Verlag). Second enlarged edition, 2007.

- Salingaros, N. A. (2005) *Principles of Urban Structure* (Amsterdam, Holland: Techne Press).

- Salingaros, N. A. (2006) *A Theory of Architecture* (Solingen, Germany: Umbau-Verlag).

- Salingaros, N. A. & Masden, K. G. II (2006a) "Architecture: Biological Form and Artificial Intelligence", *The Structurist*, No. 45/46: 54-61.

- Salingaros, N. A. & Masden, K. G. II (2006b) "Review of Christopher Alexander's 'The Nature of Order, Book Four: The Luminous Ground'", *The Structurist*, No. 45/46: 39-42.

- Salingaros, N. A. & Masden, K. G. II (2007) "Restructuring 21st-Century Architecture Through Human Intelligence", *ArchNet International Journal of Architectural Research*, 1, Issue 1: 36-52. http://archnet.org/library/documents/one-document.tcl?document_id=10066.

- Squire, L. R. & Kandel, E. R. (1999) *Memory: From Mind to Molecules* (New York, NY: Scientific American Library).

- Taylor, R. P. (2006) "Reduction of Physiological Stress Using Fractal Art and Architecture", *Leonardo*, 39, No. 3: 245-251.

- Taylor, R. P., Newell, B., Spehar, B. & Clifford, C. (2005) "Fractals: A Resonance Between Art and Nature?", in: Michele Emmer, Editor, *Mathematics and Culture II: Visual Perfection* (Berlin: Springer-Verlag): 53-63.

- Tse, M. M. Y., Ng, J. K. F., Chung, J. W. Y. & Wong, T. K. S. (2002) "The effect of Visual Stimuli on Pain Threshold and Tolerance", *Journal of Clinical Nursing*, 11: 462-469.

- Tsunetsugu, Y., Miyazaki, Y. & Sato, H. (2005) "Visual Effects of Interior Design in Actual-size Living Rooms on Physiological Responses", *Building and Environment*, 40: 1341-1346.

- Turing, A. A. (1950) "Computing Machinery and Intelligence", *Mind*, 59: 433-460.

- Ulrich, R. S. (1984) "View Through Window May Influence Recovery From Surgery", *Science*, 224: 420-421.

- Ulrich, R. S. (2000) "Evidence Based Environmental Design for Improving Medical Outcomes", in: *Healing By Design: Building for Health Care in the 21st Century* (Montreal, Canada: McGill University Health Center).

- Valentine, J. W., Collins, A. G. & Meyer, C. P. (1994) "Morphological Complexity Increase in Metazoans", *Paleobiology*, 20: 131-142.

- Weizenbaum, H. (1976) *Computer Power and Human Reason* (San Francisco: W. H. Freeman).

- Wilson, E. O. (1978) *On Human Nature* (Cambridge, Massachusetts: Harvard University Press).

- Wilson, E. O. (1984) *Biophilia* (Cambridge, Massachusetts: Harvard University Press).

- Wilson, E. O. (2006) *The Creation* (New York, New York: W. W. Norton).

- Wise, J. A. & Leigh-Hazzard, T. (2002) "Fractals: What Nature Can Teach Design", *American Society of Interior Designers ICON*, March: 14-21.

# 19. Lecture Notes, Seventh Week. Alexander's Fifteen Fundamental Properties

## Readings for the Seventh Week:

- Alexander, *The Phenomenon of Life*, Chapter 5, "Fifteen Fundamental Properties".

We have come to the point in this course when we need to present the geometric properties responsible for the deep connectivity that we have been talking about. Christopher Alexander has derived a set of 15 properties that all structures that we perceive to have "life" possess.

Note that it is only after separating what has qualities of "life" from what does not that we have a body of examples from which to extract the sought-for geometric rules. Those rules are discovered by observation from these objects, as was achieved by Alexander. Once written down, we can then verify that all objects with the quality of life satisfy these rules.

The 15 fundamental properties of Alexander are the important beginnings of a massive ongoing investigation into the properties of matter. The 15 properties are phenomenological, yet we know from experiments that the phenomenon of life is based upon our biology and the physical properties of matter itself.

Therefore, starting from the 15 properties opens up a research program to discover why these geometrical rules are so important, and to explain them. It also drives us to seek further complementary factors that refine and improve our understanding of the phenomenon of life. Alexander himself has done this in the other volumes of the "Nature of Order", and I have also been responsible for results in this topic.

I am going to use some notes on the fifteen properties from Lecture 6 of my book *Twelve Lectures on Architecture: Algorithmic Sustainable Design*, 2010. Here is a list of the fifteen properties:

1. Levels of scale

2. Strong centers

3. Thick boundaries

4. Alternating repetition

5. Positive space

6. Good shape

7. Local symmetries

8. Deep interlock and ambiguity

9. Contrast

10. Gradients

11. Roughness

12. Echoes

13. The void

14. Simplicity and inner calm

15. Not-separateness

1. Levels of scale exist along with a scaling hierarchy. Repeating components of the same size and similar shape define one scale. Levels of scale have to be spaced closely enough in size (magnification) for coherence, but not too close to blur the distinction between nearby scales. [Thus, a jump in scale by a factor of 15 is disorienting, whereas a factor of 1.5 is too close to distinguish one scale from another]. A mathematical rule generates a distribution of scales via the logarithmic constant $e \approx 2.7$ and the Fibonacci sequence. The whole point of adaptive design is to satisfy needs on the human scales, which range from 2 m down to < 1 mm. The rule only says that you must accommodate all these scales.

2. Strong centers are formed when a substantial region of space is tied together coherently. It is useful to distinguish two types of centers — "defined", and "implied" — that overlap and interact. A "defined" center has something in the middle to focus attention. An "implied" center has a boundary that focuses attention on its empty interior. Visual focus is

a precondition for the use of spaces. Each center combines surrounding centers and boundaries to focus on some region. Centers support each other on every scale: this is a recursive hierarchical property.

3. Thick boundaries (Alexander has revised the title to emphasize the thickness). A thick boundary is an "implied" center. According to the scaling hierarchy, a thick boundary arises as the next smaller scale from what is being bound. For this reason, thin boundaries are ineffective, because they skip over one or more terms in the scaling hierarchy, so the boundary is not connected by scaling to what it bounds. An "implied" center is defined only through its own thick boundary. Therefore, thick boundaries play a focusing role as well as a bounding role.

4. Alternating repetition helps in the informational definition of repeating components. Simplistic repetition is collapsible information, because what repeats is trivially coded (for example, take an empty or plain module $X$ and repeat it 100 times). Contrast, acting together with repetition, reinforces each component through alternation. This alternation helps to better define essential translational symmetry.

5. Positive space refers to Gestalt psychology, and links geometry with the basis of human perception. Convexity plays a major role in defining an object or a space (area or volume). We feel comfortable or not in the spaces we inhabit for mathematical plus psychological reasons. We strongly feel a threat from objects sticking out. We need to apply the positive space concept to both figure and background. Not only the building's interior space but also urban space must be positive.

6. Good shape arises when symmetries reduce the information overload. Perceivable objects produce a represented shape from many separate 2-D views, which the brain can computationally manipulate in 3-D. "Good" means "easily graspable", satisfying the brain's innate need to compactify information. Shapes that are not easily represented strain mental computation, hence they induce anxiety.

7. Local symmetries are symmetries within the scaling hierarchy. Symmetries must act on every distinct scale. "Symmetry" does not mean overall symmetry on the largest scale, as is usually understood. In organized complex structures, we have multiple subsymmetries acting within larger symmetries. All the symmetries should be nested hierarchically.

8. Deep interlock and ambiguity are other strong ways of connecting. Forms interpenetrate to link together. An analogy comes from fractals, where crinkled lines tend to fill portions of space, and surfaces grow with accretions. Two regions can interpenetrate at a semi-permeable interface, which enables a transition from one region to another. There is ambiguity as to which side of the interface one belongs while inside

the transition region, and this is a good feature. Abrupt transitions such as a clean straight line, however, do not bind objects coming up to each other.

9. Contrast is necessary to establish distinct subunits and to distinguish between adjoining units. Contrast is also needed to provide figure-ground symmetry of opposites. Strongly contrasted regions can also be strongly connected. For example, the space under an arcade contrasts with open street space. False transparency reduces contrast, and reduced contrast weakens the design. An example of weak (ineffective) contrast is inside versus outside space separated by a glass curtain wall.

10. Gradients represent controlled transitions. They provide a method of getting away from uniformity, because that is a non-adaptive state. Subdivision also does this, but sometimes we should not divide a form into discrete pieces, and instead need to change it gradually. Examples include the urban transect: city transitioning to countryside, and in interior spaces: public transitioning to private realms.

11. Roughness. A fractal structure goes all the way down in scales — nothing is smooth. Ornament can be interpreted as controlled "roughness" in a smooth geometry. The relaxation of strict geometry to allow imperfections makes it more tolerant. So-called "imperfections" differentiate repeated units to make them similar but not identical — for example, hand-painted tiles. There is deliberate roughness in repetition that avoids monotony. Approximate symmetry breaking prevents informational collapse. Adaptation to local conditions creates roughness, since it breaks regularity and perfect symmetry.

12. Echoes. There are two types of echoes in design. First, translational symmetry — similar forms found on the same scale but at a distance. Second, scaling symmetry — similar forms existing magnified at different scales. Mathematical fractals are exactly self-similar. But all natural fractals obey only approximate, or statistical self-similarity — not exactly the same when magnified, but only "echoes".

13. The void can be identified with plain structure at the largest scale of a fractal. The largest open component of a fractal survives as the void. It is not possible to fill in all of a fractal with detail. In "implied" centers, a complex boundary focuses on the open middle — the void. Therefore, an empty portion in necessary to balance regions of intense detail.

14. Simplicity and inner calm. This is a more subtle quality. Balance is achieved by an overall coherence and lack of clutter. Symmetries are all cooperating to support each other, with nothing extraneous or distracting. Coherent design appears effortless (but is in fact very

difficult to achieve). We see this simplicity in nature, though it is never actually "simple" in the sense of being minimalist. "Simple" in nature means extremely complex but highly coherent. A system appears "simple" to us because it is so perfect.

15. Not-separateness comes after achieving coherence. Coherence is an emergent property — not present in the individual components. In a larger coherent whole, no piece can be taken away. Decomposition is neither obvious, nor possible. When every component is cooperating to give a coherent whole, nothing looks separate, and nothing draws attention to itself. This is the goal of adaptive design: a seamless blending of an enormous number of complex components. This is the opposite of willful separateness. Not-separateness goes beyond internal coherence, because the whole connects as much as possible to its environment.

The fifteen properties give rise to coherent form, which is so natural that it is hardly noticed — like nature herself! But we do perceive this coherence subconsciously, and it affects us deeply. Coherence is healing. We also immediately notice incoherence, in which the fifteen properties are absent. It disturbs, alarms, and excites us at the same time. This type of excitement is unhealthy in the long term. Architects and students most often wish to draw attention to their designs, and accomplish this by violating the fifteen properties. Doing so causes physiological anxiety for the users.

Whether consciously or unconsciously, architectural design since the beginning of the 20th century has cultivated the absence of the 15 properties. As a result, students and architects respond emotionally (very negatively) to them, reacting from their image-based conditioning. One cannot hide behind the excuse that what I'm talking about is only very recent knowledge, because architects have always been aware in some way of the fifteen properties. Form languages that we use widely today were developed to contrast with traditional form languages, and thus to deliberately break the 15 properties.

Since architects have avoided the 15 properties for one century, why apply them today to design the built environment? The reason is that we are still part of nature: human biology has not changed in one century. Yet during that time, we have been desensitized to go against nature and our reactions to natural and unnatural forms, denying our own biological makeup. Everybody agrees that our society is stressed, and that it would improve our health to go back to building structures and environments that help us to heal. This type of architecture can make a significant contribution to raising the quality of life.

It is true that part of the motivation for abandoning design according to the 15 properties was for practical reasons: a more rapid design process, standardization, manufacturing efficiency, strictly generic spaces to allow maximum flexibility of use, a "sleek, modern look", etc. But now it's time to recover what we have lost. It's time to become reconnected with nature directly, as well as through the geometrical properties of what we build. With present-day technological sophistication, it is just as easy to implement architectural solutions that exemplify the 15 properties, as it is to continue to disregard the problem.

The question of styles needs some clarification. People grow tired of a style, then adopt another different one. But what we observe since the introduction of modernist architecture is a cycling through a related group of styles, all of which violate the 15 properties. Form languages did indeed change during the last several decades, but what they have in common is that they avoid the 15 properties. Innovative form languages have not come back to adopting the 15 properties, but remain in a geometrical domain of violation. This cannot be accidental — there is a meta-selection rule that keeps architects from using the 15 properties for design, considered as somehow "improper". But we wish to focus on and implement what's best for people, not to continue a biased stylistic dictate.

# 20. Lecture Notes, Eighth Week. Fractals and Hierarchical Scaling

## Readings for the Eighth Week:

- Alexander, *The Phenomenon of Life,* Chapter 6, "The Fifteen Properties in Nature".

- Salingaros, *A Theory of Architecture*, Chapter 2, "A Scientific Basis for Creating Architectural Forms" & Chapter 3, "Hierarchical Cooperation in Architecture: The Mathematical Necessity for Ornament".

We might now believe the utility and the importance of the fifteen fundamental properties, yet there is one more obstacle to overcome. Architects are used to alliances with the fine arts, where the perceived effects are aesthetic ones, and concern only our psychology. As such, those are valuable but their importance is limited to human emotions.

The fifteen properties are something different altogether. Their importance lies in physics, and thus goes far beyond any human interpretation. They exist even if we humans never evolved — they are not a human creation.

I am going to spend some time developing one of the fifteen properties further, and give a theory to support it. "Levels of scale" applies to decide scaling relations among design components. It says very little about the forms themselves. Scaling coherence is achieved when, first, the scales exist in the correct hierarchy, and second, when all the distinct scales are made to relate to each other. The entire system then ties together through this process.

Let us choose a convenient scaling factor of $e \approx 2.7$, the logarithmic constant from mathematics. Then, we claim that many natural structures (though not all) obey an approximate scaling rule: "Starting from the largest dimension $X$, there exists perceivable structure of size $X/e$, again of size $X/e^2$, all the way down to the microstructure of the materials." This is a manifestation of the scaling rule from the larger to the smaller.

We can also analyze a form by going the other way, from the small to the larger dimensions. Suppose there exist components of a very definite small size defining a scale $Y$. Then, we should expect to see larger sizes defined at $Ye$, $Ye^2$, etc. going all the way up to the largest scale.

It is important to point out that the scaling factor of $e$ is simply a convenient number to formulate the theory, and is not exact. Empirical measurements show a variety of scaling factors that we observe in nature, ranging from about 2 to about 5. Thus, $e \approx 2.7$ represents a sort of global average based upon experience.

However, a scaling factor of, say, the Golden mean $\Phi \approx 1.6$ is too small, and a scaling factor of 10 is too large. So at least the choice of $e$ is useful for illustrating the existence of a scaling hierarchy. That is the important point.

A scaling hierarchy is made up of distinct levels of scale. Each level of scale is defined by having several objects of approximately the same dimension. When there exist clear jumps from one scale to another, we could have a scaling hierarchy. Modernist buildings tend to have scaling hierarchies, since dimensions can jump from, say, detail at 1 cm, up to a wall panel of 4 m, with no other intermediate scales. But the scaling factor here is 400, which is far too large according to our theory. There is nothing in-between.

The scaling property described here is an intrinsic feature of fractals. A fractal has some well-defined structure at every magnification. What is remarkable is that mathematical fractals are self-similar: they look the same when magnified by the appropriate scaling factor. This, in the commonest examples of fractals, equals two or three, or values between these numbers.

Exactly how the scales in a scaling hierarchy are spaced is the topic of "scaling coherence". This is the cognitive distance between one well-defined scale and the next scale. If this cognitive distance is too small (as happens when the scaling ratio is small), we cannot perceive the two scales as really distinct. If the cognitive distance is too large (when the scaling ratio is large), then we do see two distinct scales, but they are unrelated to each other because too far apart.

Psychological tests of how faithfully mathematical fractals resemble natural scenes such as coastlines, mountain ranges, snowflakes, etc.

have been performed by adjusting their scaling ratio. Similar visual scenes are generated by computer, with each one produced by the same fractal algorithm but using a different scaling ratio. It turns out that those artificial scenes appear most natural when the scaling ratio is close to the value that we propose: in the range from $\sqrt{7} \approx 2.65$ to 3. This is consistent with $e \approx 2.7$.

Nature herself will impose fractal weathering patterns on materials, which turn "pure" forms into ones with a scaling hierarchy. This shows that fractal forms are more natural than pure, mechanical forms, since any non-fractal object will eventually become fractal. (Maybe that's why architects like to use titanium — in order to delay the fractal transformation by a few centuries. But this practice is extremely expensive and energy-wasteful). Modernist architects have resisted the weathering process as it ruins their pristine designs, whereas traditional architects always design in a scaling hierarchy to begin with. Those buildings weather much better.

An emotional connection occurs with surfaces, but only when they have a nicely ordered microstructure. I am referring to patterned scales of 1 mm to 1 cm. Going up in scales, traditional architecture used moldings and ornament to define additional scales from 1 cm to about 30 cm or even 1 m. Even larger scales, from 30 cm up to the overall size of the building, are fixed by the spaces, tectonics, and structural dimensions.

With the idea of a scaling hierarchy, we can see that all of these observable architectural features, from the smallest to largest scale, together form a mathematical hierarchy. The cognitive distance between scales determines the effectiveness of the hierarchy, which could be made either empty, or cluttered, or unbalanced, or nicely coherent. It is the architect's choice, working with appropriate materials.

A building with scaling coherence has a great feature for its user: it makes sense at any distance. This occurs because only some of the scales in the scaling hierarchy will be perceivable at any particular distance, yet other scales will come into view as one gets closer, or as one moves away. There is always a balanced hierarchy of scales at every distance, right up to touching its surface.

I will now outline how scales in a design become coherent.

(1) Objects on the same scale bind together through similarity and contrast.

(2) Objects on a lower scale combine into an ensemble having higher symmetry that exists on a larger scale. This more complex object is dependent upon its smaller components.

133

(3) Scaling similarity links objects on distinct scales.

I claim that a building's scaling coherence is severely compromised if one or more of its scales are missing (as determined by gaps in a scaling hierarchy). Similar destabilization occurs in natural systems. The clearest example is an ecosystem containing animals of different mass. It is found that the distribution of the masses of different animals obeys a clear scaling hierarchy. Furthermore, removing one species of animal endangers the entire ecosystem. Nature solves the problem by re-establishing the scaling hierarchy as quickly as possible. Either another animal will evolve to take its place in the hierarchy, or all the larger animals will die out.

Let us now leave "levels of scale", and look for the other fifteen properties in nature. Alexander gives countless examples, demonstrating that they are part of science, and not human aesthetics or psychological response or preference.

All the instances where the fifteen properties appear in nature should convince us that something important is taking place. Also, try as one might, an architect is foolish to ignore natural processes. I already noted how weathering creates fractal patterns. Buildings become part of nature whether we like to admit it or not.

Architecture students can read the very interesting examples showing how the fifteen properties occur throughout the universe, in systems of all scales in space and time, and in all sub-disciplines of science. They are indeed universal. Each example, in fact, has its own separate scientific explanation for why it occurs. An explanation for the growth of a crystal does not apply to explain the shape of a flower. And yet, the overall geometric rules appear the same!

All of these different scientific explanations do not concern architecture — they are chiefly of general interest. What is crucial is that the fifteen properties are higher-order rules for coherence in nature. They indeed cross different scientific disciplines, and are not dependent upon the detailed explanations for each occurrence. Those explanations merely support a phenomenon that occurs, and which repeats throughout space, scale, and time.

We see the fifteen properties everywhere in nature. But, as Alexander points out, the configurations that exist are only an infinitesimally small portion of all possible configurations. So, why don't we see in the universe the vast number of physical configurations that would violate the fifteen properties? Clearly, natural mechanisms select those structures that have these properties, from a vastly greater number of possibilities that don't. We don't know the reason for this selection.

One could conjecture that possible universes that violate the fifteen properties would be unstable, and cannot form for some basic reason. This is sheer speculation, of course. Yet there is no other explanation for why our universe displays these fifteen properties so prominently.

The same is not however true of human creations. Yes, the fifteen properties are satisfied by what is generally agreed to be the corpus of the greatest human creations of the past, as well as by un-selfconscious artifacts and buildings. That is where Alexander discovered the fifteen properties in the first place. Yet there exist a very large number of objects and buildings that violate the fifteen properties. Artifacts, buildings, and pieces of urban fabric that do not satisfy the fifteen properties don't automatically disintegrate: they are physically stable. We have them all around us today.

If we take the fifteen properties as defining what is natural structure, then we conclude that humans, unlike nature herself, have the freedom to be unnatural. There does not exist an automatic selection process that erases unnatural artificial products. And yet, we mostly connect to precisely those human creations that are more natural in the sense of satisfying the fifteen properties.

# 21. LECTURE NOTES, NINTH WEEK. ORGANIZED COMPLEXITY AND A MODEL THAT ESTIMATES LIFE IN ARCHITECTURE

## Readings for the Ninth Week:

- Alexander, *The Phenomenon of Life*, Appendix 6, "Calculating Degree of Life in Different Famous Buildings".
- Salingaros, *A Theory of Architecture*, Chapter 5, "Life and Complexity in Architecture From a Thermodynamic Analogy".

The time has come to begin estimating qualities of buildings that can provide a theoretical measure for their perceived degree of "life". If the theory is sound, then the theoretical result computed for "life" ought to correlate rather well with the result obtained directly from the "mirror of the self" test.

First, let us define a theoretical measure $L$ as the degree of life perceived in the building. I will present a model that computes $L$ as a percentage value. It works by estimating some of the fifteen fundamental properties statistically on a scale of 0 to 2 as follows: 0 if there is none present, 1 if that a quality is partly present, and 2 if it is strongly present.

I introduced the Architectural Temperature $T$ as an easily-measurable quality of a structure. It estimates several of the Fifteen Fundamental Properties, such as Levels of Scale, Thick Boundaries, Alternating Repetition, and Contrast, though in a much-simplified manner. The Temperature $T$ is supposed to measure the departure of a form or structure from total uniformity, which is empty, featureless, flat, grey or white, or transparent. We normally feel that such a minimalist form is "cold". I imagine that, as a form is made more interesting, it becomes "hotter". Color is included here because of the analogy with physical objects that begin to glow when heated up. $T$ will provide us with a statistical measure of a structure's informational richness.

Five different measures $T_1$ to $T_5$ contribute to the Architectural Temperature $T$. Each is estimated on a scale of 0 to 2 according to a rough judgment: very little or none = 0, some = 1, considerable = 2. The first three contributions come from geometrical substructure, whereas the last two come from color:

$T_1$ = intensity of perceivable detail (strictly small scale);

$T_2$ = density of differentiations, on every scale;

$T_3$ = curvature of lines and forms on every scale, with a higher value for a smaller radius of curvature, and for more curves present;

$T_4$ = intensity of color hue, high for a vivid color with high chromatic depth;

$T_5$ = contrast among color hues, complementary colors, and black-and-white contrast.

The architectural temperature $T$ is the sum of all these estimates (the subscripted quantities). Each component assumes values between 0 and 2, therefore the total quantity $T$ will range from 0 to 10.

Now we need to incorporate some of the other Fifteen Fundamental Properties, such as Strong Centers, Local Symmetries, Deep Interlock, and Echoes. Again, I define five different components, this time of the Architectural Harmony $H$ to measure obvious features of a structure that are responsible for coherence and unification. I use the façade of buildings, which is what users experience, and not the plan, which is perceivable in only very few instances (except on aerial photos, which are irrelevant to a user inside the building).

$H_1$ = reflectional symmetries on all scales, with a preference for a vertical axis of symmetry

$H_2$ = translational and rotational symmetries on all scales, or the degree to which forms at different locations have similar shapes

$H_3$ = scaling symmetries, or the degree to which forms at different magnifications have similar shape

$H_4$ = geometrical connections, or the degree to which forms are joined to one another

$H_5$ = degree to which different colors harmonize, lower for garish combinations

The architectural harmony $H$ is then the sum of these five estimates, and takes values from 0 to 10.

I now combine the Temperature and Harmony into a product $L = TH$, which is a measure out of 100. In this way, we can actually estimate some of the fifteen properties of an object in a rather easy manner, and get a total as a convenient percentage value for each case. Despite the extreme simplification of this model, it turns out to be remarkably accurate in predicting more or less what the "mirror of the self" test tells us. It is therefore quite valuable. This strong correlation permits me to call the measure $L$ the "Architectural Life".

Note the differences, however: the "mirror of the self test" lets us compare two buildings or artifacts and judge which of them has more "life". It doesn't give us an objective measure on a definite scale, which is what $L$ does. For example, we could measure the $L$ values of two objects at 50% and 80%, respectively, and this would correlate independently with our discovered preference of the second one according to the "mirror of the self test".

To illustrate how the model works with actual examples, I have estimated the architectural temperature $T$ and harmony $H$ of twenty-five famous buildings covering a spectrum of architectural styles and traditions spanning the entire world over several centuries. The numbers given are very approximate. To obtain these estimates, I have used a variety of published photographs, coupled in some cases with my personal recollection of those buildings in the list that I have experienced first hand. The table includes computed values for the architectural "life" $L$.

*Twenty-five famous buildings and their values of architectural life. Buildings are numbered in chronological order. The third column is computed from the first and second columns as L = TH.*

|     | Building | Place | Date | T | H | L |
|-----|----------|-------|------|---|---|---|
| 1.  | Parthenon | Athens | −5C | 7 | 8 | 56 |
| 2.  | Hagia Sophia | Istanbul | 6C | 10 | 8 | 80 |
| 3.  | Dome of the Rock | Jerusalem | 7C | 9 | 9 | 81 |
| 4.  | Palatine Chapel | Aachen | 9C | 7 | 9 | 63 |
| 5.  | Phoenix Hall | Kyoto | 11C | 7 | 9 | 63 |
| 6.  | Konarak Temple | Orissa | 13C | 8 | 8 | 64 |
| 7.  | Cathedral | Salisbury | 13C | 7 | 9 | 63 |
| 8.  | Baptistry | Pisa | 11/14C | 7 | 8 | 56 |
| 9.  | Alhambra | Granada | 14C | 10 | 9 | 90 |
| 10. | St. Peter's | Rome | 16/17C | 9 | 6 | 54 |
| 11. | Taj Mahal | Delhi | 17C | 10 | 9 | 90 |
| 12. | Grande Place | Brussels | 1700 | 9 | 7 | 63 |
| 13. | Maison Horta | Brussels | 1898 | 8 | 7 | 56 |
| 14. | Carson, Pirie, Scott | Chicago | 1899 | 7 | 8 | 56 |
| 15. | Casa Batlló | Barcelona | 1906 | 8 | 5 | 40 |
| 16. | Fallingwater | Near Pittsburgh | 1936 | 4 | 5 | 20 |
| 17. | Watts Towers | Los Angeles | 1954 | 10 | 4 | 40 |
| 18. | Corbusier Chapel | Ronchamp | 1955 | 3 | 2 | 6 |
| 19. | Seagram Building | New York | 1958 | 1 | 8 | 8 |
| 20. | TWA Terminal | New York | 1961 | 3 | 4 | 12 |
| 21. | Salk Institute | San Diego | 1965 | 1 | 6 | 6 |
| 22. | Opera House | Sydney | 1973 | 4 | 5 | 20 |
| 23. | Medical Faculty | Brussels | 1974 | 7 | 4 | 28 |
| 24. | Pompidou Center | Paris | 1977 | 6 | 4 | 24 |
| 25. | Foster Bank | Hong Kong | 1986 | 3 | 7 | 21 |

The precise formulation of this model tries to take into account two complementary processes that drive design. Even though each process depends upon some of the fifteen properties, they are in a way oppositional — yet it is precisely this opposition that, when controlled, creates the phenomenon of life.

Architectural temperature inserts information and sometimes disorder into a design. For the architect, this means freedom and exuberance in expressing ideas and, quite frankly, inserting elements that create a positive emotional feedback. Raising $T$ can result in interest but also in disorder. Now the complementary task of raising the architectural harmony has to be achieved.

All the elements that were just added in order to raise $T$ have to be further ordered and coordinated into a coherent whole. And yet, the tension between $T$ and $H$ can never be resolved in a one-sided manner without ruining the process. The designer therefore has to understand this delicate balance and work carefully.

Either $T$ and $H$ can be raised by steps, going through iterations of raising $T$ then $H$, then $T$, then $H$, and so on. Or $T$ and $H$ could be raised simultaneously, in a process that is more tightly controlled at all times. Either way, the product $L = TH$ is increased.

Coming back to the necessary compromise between $T$ and $H$, the quest of designing a building with "life" has to accept certain basic consequences of the model. Firstly, high $L$ is dependent upon high $T$, and so it makes sense that there will be some degree of randomness and even garishness, though that has to be relatively small. Secondly, a building with "life" could never be totally symmetric in a simplistic sense. But neither can it be done without a strong basis of overlapping, nested symmetries. In actual practice, we find a wealth of symmetries contributing to $L$, although they will be broken in some minor way. (This is the fascinating topic of "symmetry breaking").

In the past, architecture included sculptures, reliefs, representational murals and mosaics, and calligraphy. These smallest-scale elements help to raise $T$. The key to traditional design is that known harmonization techniques for raising $H$ kept a balance so that neither factor was compromised. The contemporary environment, however, makes absolutely no effort to coordinate visual clutter contained in signs and commercial billboards. This is the consequence of ignoring the link between information and architectural design. By accepting the false ideological statement that humans don't need color and ornament, our society didn't develop techniques for nurturing their proliferation in the environment, and thus we are at a loss to make order out of the garish commercial landscape of billboards and signs.

By understanding what design factors lead to a high $L$ environment, we are in a position to relate a building better to nature. By appreciating the intimate relation between the built and natural environments through this model, we can better appreciate the latter, and save it from destruction. Our design system can profit from using natural analogies understood deeply, and not just copied superficially. This leads to a higher level of comfort, because architectural life is an indicator of the positive experience of a building.

Questions raised concern famous buildings with low values of $L$. Are these to be considered as being deficient in some manner? There are two points to keep in mind here. First, the model for architectural life based on estimating values for $T$ and $H$ is a simplification of the fifteen fundamental properties. Therefore, for a more complete understanding of a building's value, we need to consider how well it satisfies all of the properties.

Second, a reader will correctly conclude that the ideal built environment will look very different from what is preferred today by trendy architects. New high $L$ buildings will remind us of a variety of traditional architectures, Art Nouveau, Art Deco, etc., which represent the opposite of minimalist concrete and glass boxes. Can we imagine a world like this? Yes, and it will likely be a positive experience and immensely comfortable!

Those who prefer the early 20th century form languages of Bauhaus Modernism might object to our model, because it rules out their favorite styles. But then, how did our present-day built environment originate? It was decreed that high $L$ buildings should no longer be erected, and that the only acceptable construction had to conform to a minimalist aesthetic. This decree was universally adopted, in my opinion without any valid justification.

# 22. LECTURE NOTES, TENTH WEEK.
# WHOLENESS AND GEOMETRICAL COHERENCE

## Readings for the Tenth Week:

- Alexander, *The Phenomenon of Life*, Chapter 3, "Wholeness and the Theory of Centers", Chapter 4, "How Life Comes From Wholeness" & Appendix 3, "Cognitive Difficulty of Seeing Wholeness".
- Mehaffy & Salingaros, "The Transformation of Wholes", *Metropolis*, 13 April 2012.

The phenomenon of life in the environment depends on the perceived coherence, what Alexander calls "wholeness". In practice, coherence is achieved through an iterative design process, i.e. after a sequence of adjustments. It is experienced all at once, however. Coherence or wholeness emerges from a dense packing of overlapping design components, which Alexander calls "centers".

A "center" is a visual region that, through its structure, focuses attention into itself, ties its region (neighborhood) together, and thus increases the overall coherence. At first this effect seems merely a psychological response of our visual system, but the phenomenon turns out to have connections with the wave functions of Quantum Mechanics, so it crosses over into physics. Alexander argues that for a configuration to be perceived as a "center", it must satisfy certain very precise qualities. Furthermore, one cannot obtain a center randomly — by chance — because the number of configurations without coherence is infinitely more numerous than those with coherence. A center is therefore a relatively rare occurrence, and must satisfy some very definite constraints. This also means that the creation of centers has to be deliberate, and follow certain specific rules.

For a region of space to be perceived as a strong center, it has to obey the most primitive version of the fifteen fundamental properties. I have found it useful to distinguish between two complementary types of center: (1) a defined or explicit center has something right in its middle that serves as a focus for the structure; (2) an implied or latent center has an empty middle, but the boundary is directed inwardly and focuses attention on its central point.

We normally experience combinations of centers wherever we perceive structure that has "life". Among artifacts and in the built environment, isolated centers are hard to find because coherent structures and regions are composed of many nested centers. Incoherent or empty structures contain few or no centers.

Part of the meaning of the term "center" to denote a coherent region of space is that it does not have an isolating outer boundary. In a system of nested centers, every such local center will be part of — and be contained in — a larger center. For this reason, it is necessary to describe coherence through its function of local focal points, rather than by referring to a definite region. We actually want coherence to extend as far beyond any local region as possible: there are boundaries within boundaries.

A system with wholeness is a combination of many overlapping, interacting centers. But those cannot be separated like simple components: the system is indecomposable. Simple machines can be assembled from components, but living organisms cannot. Architecture that exhibits the phenomenon of life is much closer to a biological system than to a crude mechanical system.

It helps in working with whole systems to approach them using transformations instead of decomposition and re-assembly. That is, we hopefully transform something that exists into a system that has more wholeness. Every step we take is guided by this concept. There is a basic rule for doing this: consider all components as inter-related and inter-connected. Thus, we evolve the system by transforming it in a way that its necessary connections are preserved (augmented, reconnected, but not simply cut) and its wholeness is increasing at each point.

Living systems routinely use transformations to create complex wholes out of other, simpler wholes. Life itself depends upon maintaining an organizational pattern, but not the actual matter of an organism, since metabolism is constantly replenishing cell material. It's the structural and metabolic pattern that survives, not the atoms that make it up. A highly successful design, whether it is a building or designed machine, shares this process of pattern generation via transformation. We can list three key ingredients for optimal designs:

(1) The final result arises by transforming relationships.

(2) Many of the patterns that make the product work existed before the transformations.

(3) The transformations will hopefully increase the coherence of the patterns. In the many cases they don't, we have a non-optimal product.

The transformation of the embryo is an excellent example of the transformation of wholes, with the aim of increasing complexity. As is well known, this transformation recapitulates the evolution of a species. Animal embryos all look very much the same until late in their development; there is an obvious re-play here of the selection process and how that triggers morphogenesis. For example, bones and organs from our fish ancestors transformed to provide very different uses for our own body (such as the bones of the inner ear).

Trying to perceive and build wholeness forces us to concentrate on the duality between the centers making up a whole, and the whole itself. This is not easy to do, as people tend to think of design as an act of assembling parts. Far from the picture of isolated pieces coming together into a whole, however, we find an interdependence between a whole and its constituent centers. Alexander illustrates this phenomenon visually by sketches on paper, but the same process occurs in solid examples like room sequences, or urban open spaces.

The wholeness is created from the centers, and conversely, the centers are created by the wholeness. Simple sketches on paper reveal how extremely sensitive these centers and the wholeness are to very minor variations: the same is true for large-scale structures, yet architects don't currently take this effect into account. A side lesson of this dependence of the large scale on what are minor variations on the smallest scale reveals the importance of ornament. It certainly does make a difference to our perception of the large-scale structure, so we cannot ignore it.

We should approach design by using full-scale mock-ups to experience volumes, surfaces, and spaces directly. Alexander builds in precisely this way: mock-ups made using temporary materials are adjusted until the group of architect/builders feel that the spaces and dimensions are comfortable, then those are measured and the drawings prepared, NOT THE OTHER WAY AROUND. In this way, the wholeness of the configuration creates the parts necessary to maintain that wholeness. In nature, for example, the petals of a flower are created from their role and position in the flower — the petals do not create the flower!

Such a direct interpretation of the experience of space reverses some aspects of our usual approach to design. First, what seems important

144

in present-day design (formal geometries; an "inspired" conception of form) turns out to be minor, while things that are normally ignored (how the spaces, surfaces, and volumes affect human beings) are really responsible for the life-affirming wholeness. If we ignore the latter, we will never achieve wholeness. Second, even the way we are used to describe the built environment in terms of architectural elements turns out to impede our perception of wholeness. And, of course, if we cannot perceive it, or describe it, we cannot generate it.

Centers and the wholeness of a physical region control our behavior in that structure. They influence the life that can develop there, and the feelings we have about that place. In this manner, they eventually control the human events that could and will happen there. This may not be obvious immediately, but will determine the long-term situation.

Alexander goes through several examples of how wholeness is built up by working on creating centers sequentially. The important lessons are: (1) this cannot be done all at once, but needs a step-by-step process; (2) the process is not additive, but transformative. Each step does not add entirely different components, but instead evolves what is already there towards increasing coherence. Transformations towards increasing wholeness end up adding new centers, yet those are generated internally and reinforce the existing centers. The greater the density of overlapping centers, the more we experience that structure as having qualities of "life".

Alexander points out that perceiving wholeness is extremely difficult, and especially so for adults in today's culture. It is not so in traditional societies, or in our own pre-industrial past, and children everywhere possess this gift. One experiment that demonstrates how adults have lost the ability to see wholeness is to ask students to draw an intricate design with overlapping centers. They will do a very poor job if they merely copy the pieces of the design. The only way to do it right is to try and draw the wholeness of the configuration: paying attention to the relationships among the parts just as much as to the shape of the parts themselves.

It turns out that this is also the secret of drawing an accomplished portrait of someone. The wholeness of the person's face will convey the personality of the sitter. This goes far beyond a faithful (near-photographic) copying of the face's features. Even if it has great accuracy, a portrait not based on wholeness will look dead and artificial.

Alexander performed an experiment using 35 distinct strips of seven black and white squares. Each pattern has an intrinsic wholeness that corresponds mathematically to the density of centers on that strip. Since the internal symmetries can be counted, we have here a "measure" of the number of overlapping centers. Untrained adults tended to see the patterns but not their wholeness, because they are used to interpreting information sequentially, not all at once: 80% interpreted the patterns sequentially, just like reading a line of text, and only 20% saw their wholeness. Yet young children routinely saw the wholeness.

Alexander discovered a method of training people to see the wholeness of these strips. He would flash on a screen all the strips shown together, randomly positioned, and the subject had to identify one specific strip instantly. Sequential searching doesn't work here because there is not enough time to compare one strip at a time — the observer has to figure out how to see the entire configuration. This is doubtlessly the same skill acquired when showing a number of coins on a table and asking for their number, but without giving enough time to count them. Untrained adults cannot do it, yet children and some autistic individuals can. Children can be trained to count a random distribution instantly, yet few ever are. Instead, we train our children to count sequentially — an important skill, but the other global quantitative skill is lost.

With both global training methods, after a while, the subjects increase their ability to see wholeness everywhere — the world becomes more and more the conveyor of configurations with wholeness. This wholeness cannot be perceived by a sequential, analytical search for information.

How can architecture benefit from designing through wholeness? Instead of viewing individual pieces and components, we could design the general experience of the entire building. Wholeness creates better geometrical transitions between diverse forms. If done correctly (paying attention to human sensibilities), the user will benefit from the geometrical organization. Coherence makes it easier to understand a complex building: we don't have to resort to reductive simplicity to achieve the same goal.

Wholeness can attach a building to its surroundings, if the design technique is applied to a scale larger than the footprint of the building itself. In this way, we can bring nature to connect better to a building situated next to nature. We can also provide a better experience for the exterior spaces. A complex built environment with wholeness is more lively.

# 23. THE TRANSFORMATION OF WHOLES

*By Michael W. Mehaffy and Nikos A. Salingaros*

*Metropolis, 13 April 2012. Reprinted by permission.*

The most commonly held and influential idea about design is that it's the art of bringing essentially unrelated parts into a "composition" or an "assembly". The funny thing is, from a scientific point of view, this idea is entirely wrong. A much better idea about design is that it's the transformation of one whole into another whole. Not only is this definition more accurate, it's also crucial for achieving an adaptive design.

Let's talk about the important implications of this distinction between *assembly* and *transformation*.

Why is it scientifically wrong to say that design is the "composition" of essentially unrelated elements? Because nothing that works as a complete system is really "essentially unrelated" — though the sciences used to operate more or less successfully from that abstract premise, and much of technology still does. By contrast, the sciences of the last century have taught us more and more about the essential inter-relatedness of the Universe, from the largest scales of the space-time continuum, to the push-pull world of the quantum. In the biological sciences, we've come to understand the multi-layered, historical interdependence of systems, especially evident in the web-like relationships of ecological systems. Wherever we look in nature, we find vast and intricate networks of connections.

This "essential inter-connectedness" matters because it can have big consequences when it comes to complex systems like human bodies, ecologies, or cities. We can't treat the parts of these complex systems as separate and interchangeable, without generating unintended consequences. (Think of a doctor who would do a heart transplant without bothering to find a careful tissue match!)

For the simplest problems, we can usually consider parts as if they were unrelated, and there is little harm in doing that. We profit from the procedural advantage of (over)simplifying our problems, and understanding them as made from separated and interchangeable components. But at a certain threshold of complexity, this useful little fiction starts to create a serious risk. At the level of a civilization, the risk becomes unacceptable. Then we have to start looking at other ways to deal with nature, and other ways to approach our design technology. That, in a nutshell, is where we stand today.

So it is "technology" — the knowledge of making things — that's really at the heart of the question. We sometimes think of technology as comprising powerful machines and big abstractions, but it is nothing more than our strategy to get natural processes to do the things we want. That's true whether it's striking the flint from an arrowhead, or sending a rocket to the Moon.

From the very beginning, members of our species have interacted with nature to create tools that achieve what we want and need. For almost as long, it seems, we have struggled to conceptualize what was going on. At the putative birth of the Western scientific tradition, Plato and his pupil Aristotle posed questions about *mereology*, the question of how parts relate to wholes — and to what extent we humans create wholes by combining parts, or by transforming other wholes.

It turns out that living systems routinely use transformation to make new wholes. In fact, one definition of life is simply this: "Life is the transformation of energy into information". Solar energy captured on the Earth's surface is converted into genetic information. Because of the impermanent nature of organic matter, this information has to be passed on to offspring through reproductive strategies. Each living entity assembles itself — and replenishes its worn-out components over its lifetime — out of chemicals.

Nevertheless, the crucial part of the mechanism is the genetic information and the complex organic structure that it grows and maintains — but note that the structure that is maintained is in the *pattern*, not the materials, which are constantly discarded and replaced. Furthermore, the more advanced life forms such as multi-cellular organisms don't live from just any simple chemical elements, but require the ingestion of complex compounds for their metabolism. Plants need organic nutrients, and animals need proteins that can only come from other organisms.

This means that transformation is key to the rich complexity of living structures — and an important clue for human designers. Certainly, we are arguing for the need to understand design in a manner that actually represents reality, not wishful thinking. Since this amounts to an entirely new theoretical discipline — and a very promising one at that, given our challenges — we cannot be haphazard about it.

Looking around us at the vast production of the 20th and the 21st centuries, we see an overwhelming number of "designed" objects that show only surface effect. They focus on components and "style", and not on essential wholeness, adaptivity, and function. Yet we find those latter, essentially "living" features produced routinely during the millennia of human inventiveness prior to modern industrialization. The question is, therefore, how can we integrate these more resilient qualities into our failing modern technologies?

The answer is closely related to what we think of as "classic" design. As we have discussed elsewhere (see our essay "Science for Designers: The Meaning of Complexity"), a truly classic style arises when a product attains its highest point of adaptation and functionality — and this achievement has nothing to do with visual fashion or a predilection for any particular "look".

Here, then, are three key ingredients of such an optimal design:

1. The transformations are not of "things", but of patterns — that is, relationships.

2. The patterns existed (at least in part) before the transformations.

3. The transformations either increase the degree of order of the patterns, or decrease it (or in some cases, keep it about the same).

Generally speaking, as designers, we are more interested in the kind of transformation that increases the complex order of the pattern. We especially value the kind of transformation that creates more variety, but preserves an essential unity, or what we might rightly call (as some physicists do) "wholeness". Wholeness in this context is not some vague mystical quality, but a definable characteristic of a system, just like the health of an organism. (And indeed, the two words share the same etymological root.)

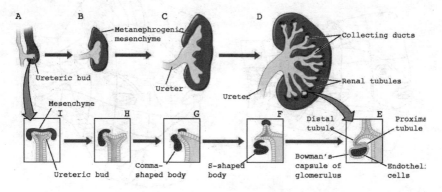

*Figure 1. The transformation of whole structures within the complex morphogenesis of a kidney. Image: R. V. Sampogna and S. K. Nigam, American Physiological Society.*

We can see the evolution of complexity in the process of "embryogenesis", where each multi-cellular organism (plant or animal) grows from a fertilized seed or egg through embryonic development. This process is definitely *not* an assembly of unrelated material, but is instead a transformation of the initial seed or egg through cell division and morphogenesis. The form-pattern at each stage of the embryo is transformed and further developed as it increases its complexity towards a final goal, the independent organism (which is encoded in its particular DNA).

Nature re-uses and re-combines working wholes into new uses, which is the most efficient method of building novel applications. For example, the auditory ossicles (bones) of our middle ear were adapted from an older use as the gill bones in early fish.

On another scale, organisms that are nearby on the evolutionary tree can be interpreted as variants of one basic organismic template. Members of such a family are simply morphological transformations of one pattern into another. This was beautifully explained by the pioneering mathematical biologist D'Arcy Wentworth Thompson. Going further away in structural space involves more transformational steps, until the forms seem hardly related to one another. Still, the hugely diverse evolutionary tree begins with only a few common ancestors — and achieves its complexity through this transformation process.

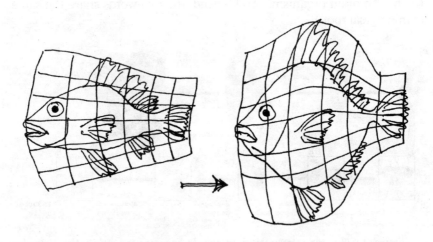

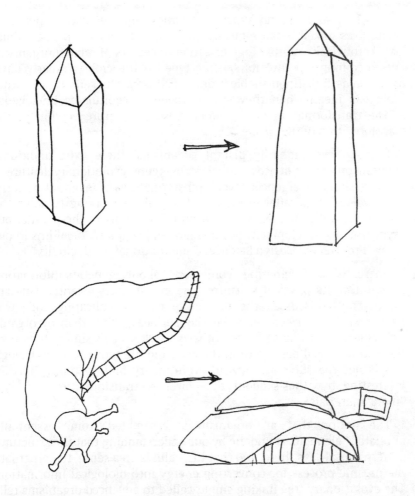

*Figure 2. Three examples of transformations. Top, geometric transformation of the external form of two different fish having the same internal wholeness, re-drawn from D'Arcy Wentworth Thompson's book "On Growth and Form" (page 1063). Middle, crystal transformed into a skyscraper loses its wholeness. The crystal's 3-dimensional atomic lattice gives it structural wholeness, whereas the hollow building's supportive steel framework does not extend to its volume, or to the transparent curtain walls. It is fine as a monument, only meant to be observed at a distance. Bottom, banana slug (Ariolimax) transformed into a Museum of Contemporary Art — an example of informational collapse. None of the animal's complex internal structure gets transformed. The building is just an empty shell, without any transformation of its internal structure. Drawings by Nikos Salingaros.*

The first and second types of relationship we discuss here are themselves linked because during embryonic development, the animal goes through the morphology of earlier ancestors of related organisms before coming out into its specific type. In the embryo's early days, a human is indistinguishable from a fish or a chicken. This is what biologists mean when they say "ontogeny recapitulates phylogeny" — the transformation of the embryo is a miniature version of the transformation of the species.

Even in evolutionarily distant organisms, there exist additional spontaneous coincidences, called "convergent evolutionary features". These design convergences reveal transformations of invariant patterns that evolved in parallel in unrelated organisms working to solve the same invariant problem. (We mention the example of the parallel but asynchronous development of the Shark and Dolphin dorsal fins in our essay "Frontiers of Design Science: Computational Irreducibility".)

There is a fascinating conjecture about genetic information substituting its physical platform. The evolutionary scientist Graham Cairns-Smith discussed the possibility that a replicating code was itself first developed on exposed clay surfaces rather than by organic molecules. According to his hypothesis, nucleic acids simply took over the informational pattern from the clay, and life took off! Even though this is not the standard view in evolutionary biology today, it is an interesting hypothesis about the power of transformations in even "inert" materials.

The notion that an organism is assembled from "essentially unrelated" elements is undone by our understanding that the structural pattern was always there, and that life's aim is, in a sense, to perpetuate the organic process for converting energy into biological information. The evolutionary tree linking single-celled to advanced organisms tells us that there are really not that many basic patterns of organisms, but those give rise to an almost infinite number of transformations.

We can find the same hallmarks of transformation in the most advanced design work today. You may have heard the story of how the interface pattern of Douglas Engelbart in the Stanford On-Line System transformed into Xerox PARC and then into the Apple Macintosh. In that sense, the Mac did not assemble essentially unrelated elements. Taking a broader view, the vast majority of computers today also represent a transformation — certainly, a very sophisticated one — of the original machines that first applied the computer architectures of Alan Turing and John von Neumann. But this common evolutionary origin also embodies their fundamental restriction. In an article entitled "The Information Architecture of Cities" co-authored with L. Andrew Coward (reprinted as Chapter 7 of our book Principles of Urban

Structure), one of the authors argued that a computer can never think, precisely because its architecture is distinct from that of the human brain. To make a thinking, and thus conscious computer, requires implementing a basically new computer architecture.

In product design, design theorist Jan Michl has argued — brilliantly, in his essay "On Seeing Design as Redesign" — that all successful design is a transformation of existing patterns, with much less innovation and assembly than is frequently realized. Thus, a mechanical watch represents a transformation of complex schematic mechanisms and partial solutions dating back to ancient Greece (for example, the Antikythera Mechanism from around 130BCE, despite a thousand-year gap when the science and technology were lost and had to re-evolve from scratch). It is not an *ex nihilo* creation. This interpretation of design was put forward by George Basalla, among other authors.

Thus we come to a core principle governing all design: the components to be assembled into the final product are not themselves the only things of importance; it's the pattern of how the structure works as a whole that's primary. This realization re-orients the designer's focus from visual "design" defined by components, to the essential connective wholeness of a product. The issue here is the connections and how they facilitate its function and adaptivity. And those connections are a transformation of something that may well be just as complex.

Buildings and cities of course follow the same general schematic rules. Despite human arrogance (and ignorance) in wishing to create — or, more accurately, impose — artificial environments, the basic processes of design as transformation still rule everything we do. Whether we admit it or not, the best products are transformations of whole patterns. On the other hand, products that are created arbitrarily tend to be at best deficient, or at worst dysfunctional in practice.

For example, much of the building stock erected during the 20th century has been a transformation of the concrete and glass cubes, planes, and cylinders of early Modernism. Other kinds of product design have followed suit, adapting tools to an essentially industrial visual aesthetic rather than to fundamental human needs, or even to any genuine "functionalism". Since only limited transformations are possible for the primitive geometries of cubes and the like, the result has been a limited architectural vocabulary with repetitive variations of the same result over and over again. Lately, the cubes have been transformed by squashing and twisting their sides, and even replacing their edges with spline shapes. Formerly glass walls now almost disappear by transforming into "trendy" wire meshes. Yet for all the apparent novelty, the result is still a transformation of a relatively primitive early industrial pattern.

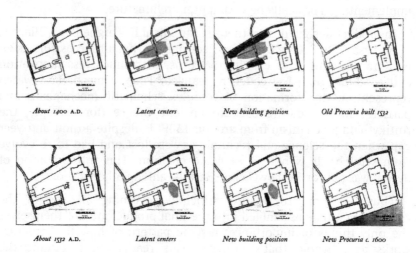

*About 1400 A.D.*     *Latent centers*     *New building position*     *Old Procuria built 1532*

*About 1532 A.D.*     *Latent centers*     *New building position*     *New Procuria c. 1600*

*Figure 3. Transformations of the Piazza San Marco in Venice that preserve structural wholeness over about 200 years, part of a larger series over 1,000 years as shown by Christopher Alexander in his book, "The Nature of Order" (Volume 2, page 254). At every step in its history, the city was a complete whole — not an incomplete set of parts waiting to be assembled.*

To attain an innovative, adaptive architecture, therefore, designers have to abandon the old "geometrically fundamentalist" patterns. But like other kinds of fundamentalism, this way of thinking is extremely seductive. It's difficult for practitioners and students trained in an ideology of "neophilia" within the Modernist typological straitjacket to recognize, or even accept, the value of transformation from older precedents. (We have discussed fascinating research that helps to explain this phenomenon in our essay "Architectural Myopia".)

This point bears emphasis, since it has important implications for sustainable design. It is ironic that many designers today (especially architects) believe it is automatically "reactionary" and "not creative" to use transformations from the vast pool of precedents before about 1920. But as this discussion suggests, such a prohibition mistakes creativity for novelty. It does so on the basis of an almost century-old (and as we now see, scientifically unsound) theory of design. In fact, recapitulation is precisely the way that natural systems achieve their high degree of diversity, adaptation, and resilience in the face of environmental shocks. We suggest that the most radical advancement now, in an age of biological complexity, is to use the best precedents from any source freely, and then to apply the processes of creative transformation. Indeed, there is reason to believe that the greatest design renaissances in history did exactly this.

And yet, contemporary design seems focused upon transformations that drastically reduce the degree of order — a *contraction* or *collapse* in mathematical terms. Our world is full of examples: replacing dense 19th century urban fabric of four-storey buildings with "towers in the park"; "renovating" a historic urban space by inserting a "contemporary" pavilion, concrete benches, and a giant abstract sculpture; cutting down century-old trees to widen a road or lay down a parking lot; replacing thriving integrated cities with sprawling landscapes of mechanical, "composed" objects.

The lesson is that if we want an environment with life — one that in turn nourishes our own life — we need new design skills and methods for transforming wholes, and, where possible, for enhancing the degree of complex order. This is the way natural systems "design" — and it appears, this is the way we had better learn to design too, if we want to be a healthy species in the future.

# References

- L. Andrew Coward & Nikos A. Salingaros, "The Information Architecture of Cities" *Journal of Information Science*, Vol. 30 No. 2 (2004), pages 107-118. Reprinted as Chapter 7 of Nikos A. Salingaros, *Principles of Urban Structure* (Techne Press, Amsterdam, Holland, 2005).

- M. Mehaffy & N. A. Salingaros, "Architectural Myopia: Designing for Industry, Not People", *Shareable*, 5 October 2011.

- M. Mehaffy & N. A. Salingaros, "Frontiers of Design Science: Computational Irreducibility", *Metropolis*, 12 January 2012.

- M. Mehaffy & N. A. Salingaros, "Science for Designers: The Meaning of Complexity", *Metropolis*, 30 March 2012.

- Jan Michl, "On Seeing Design as Redesign", *Scandinavian Journal of Design History*, Vol. 12 (2002), pages 7-23, available from <http://www.designaddict.com/essais/michl.html>.

# 24. Lecture Notes, Eleventh Week. Recursion and Stress Reduction Through Fractals

## Readings for the Eleventh Week:

- Mehaffy & Salingaros, "Scaling and Fractals", *Metropolis*, 28 May 2012.

- Salingaros, *A Theory of Architecture*, Chapter 6, "Architecture, Patterns, and Mathematics" & Chapter 7, "Pavements as Embodiments of Meaning for a Fractal Mind".

- Salingaros, "Fractal Art and Architecture Reduce Physiological Stress", JBU — *Journal of Biourbanism*, No. 3, March 2013.

Fractals are patterns or structures that are partly or entirely self-similar on different scales. Similar geometric patterns repeat at different sizes in a fractal. This means that fractals exhibit perceivable structure at every magnification. Some natural fractals such as fern leaves, lungs, cauliflowers, and nervous systems are ordered, whereas others such as coastlines and clouds are more random.

The point is that nature turns out to be almost exclusively fractal. Computer graphics can mimic natural objects or scenery by generating an artificial fractal. We connect emotionally with such an image because our neurophysiologic system is tuned to connect to fractals. The natural environment that shaped human evolution was fractal, and therefore we respond to it, as we respond to other biological forms having fractal properties.

Since a fractal has structure at every scale, we can see the different scales and are able to judge distance much better in a fractal environment. It follows that we feel better situated and more comfortable there. This phenomenon goes beyond aesthetics; it is a key survival advantage.

We apply our innate perception apparatus to negotiate the built environment — there is no physiological difference in the mechanism we use to register our surroundings, whether a forest or a city. We search for fractal structures to systematize ambient information. How we interpret these relationships determines whether we can successfully operate in our environment or not. That rubric for interpreting complex relationships among environmental elements is a fractal one.

On the scale of the city, fractality in paths means having roads and paths that branch and are layered, and go down in capacity in a connected hierarchy of scales. The network begins from highways, and distributes to roads, footpaths, and sidewalks. "Fractal loading" occurs when information exchanges on different scales can occur simultaneously: for example, being able to physically meet with people informally while walking to some task. Unexpected spillovers of positive exchanges make daily life more pleasurable.

Fractal loading also makes information exchange more efficient, since more gets done at once. It's difficult to see this from the perspective of mechanization, however, which assumes that every task has to be isolated. But human nature doesn't work in this mechanized manner, despite the huge efforts to force workers into assembly lines.

Fractal loading is especially important at the range of scales of the human body and its easy physical reach, 1 mm to 10 m. When we are presented with structural choices on all these scales, we can build synergies between them on the same scale and across different scales. The same mechanism holds true for events occurring on a temporal range of scales: we can negotiate and enjoy events on many different time scales simultaneously.

Well-structured pedestrian networks connected to higher-level movement networks are important because they help to preserve the fractal nature of the built environment by filling the lower scales. An existing physical urban infrastructure either encourages, or inhibits multi-scale information exchanges. Most important, it has to protect the weaker or lower-level events from being squeezed out by the stronger, higher-level events. Post-war modernist cities fail to do this, however.

Fractals are generated by an algorithmic process that produces related structure on all scales. Geometrical fractals illustrate this process, which can vary in two ways: (1) lines are crinkled or folded, and thus tend to fill in some of the space next to them, or (2) lines are perforated, broken all along their length like a sieve. Both cases represent departures from a continuous smooth line.

Traditional urban environments and architectures utilize fractal ideas, while not copying any particular fractal. (One exception is found in Cosmati stone pavements in 12th to 13th century Italian churches, which represent the Sierpinski fractal discovered by mathematicians only in the 20th century.) Both architectural and urban boundaries are necessarily wide and complex, nothing ends abruptly, and there is everywhere a gradated transition from large to small scales. These design forces, arising from fractal expression in the urban dimension, generate porticos and colonnades, porches and shared public space, etc.

Anticipating our later discussion on ornament, the smaller fractal scales represent exactly that. Removing them because of an ideological aversion to ornamentation destroys the fractal scaling, and hence the fractal. And doing this damages the natural experience that users demand from complex environments, turning them instead into an alien experience. It makes the environment less intelligible and less beautiful.

Stripping buildings and urban environments down into minimalist compositions is an explicitly anti-fractal action. Moreover, the results are mathematically crude, consisting of elementary solids and surfaces. An enormous amount of rhetoric argues for such simplification, but none of the reasons offered is architectural. It all boils down to a very narrow aesthetic preference for a sleek mechanical "look".

The presence of complex ordered patterns in our immediate environment is reminiscent in some essential manner of the natural fractal patterns of the natural environment in which we evolved as humans. Those patterns are a necessary part of our experience and sensory grounding in the world. It could be argued that there is too much of a cognitive shock to find ourselves in a minimalist world built in the pursuit of that specific style. Since the ability to process information is linked to our ability to reason and do mathematics, the environment could be affecting those capabilities negatively.

Architecture originally developed alongside mathematics, and for centuries, architects were also practicing mathematicians. Mathematics was for this reason made visually explicit, not only in the forms of buildings, but especially in the complexity of all their smaller scales. For unschooled people, this visual display of mathematical patterns on buildings was an important part of their education.

Post-modernist and deconstructivist form languages react to an empty minimalism. Are those styles fractal? Usually not. Fractals possess an internal organization of patterns, absent in both these styles. In post-modernist buildings, smaller coherent pieces are pasted haphazardly to create an incoherent whole. The different scales don't relate. In deconstructivist buildings, jarring discontinuities abound. Neither leads to the overall coherence of a fractal.

When we use a fractal template to interpret our environment, the most obviously fractal structures assume the greatest value. Those consist of trees, boulders, rivers, and natural formations. Traditional buildings and urban spaces also possess fractal qualities, and therefore couple very nicely with nature. This coupling is mathematical, is perceived with ease by our cognitive system, and provides us with a value system for judging structures that make us emotionally comfortable.

In a world that is built according to a minimalist, rectangular, and machine-like visual template, fractal natural elements appear out of place. So do buildings and urban elements from before the 20th century, because those also have obvious fractal qualities. Humankind now has other reasons for valuing nature and historical buildings, though those criteria are not always respected. But nature and the architecture of the past are not valued because they conform to the mechanical visual template that is lately used to build the world: they contradict it. For this reason, I believe that both nature and evolved architectural solutions are at great risk from an intolerant aesthetic.

Fractal loading has its counterpart in fractal image compression, a technique for reducing file size in computer science. A large quantity of information can be stored as a fractal, where pieces on different scales are attached as components of the fractal. Decompressing the fractal liberates all of its components to their original raw state.

We have hints that our mind does indeed use fractal compression to some extent. The evidence shows that a small-scale cue can trigger a hierarchical cascade of memories. For example, a certain smell could trigger recall of a place, with an enormous number of accompanying details describing the experience of a situation from the past. The information is present on many different scales. This process is known as "associative memory", which can trigger very powerful emotions. When we experience the world directly, we do so emotionally, not analytically.

People have a basic need to extend their consciousness outside their body, into their immediate environment. Fractal organization of internal thoughts and memories seeks to connect to external fractal information. This is done, we believe, through a fractal hierarchy, by connecting to a single immediate detail. Then, we connect through all the scales of the fractal to the entire external region into which it extends.

Take, for instance, patterned pavements. By perceiving a detail of a fractal at or near our feet, our mind connects to the entire hierarchy. If the design has been created correctly, we then connect instantly to the whole interior space if it's inside a church, or to the surroundings of an urban plaza if the pavement is outdoors. Connection with a complex environment, if it occurs effortlessly through a fractal hierarchy, endows meaning to it.

Richard Taylor and James Wise performed experiments that suggest that our neurophysiological system is tuned to fractals found in the natural environment. Most striking is the discovery that an observer's stress is influenced positively (dampened) by fractal scenes, but negatively (heightened) by non-fractal scenes. These effects were not based on verbal preferences, but on direct measurements of bodily indicators.

Supporting separate research on the biophilic effect, both artificial and natural fractals are shown to reduce stress. Therefore, our body apparently reacts to the fractal geometry itself, and not only to biological forms. Probably, then, humankind has always used ornamentation, building façades, and roof shapes to reduce stress through fractals. This has nothing to do with aesthetics: it is an adaptation for improving our health through shaping our environment in a particular mathematical manner.

Finally, the separate experiments of Taylor and Wise revealed that some fractals are better at stress reduction than others. The more effective ones have fractal dimension $D$ within a narrow range. In mathematical terms, this means that the hierarchical scaling factor is neither too small, nor too large, and falls within the intermediate range proposed by Alexander and myself.

# 25. Scaling and Fractals

By *Michael W. Mehaffy and Nikos A. Salingaros*
*Metropolis, 28 May 2012. Reprinted by permission.*

With apologies to real estate agents, one could say that the three most important factors in design are scale, scale, and scale. One reason is that many of the worst environmental design blunders of the 20th century have been mistakes of scale — especially our failures to come to terms with the linked nature of scales, ranging from small to large. The cumulative consequence of these failures is that the scales of the built environment have become highly fragmented, and (for reasons we detail here) this is not a good thing. Can we correct this shortcoming?

Most designers know something about "fractals," those beautiful patterns that mathematicians like Benoît Mandelbrot have described in precise structural detail. In essence, fractals are patterns of elements that are "self-similar" at different scales. They repeat a similar geometric pattern in many different sizes. We see fractal patterns almost everywhere in nature: in the graceful repetition at different scales of the fronds of ferns, or the branching patterns of veins, or the more random-appearing (but repetitive at different scales) patterns of clouds or coastlines.

*Figure 1. The beautiful structure of fractals, patterns that are repeated and sometimes rotated or otherwise transformed at different scales. Left, a natural example of ice crystals (Photo: Schnobby@wikimediacommons). Right, a computer-generated fractal coral reef that, helped by color and shading effects, could be mistaken for a natural scene (Photo: Prokofiev@ wikimediacommons).*

We can also reproduce fractal patterns in a computer, often with strangely beautiful results. Some graphic designers use fractal methods to reproduce very realistic-looking landscapes and other natural phenomena. These, too, seem to trigger something in our perception. We somehow recognize them as being "natural" and connect with them emotionally.

We seem to be wired to "read" fractals in our environment, probably for two key reasons. One is that biological structures are largely fractal in their patterning, and we are innately interested in other biological structures because they might be food, or predators, or other people, or just a key component of the biologically supportive environment.

The other reason goes deeper into geometry. When we look at a long vista, structures that repeat (trees for example), repeat at smaller apparent scales when they are farther away. This fractal information helps us read distances and depth in the environment. Doing so gives us an effortless understanding of the geometrical order of our environment. We're aware of this only as a pleasurable sense and not, coincidentally, as an important survival need, from an evolutionary point of view.

Fractal structures also give us other kinds of useful information, like complex relationships among environmental elements. The order of an essential but non-graspable structure, like an ecosystem, is more intelligible to us because we can detect the symmetrical fractal patterns of its plants and animals — another important evolutionary need. In modern times we have a greater need for urban environments to be legible to us, and there is evidence that we do this by reading fractal relationships in buildings and details (after all, we have evolved with this sense).

From an evolutionary point of view, it's evident that we perceive these relationships because they are supremely useful to us. They help us understand the structure of choices that our environments present, and how the different alternatives might offer us different benefits. It is an innate skill.

Importantly, fractal urban structures typically provide multiple combinations of benefits that work in synergy. And our pleasurable perception of fractals is probably related to this too. For example, the branching, layered, fractal-like paths we can take within the city help us carry out many different tasks simultaneously. People moving along such paths for the purpose of higher-level information exchange (going to a business meeting) can thus carry out lower-level information exchange (having informal "spillover" exchanges with other people, or perceiving pleasurable scenes). The time required for higher-level exchange is therefore used more effectively, and the net effect is a synergy of activities which often translate into economic, social, and other benefits.

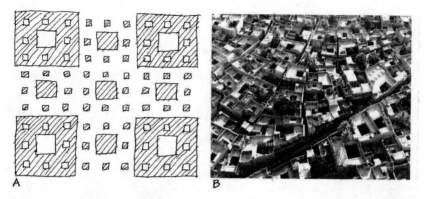

*Figure 2. The fractal pattern of self-organizing urbanism. On the left is a simple fractal pattern called a "Cantor Gasket" (Drawing by Nikos Salingaros). On the right is a much more complex and irregular pattern with recognizably similar fractal properties, a traditional urban neighborhood in Baghdad, Iraq. Notice the similar patterning at different scales of bordering spaces and alternating patterns of indoor-outdoor space (Photo: G. Eric and Edith Matson Photograph Collection, Library of Congress).*

This "fractal loading" means that each high-level exchange carries with it simultaneous exchanges on many smaller levels. An ensemble of exchanges on different scales is supported by a physical infrastructure that permits mixed information exchanges, but does not let other competing exchanges squeeze out the weaker or lower-level exchanges.

Fractal loading is important at all scales. But it becomes especially important at the scale of a human being. For instance at the scale of a region there are not that many structural choices that are relevant to an individual person going about his daily activities. But as we approach the scale of a human being (in fact, a group of scales ranging from 1mm to 10m), more and more structural choices begin to crowd into the picture, so that by the time we are at that scale, the environment often presents a rich set of structural choices that a person might make on a daily, hourly, and even instantaneous basis.

At this scale, the fractal loading of our environment vastly expands the structural options, and builds synergies between them. If I am in a well-connected, fractal-loaded spot at this human scale, I can read the newspaper, I can talk to a friend, I can say hello to a passerby, or I can run one errand or more. And I can easily connect these activities into a web of choices.

This is very likely a key reason that, within urban systems, well-structured pedestrian networks are so important. As our work has shown, there is reason to believe that there are important synergies of economics, resource conservation, psychological health, and other benefits, which are only provided by pedestrian networks that have this key property of fractal loading.

*Figure 3. The pedestrian networks of medieval Rome have a fractal structure, extending into the buildings and even the rich ornamental details of the buildings themselves. These "place networks" offer pedestrians a dense and overlapping set of choices of movement, views, and other enriching experiences (Drawing using the plan by Giambattista Nolli/ Photos: Michael Mehaffy).*

Fractal loading is one example of a "scaling phenomenon" in complex network structures like cities, and an active area of urban research. Another related phenomenon is that as the scale of a structure like a network increases, the phenomena that happen at a smaller scale often do not increase at a linear (proportional) rate. Often they are "super-linear" (they increase more than proportionally) or "sub-linear" (they increase less than proportionally).

These phenomena, such as economic growth and resource use per person, are very important to us. If we get more economic growth per person at a larger scale, or less resource use per person, then our quality of life can improve. This may be one important reason why people are attracted to large cities. Dense settlements really do offer more quality of life for proportionally less cost than sprawl does. And by understanding scaling, we can deal better with challenges like resource depletion and climate change.

But notice that this phenomenon occurs as a result of the specific network structure of the city, and its "metabolic" interactions and synergies (such as fractal loading). A collection of entirely separate individuals all "doing their own thing" would likely not benefit from such scaling phenomena. It is in the multi-scale interactions that these phenomena, and the synergetic benefits they bring, come about.

Interestingly, this characteristic of fractal loading tends to emerge spontaneously within urban systems that are allowed to self-organize within the natural processes of human culture — that is, within traditional urban environments. We all recognize this intuitively in the fractal-rich environments of popular tourist destinations like Bruges or Edinburgh. (And we recognize its absence in engineered environments that are decidedly *not* tourist destinations, like London's Docklands, or Paris' La Defense.)

*Figure 4. On the left is the highly fractal structure of urbanism in Bruges, Belgium. On the right, a much more sparse, fractal-free environment in the modern suburbs of Bruges — which is also far less walkable, and has other negative impacts (Photos: Michael Mehaffy).*

What does this tell us? Are fractal urban structures just nostalgic remnants of an obsolete pre-modern era? Or do they offer crucial lessons for designers today?

While there are certainly ideologically dogmatic theories of style and history that support the nostalgic remnant proposition, they are unsupported by real scientific evidence. And, critically, there is important evidence for the crucial lessons for today's designers proposition. To see what these lessons might be, we will discuss how fractal structures are formed in nature — and, it appears, in human nature — and why they might be such important attributes of a well-functioning environment.

Fractals have two related characteristics: They show complexity at every magnification. Their edges and interfaces are not smooth, but are either crinkled or perforated.

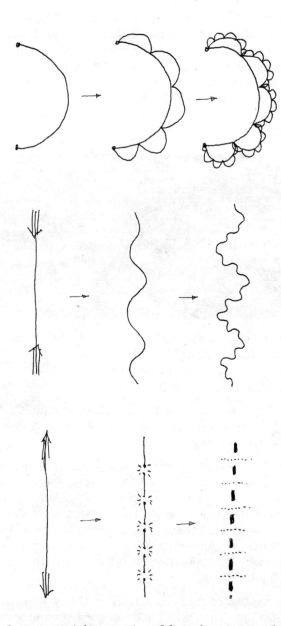

*Figure 5. Some essential properties of fractals. (a) Fractal loading uses a basic scale as a carrier for other successively smaller mechanisms and structures. Far from being monofunctional and simplistic, every structure becomes richly complex and carries information on several distinct scales. (b) Longitudinal compression forms a "folded" fractal, creating a crinkled line that then generates crinkles on its crinkles. This interface can catalyze*

*urban interactions, mimicking the non-smooth surface of a chemical catalyst. (c) Longitudinal tension and breaking along the entire line form a "perforated" fractal, here shown at its first stage. This is a natural mechanism for defining an urban colonnade and any semi-permeable urban boundary, such as a row of bollards that protect pedestrian from vehicular traffic (Drawings by Nikos Salingaros).*

Fractal patterns tend to form naturally for one simple reason: there is a "generative process" that creates the geometric pattern, and it does so at more than one scale. For example, in a blooming flower, the genetic code that creates the pattern does so in a time sequence, while the previously generated patterns grow larger.

In a computer-generated fractal, the generative process is called an "algorithm", a bit of code that generates the pattern from a complex interaction with what has been generated previously. In a city, the generative processes are carried out by people doing what people do in making cities. They articulate spaces with boundaries that are shared to varying degrees. They create spaces that have degrees of publicness, somewhere along the spectrum ranging from public to private, from the most public streets and squares to the most private bedrooms and baths.

The boundaries of living spaces are not simple structures either, but complex membrane-like structures offering their own set of structural choices, either to maximize privacy (by closing a curtain) or publicness (by opening a door). These boundaries are wonderfully complex structures in themselves and self-organize into larger patterns (doors or windows that become shared types over time, and neighborhoods that develop characteristic interface patterns of porches or colonnades).

How are the different scales linked? Just as biological structures and computer algorithms spontaneously repeat their geometric patterns at different scales, so do we, unless we're forced to do otherwise either by legislation or by ideology. Individuals might make small repetitions of a pattern (a rectangular room shape) while groups might make larger versions of the same pattern (a courtyard) and larger groups might make a still larger one (an urban plaza).

But as with biological and computer structures, the story does not end at any particular scale. The boundary of a room is perforated with smaller structures like rectangular doors and windows. The boundary of larger spaces might be perforated with colonnades (we are talking about living spaces and not the dead spaces characteristic of post-war architecture and urbanism).

These repetitive perforations at smaller scales — the fractal loading that results from the characteristic "generative algorithm" of fractal

167

structure — will often continue on down to the scales of detail and ornament. Why is this? It seems likely that we, the users, making our way through these places find such complex environments (complex in a very precisely ordered sense) easier to comprehend, more intelligible, more usefully organized, and more beautiful. We are very good at reading the multiple scales of these "place networks".

But there is a serious problem. If we are not users, but designers educated in our industrial/artistic culture, we might have another agenda: to impose another kind of order on the built environment. And that agenda might come from a very different set of criteria than the environmental experience of humans.

Such is indeed the case. To put it simply, our current methods of making cities are over-reliant on economies of repetition and scale, which do offer narrow advantages but are also extremely limited, and from a human perspective, very crude and destructive. Natural systems never use those strategies in isolation, but always combined with economies of differentiation and adaptation. Surprisingly, we haven't really figured out how to employ these in our current strategies (though many people are working on this problem, and our own work takes up this challenge).

Choosing to work with a severe technological limitation, modernist designers argued that a more sophisticated approach was to strip down buildings into "minimalist" compositions, much easier and cheaper to produce under the crude industrial processes of the early 20th century. It was the compositions of these elementary "Platonic" solids that were most beautiful, postulated architects like Le Corbusier, because they were "pure" expressions of form. The old Gothic cathedrals, with their fractal tracery, were "not very beautiful", he said infamously. Nor were the lively streets that he despised! Indeed, he and other designers made a strong ideological case (still persuasive today) that the old ornamented designs were bourgeois, contemptible, even (in the famous words of Adolf Loos) "a crime".

In this ideologically driven design movement, we have come to accept the incorrect idea that fractals are somehow primitive, whereas smooth, undifferentiated "Platonic" forms are "modern" and sophisticated. Ironically, the opposite is the case: The most advanced theories of today's science are all about complexity, differentiation, networks, and fractals — a dramatic contrast with the straight, smooth industrial geometries of early modernism.

Recognizing this, many architects and urban designers are speaking in terms of fractals, scaling laws, and "morphogenetic design". But the question remains: Are these individuals really engaging such principles to create human-adaptive structure? Or are they only using them to create attention-getting aesthetic schemes, tacked onto what is essentially the same failing industrial model of design? These questions are at the heart of the debate on the future of the built environment.

What, then, are the lessons to be drawn? Fractal structure is not just an aesthetic gimmick. It is an important characteristic of sustainable human environments. And this structure does not arise from the well-meaning top-down schemes of old-mode art-designers, but from those with a skilled application of processes of self-organization, as part of a new way of thinking about what it is to design.

And yet, we designers have been exceedingly stubborn in taking on this lesson. Under a misguided theory of environmental structure that confuses simplicity with order, we have been stripping away the critical connected scales and fractal relationships within our environment. We have replaced a world of richly connected urbanism with a disordered geography of artfully packaged, catastrophically failing art-products.

# 26. FRACTAL ART AND ARCHITECTURE REDUCE PHYSIOLOGICAL STRESS

*By Nikos A. Salingaros*

*JBU — Journal of Biourbanism, No. 3, March 2013.*

Human beings are apparently tuned to prefer an environment that has the self-similar properties of a fractal. Furthermore, as different types of fractals are characterized by what is known as their "fractal dimension" $D$, we respond best to "mid-range" fractals where $D$ is between 1.3 and 1.5. In such fractal environments, our body automatically dampens its response to stress induced by intensive tasks and reaction to external forces. This implies that particular fractal environments are healing, or at least buffer us from life's stresses. The remarkable fact is that this response is independent of what the fractal designs around us actually look like: they can be either representational or abstract. Altogether, we have here the beginnings of a new way of interpreting how the visual environment affects our health.

## Introduction

The term "fractal" refers to "broken"; that is, fractal designs are not geometrically smooth or pure, but are defined by components on a hierarchy of different scales. Fractals can be either built with accumulated accretions (patterns of ordered heterogeneity, spikes, granulations, "hairiness"), or instead have gaps or holes (perforations, sieves, hierarchically-ordered spacings). In either case, fractal structures depart from smoothness and uniformity by breaking geometrical linearity. Their name, however, tends to emphasize the "jaggedness" aspect that is characteristic of only one group of fractals. Fractals could be curved: a cauliflower is composed of superimposed whorls of ever-decreasing sizes, so there is nothing "jagged" here.

A key property of fractals is their self-similarity, where a similar structure is apparent at increasing (or decreasing) magnifications. Each perfect fractal can be magnified repeatedly by a specific scaling ratio, and will appear the same every time. Among the few natural fractals that are obviously and remarkably self-similar are cauliflowers and the mammalian lung. In a mathematical fractal, scaling similarity shows for any number of successive magnifications while for natural fractals, the basic structure eventually changes: for example, successively magnifying the bronchial tree of a mammalian lung eventually gets down to the cellular level, which shows no branching structure (West & Deering, 1995; West & Goldberger, 1987). Many natural fractals such as plants and other biological structures tend to be only statistically self-similar. In that case, a magnified portion of the fractal will resemble but not be identical to the original.

Architects are increasingly interested in fractal patterns and shapes, and are beginning to use them in their designs. Applications tend to be restricted to fractal building plans and fractal decoration on façades. The fractal forms that have been built recently, however, contrast strikingly with traditional fractal architectural expressions such as the Gothic form language (Joye, 2007). Even so, this trend moves away from the uncompromisingly "pure" forms favored by twentieth-century modernism, which insisted upon simple and empty geometrical shapes such as squares, rectangles, or regular curves such as semicircles or parabolas. Elementary pure solids and fractals represent opposite ends of the design spectrum: the former express reductionist design, while the latter express ordered complexity that is a result of mixing a hierarchy of linked scales. There is no reason why contemporary architects should not use fractals in their designs, but those should be more than just motifs.

We are commonly exposed to both natural and artificial fractals in our everyday experience. It turns out that much, if not all of natural structure is fractal. Natural forms exhibit complex geometrical structure on a hierarchy of scales, from the large to the small, going down to the microscopic scale. Artificial fractals have always been produced as part of traditional artifacts and buildings (Goldberger, 1996). Computer-generated fractals are now common in our everyday environment because of our pervasive digital technology. They are generated by recursive algorithms, which create substructure on a frame on increasingly smaller scales, or build up a complex whole by progressively adding contributions that create the whole out of smaller components.

I am interested here in knowing how the human perception system responds to fractals. We can begin with the conjecture by Ary Goldberger (1996) that our mind somehow has an intrinsically fractal structure, and therefore more readily accepts fractal information (Mikiten et al., 2000). As a consequence of this anatomical trait — and this point is crucial to architecture and design — we tend to imagine fractal forms as the most "natural". While this hypothesis is not yet proven, it does contradict the often-made claim by modernist architects that humans have a predilection for crude geometric forms. Indeed, it implies quite the opposite. Let us consider the experimental evidence on exactly what type of form makes human beings feel more comfortable, which should resolve this issue. Before doing so, it helps to remember that the modernist architects' assertion favoring abstract geometric preferences predates this latest scientific evidence by many decades, but the architecture community never went back to re-examine the original claims.

## Excitement versus stress

This paper argues that fractal images reduce stress in the workplace and living environment, and digs deeper into results that certain fractals are better than others in accomplishing this task. Experimental evidence suggests that there is an optimal fractal dimension required to reduce stress, and that being exposed to plain non-fractal shapes increases a person's stress levels. These results explain why we naturally prefer fractal images in our environment, and consequently, why humankind has produced intrinsically fractal traditional art, artifacts, and architecture. We know that we enjoy the complex patterns of woodland scenes, which are shown to be fractal. Going beyond simple enjoyment, people consider exposure to natural scenery to be restorative: it is good for our health.

In architecture, the stark modernist interiors that came of age with Adolf Loos and later with the Bauhaus have been very unsuccessful in eliciting the type of universal and visceral attraction and sense of comfort that more traditional interior environments accomplish, as witnessed by what the majority of the population chooses as their living interiors. People like to bring objects such as photographs, plants, dolls, and *objets d'art* into their living space and workplace. This practice has been condemned by a rather narrow design élite that continues to support the old minimalist design ideology against overwhelming evidence of what makes people most comfortable.

The research that provides a scientific basis for these general societal preferences would suggest that plain, empty shapes have no place in architecture; at least in architecture that has to be used by human beings (industrial buildings being a separate case altogether). Is it then the purpose of architecture to reduce stress? This is an open question that raises important issues, as some contemporary architects make it a point to induce stress in the user. Here it is necessary to distinguish between excitement that has a positive physiological effect, and stress that has the opposite negative effect on the human organism. Positive excitement is elicited by euphoria; the emotion of love; inspiration through traditional art, music, and dance; religious ecstasy; transcendental and mystical experience; sexual attraction, etc., whereas stress from negative excitement comes from physical threats (the fight-or-flight response); war; panic situations; horror and intensely violent real-world experiences and films; and prolonged exposure to environmental conditions or pollutants that wear a person out. Both groups of environmental factors disturb homeostasis (an equilibrium condition in the body), yet one is nourishing while the other is harmful (Selye, 1974).

I believe that architecture that is adapted to human physiology is nourishing because it generates positive feelings through positive cognitive response to symmetries and fractal structures (Salingaros, 2003). An artificial environment with those measurable qualities provides a better quality of life (Salingaros, 2012). By contrast, stressful environments with the opposite characteristics induce anxiety and depressive behavior, and ultimately pathology in their users and residents.

## Physiological response to fractals

Visual perception studies reveal human preferences for fractal landscapes and structures. I review material here from Richard Taylor and James Wise (Taylor, 2006; Wise & Rosenberg, 1986; Wise & Taylor, 2002). They found that people feel more comfortable with fractal images showing nature, over non-fractal images such as non-fractal abstract art. The first point to emphasize is that those research studies used physiological measures and did not depend upon responses giving the subject's preference, because that could be, and usually is, influenced by learned biases. Instead, the body's automatic responses were rated by measuring skin conductance. It is known in the medical profession that raised skin conductance (electro-dermal response) correlates very well with increased bodily stress. Therefore, the skin conductance will peak in a stress-inducing environment, and will be reduced in a low-stress environment.

The results from a 1986 study carried out by NASA (Wise & Rosenberg, 1986) strongly indicated that persons respond positively to natural scenes (either real scenes, or visual images of them), whereas they respond negatively to non-fractal abstract shapes. Subjects had to perform three types of challenging mental tasks: arithmetic, logical problem solving, and creative thinking while exposed to four different 1m x 2m images. Ordinarily, such tasks induce a degree of physiological stress, so that it was possible to measure the effect of the image on the body state while performing these tasks. The skin conduction measurements in the three different environments were compared with the same tasks performed in a control setting, which featured a pure white panel of the same dimensions. The results are as follows: the abstract non-fractal artwork *increased* the stress by 13% as compared to the control situation, whereas the two natural scenes *decreased* the stress by 3% and 44% as compared to the control (Taylor, 2006).

*Figure 1: A photograph of a forest (top), an artistic rendition of a landscape (middle), painted lines (bottom). © Richard P. Taylor, used with permission.*

A second interesting point emerges from further analyzing the data. The two natural scenes used in this experiment had a markedly different effect on reducing stress in the subject. The first image, showing a dense forest scene (top of Figure 1), lowered the stress somewhat, but the second image, showing a savannah landscape of isolated trees (middle of Figure 1), lowered stress considerably. The researchers concluded that, for some unexplained reason, persons react far more positively to a specific type of natural scenery. It's not just a question of having more nature, because the forest scene has a higher density of plants. This finding is nevertheless consistent with the biophilia hypothesis (Kellert et al., 2008), where humans feel most comfortable in environments that reproduce the mathematical qualities of ancestral human evolutionary environments. It is believed that we evolved in a savannah rather than in a forest. Thus a savannah landscape should (and does) provide the most positive response. The difference in the two natural scenes is one of fractal dimension (a mathematical measure of the fractal's internal scaling, which is described below) hence it is possible to pinpoint with some accuracy our innate biophilic fractal preferences.

There is yet a third result that comes out of these experiments. The forest scene used in the results referred to above is a photograph. It happened that the savannah landscape scene *is not a photograph, but a rather stylized drawing of a savannah landscape.* This reveals that our response is triggered by fractal properties much more than by an accurate representation. As such, the importance of the scenes in creating their physiological response relies squarely upon their mathematical content, and not in some intrinsic or mysterious vitalistic qualities of the natural scenes themselves. This result makes possible a remarkable simplification of what is at first a very puzzling effect.

In this interpretation of what is responsible for the physiological effects of fractals on human beings, I agree with my former student Yannick Joye, who attributes the mechanism to the mathematical and not the biological content of the environment (Joye, 2007). Only this assumption explains why we respond in a positive manner to artificial fractals. And, coincidentally, why humankind has produced fractal designs on artifacts and buildings for millennia (Goldberger, 1996).

## Another interpretation of the stress reduction effect

I wish to present an alternative interpretation using the same data reviewed above and draw a new conclusion. By taking the savannah landscape scene — our presumed ancestral evolutionary environment — as a fixed baseline, we can list the increasing stress conditions caused by the different experimental environments. I will use the control situation (plain white panel) as just another of the elements, giving it equal importance.

(*i*) Savannah landscape: minimal environmental stress

(*ii*) Dense forest scene: slight increase of environmental stress

(*iii*) Minimalist colorless environment: significant increase of stress

(*iv*) Abstract non-fractal design: further increase of stress

Ordering the experimental environments in this way demonstrates clearly that minimalist design is neither preferred, nor particularly good for us as far as dampening our physiological response to stress. It increases stress over our innate baseline fractal preference. When we abandon minimalism in design and create complex but non-fractal artificial environments, we actually increase our stress ever further. I'm aware that this is a disconcerting statement to designers, artists, and architects, yet it is supported by incontrovertible experimental data.

Working with Judith Heerwagen for the Herman Miller Furniture Company, Wise did a later variant of his original NASA experiment (Heerwagen & Wise, 2000). In this case, cognitive measures were used. The study used standard workstation cubicles of three different varieties, identical except for the pattern on the fabric covering their visible surface. One variety had a digital image of a savannah landscape, another variety was plain gray, and the other variety was covered with a geometrical pattern. Subjects sat in these workstations for half a day while performing a series of creative problem-solving tasks. A positive correlation was found between the scores on creative problem-solving tests and the natural-image workstation. (Since this work is proprietary, few details are available).

## We notice fractal edges and contours

It is instructive to explain how the fractal dimensions are computed for the images shown in Figure 1, above. In general, the eye forms a two-dimensional image of a three-dimensional complex of objects. Ordinarily, it focuses attention on contrasting edges in this image: a definite line, outline, border, edge where two contrasting regions meet, etc. We know that the eye scans an image by following its regions of highest contrast, called the "scan path" (Salingaros, 2003; Yarbus, 1967). Impressions of scenes are therefore determined for us by the fractal character (or not) of dominant contrasting lines within them, called fractal contours. For buildings, these dominant lines could be the roofline or skyline, borders, edges, articulated or otherwise ornamental lines, etc. The fractal dimension $D$ (explained below) is then computed for these dominant lines, with the numbers expected to lie between 1 and 2.

*Figure 2. A fractal edge defined by the repeating patterns of the Borobodur Temple, Java. © Richard P. Taylor, used with permission.*

These experiments with fractals confirm that the presence of dominant lines in our environment affects our physiological state: this effect, though subconscious, is significant. Furthermore, the effect is beneficial when such environments have a fractal property, and specifically, when they correspond to a "mid-range" fractal. People have been creating fractal art and architecture since the beginnings of humankind and civilization, which is verified by undertaking a survey of traditional art, artifacts, and architectural ornamentation produced ever since the first humans (Eglash, 1999; Washburn and Crowe, 1988). This enormous effort, concomitant with the rise of humanity and culture, may now be interpreted as the natural attempt to create stress-reducing environments using sensory feedback. This conjecture explains a great deal of anthropology and history, until we come to the 20th Century, when Art and Architecture began to diverge drastically from traditional models.

## Fractal dimension

Allow me to provide some background on what the fractal dimension $D$ represents. A smooth line (either straight or curved) has

$D$ = 1, whereas an area fills in a two-dimensional region and has $D$ = 2. However, an infinitely crinkled, meandering, and convoluted line will fill a little into its adjoining area and will have $D$ somewhere between 1 and 2. An example of this type of fractal line is the von Koch Snowflake, with $D$ = 1.26 (which is amply documented on the World-Wide Web). A mathematical object that has dimension approximately halfway between a line and an area, i.e. that has fractal dimension around 1.5, is called a "mid-range" fractal. The more convoluted and meandering a fractal line, the closer its fractal dimension will approach 2, at which point it ceases to be a line because it fills in all the area.

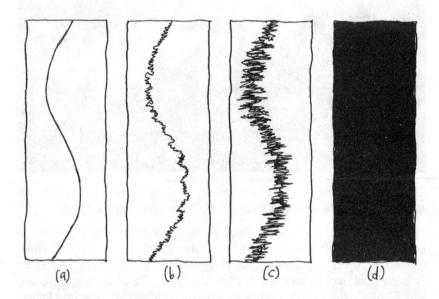

*Figure 3. Fractal lines of increasing dimension, until they become an area: (a) $D$ = 1 (not fractal), (b) $D$ = 1.2, (c) $D$ = 1.7, (d) $D$ = 2 (not fractal). Actually, these are drawings and not accurate fractals. Figures by Nikos Salingaros.*

We can also arrive at a "mid-range" fractal in quite a different manner. Starting from a filled-in plane with $D$ = 2 we begin to punch holes into it, perforating it with smaller and smaller holes. If we do this in a regular hierarchical manner, we are reducing its dimension and eventually create a "mid-range" fractal with $D$ somewhere between 1 and 2. But this object arises in a very different manner from a crinkly line: it is a sieve and did not begin as a line at all, yet it could have comparable fractal dimension to a fractal line. The triangular Sierpinski gasket, with $D$ = 1.58, is an example of such a fractal (again, see the World-Wide Web for a description).

Let us go back to the visuals used in the NASA experiment. Each of the straight parallel lines grouped in sets of three to seven (bottom of Figure 1) has dimension $D = 1$, and is not fractal. The lines being grouped together may form a visually interesting pattern, but do not contribute to any fractal structure. The groups themselves are arranged randomly without any type of scaling symmetry that might generate a fractal.

## Taylor's analysis based upon the fractal dimension of dominant lines

An analysis by Taylor using a great variety of fractal lines having different fractal dimension $D$ reveals that human beings do indeed have a preference for a specific type of fractal (Taylor, 2006). It turns out that we have a stress-reducing experience with $D$ around 1.4, i.e. for a specific "mid-range" fractal. These measurements are very approximate, yet they serve to establish a clear peak for human physiological response to fractal lines observed in scenery.

This finding helps to explain the curious and unexpected result of the original NASA experiment (Wise & Rosenberg, 1986; Wise & Taylor, 2002). The forest scene (top of Figure 1), which turned out to have a mildly positive effect, has dominant lines with fractal dimension $D = 1.6$, whereas the savannah landscape scene (middle of Figure 1), with a strongly positive effect, has lines with fractal dimension $D = 1.4$. According to this and other experiments, human beings do have an enhanced response to fractal images characterized by lines with fractal dimension nearer a preferred value of $D = 1.4$. Therefore, it should be no surprise that the subjects in the above experiment responded better to the savannah landscape scene.

Further distinct experiments by Taylor and his associates reveal a preferred value for the fractal dimension of edge lines with $D = 1.3$ (Hagerhall et al., 2008). Subject responses were evaluated this time by using Quantitative Electroencephalography (qEEG) to measure the alpha waves of cerebral cortical activity. Fractal edges having four mid-range fractal dimensions from $D = 1.1$ to 1.7 were generated by computer. (The figures were supposed to mimic fractal horizons that resemble the silhouette of the Borobodur temple shown in Figure 2, but are not nearly as attractive). By measuring the intensity of the alpha waves in the subjects, a peak preference for $D = 1.3$ was detected from among the different figures they were exposed to. Since high alpha-wave activity is known to be associated with a relaxed state, this finding is consistent with the hypothesis that such fractal edges are the most restorative and relaxing (Hagerhall et al., 2008).

# A square gasket and the relaxing effects of needlework

I will now construct a square fractal gasket, a variant of the triangular Sierpinski gasket, and compute its fractal dimension. This exercise shows that, starting from an area, one can construct a "mid-range" fractal that is no different from a fractal line. We begin with a filled-in square of side $L$, and divide it into 9 smaller squares with sides $L/3$ (Figure 4). Repeat this procedure with each of the newly-defined squares, which eventually leads to the more line-like pattern shown below in its third iteration (Figure 5).

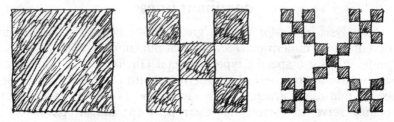

*Figure 4. Construction of a square fractal gasket with scaling factor equal to 3, by successively removing smaller squares to create a symmetrical pattern. Figure by Nikos Salingaros.*

Let me describe the iterative procedure that produces the entries shown in figure 4, above. The original filled-in square (on the left in Figure 4) is taken as the zeroth iteration: nothing has been done yet. The first iteration (in the middle of Figure 4) cuts the original black square to leave five smaller black squares each of side $L/3$. The second iteration (on the right of Figure 4) further cuts the five smaller squares into twenty-five even smaller black squares, each of side $L/9$. In general, the side $x_i$ of each square in the $i$-th iteration is as follows: $x_0 = L$, $x_i = L/3^i$. The number $N_i$ of non-empty squares (their multiplicity) at each iteration is: $N_0 = 1$, $N_i = 5^i$. From these values, we compute the fractal dimension as $D = -\Delta \ln(N_i)/\Delta \ln(x_i) = \ln5/\ln3 = 1.46$. (I refer the reader to standard descriptions for how this formula arises).

Without getting into mathematical details, the fractal dimension depends upon both the fractal's scaling ratio and the geometrical denseness/sparseness of the design. Elsewhere (Salingaros & West, 1999), I compute the fractal dimensions of the two best-known mathematical fractals in a plane: the von Koch snowflake ($D = 1.26$), and the triangular Sierpinski gasket ($D = 1.58$). The method for obtaining these results is outlined there.

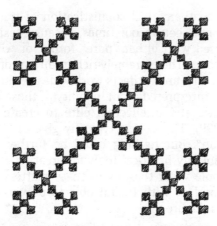

*Figure 5. Third iteration of the fractal gasket. At this stage, it resembles a fractal line, and is remarkably similar to traditional crochet needlework and cross-stitch embroidery patterns. Figure by Nikos Salingaros.*

Though evidence is mostly anecdotal, folklore tells us that stitching and creating crochet patterns such as the fractal with mid-range dimension shown in Figure 5 helps to relax a person. Indeed, for centuries before we had television and home entertainment, women did exactly that. Needlework has traditionally been identified as a particularly relaxing activity that calms the nerves, though it doesn't tell us anything about the effects of particular patterns. The American Home Sewing & Craft Association (AHSCA) commissioned a study by psychologist Robert H. Reiner, who reported that women who sew experienced significantly lower blood pressure, a drop in heart rate, and lowered perspiration rate (Reiner, 1995). (Unfortunately, no details of this experiment are available).

## Ornament generates a healing environment

A basic confusion has been encouraged in our times, by a culture that copies superficial visual traits without attempting to understand the underlying reason for the forms. This practice has led to a false understanding of what traditional artifacts and ornament represent. Many learned writers state that ornament is "imitative of nature", but this is a backhanded compliment. And it is misleading. Traditional Art, and ornament in particular, are nothing less than human mental creativity expressed in the most direct and immediate manner. Ornament is simply the first step in the generation of innovative structure towards coherently complex forms. Almost every other positive human achievement points in the same direction, and arises from the same creative process that generates organized complexity.

The incredible mathematical sophistication of traditional material culture is simply not seen in our times, because design professionals tend to be obsessed with either "pure" forms, or with the quest for innovation at all costs. The extremely rich traditions of fractal design in urbanism, architecture, and artifacts worldwide are simply dismissed as "not modern"; misinterpreted as an inability of those outside a narrow 20th century artistic and intellectual élite to create exact industrial forms (Eglash, 1999). The excuse typically given is that such objects are "not utilitarian". But nothing could be further from the truth: these are the eminently practical tools for creating a healing artificial environment. People wiser than us in these matters figured out that surrounding themselves with fractal objects provides an antidote to life's daily stresses (Figure 6).

When we confront the industrial products of the past several decades, we can hardly find a fractal. The popular interpretation for this paucity is that an anti-fractal aesthetic was necessary to reflect the needs of the machine age. But this is pure propaganda based on ideology. Late nineteenth-century and early twentieth-century industrial utilitarian designs and objects were in fact fractal, just like earlier traditional ones. Early industrial furniture and household objects and utensils were designed to also give nourishing feedback from their everyday use. The later radical simplification of forms was an ideological imposition by the Bauhaus and its successors: ever since the 1920s, people tend to judge a "modern" object by whether it conforms to this peculiar and intolerant aesthetic, not because it employs the latest technology.

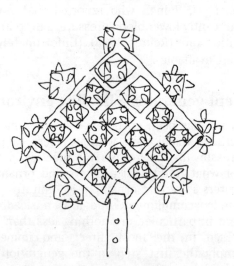

*Figure 6. Ethiopian silver cross is an obvious fractal. Figure by Nikos Salingaros.*

Taylor startled the Art world by proving that the paintings of Jackson Pollock are fractal (Taylor, 2006; Taylor *et al.*, 2011). Here we have an example of totally abstract art that is nevertheless fractal. The conjecture is that this is the reason why people find it attractive. Taylor's claim aroused excitement, with some researchers questioning whether the scaling in Jackson Pollock's paintings obeys a consistent scaling ratio, or if it extends to a sufficient number of scales for a true fractal (Jones-Smith & Mathur, 2006). Taylor's rebuttal settled the issue (Taylor *et al.*, 2006) and a number of groups subsequently performed their own fractal analysis on Pollock's paintings. This discussion encourages art historians to look at paintings and traditional products of material culture from a new, fractal perspective. Fractal art does not necessarily have to copy natural forms directly: what fractal art copies is the generative process that nature follows.

An important question raised by the discussion on Pollock is: *"how many orders of magnification are required for a self-similar visual to appear fractal?"*. It turns out that the eye can perceive fractal structures with just a few multiples of scaling. For example, the design shown in Figure 5 has only three iterations yet we respond to it as a fractal. Its scaling factor equals 3, thus two consecutive magnifications equal 9x, or approximately one order of magnitude (10x), at which one still sees the cross pattern (middle of Figure 4). At three consecutive magnifications 27x, we lose the pattern and get a square (left of Figure 4). Taylor finds that a design which is statistically self-similar at between one and two orders of magnitude (i.e., from 10x to 100x) works as a fractal.

A related but distinct question is how many orders of scaling are necessary in architecture. This time the answer is not so simple, because the user's eye perceives extremely fine detail in the materials. If a fractal structure or design is not hierarchically anchored onto the smallest scales, then any large-scale fractal will seem detached. That is, it will appear fractal but as something superimposed on the structure (and cognitively detached from it) rather than an integral part of it. Architects designing abstract fractals today don't include the number of iterations that take advantage of the stress-reducing effects. Contrast this with the fractal quality of traditional and vernacular architectural languages, right up to and including Art Nouveau and Art Deco, which do indeed connect to the materials.

## Fractal tuning and seven clues to cognitive resonance

Goldberger, Joye, Taylor, Wise, and I (and other researchers in this field) agree on one fundamental point: there appears to be a certain resonance between our cognitive apparatus and environments that possess fractal properties. Furthermore, not all fractals elicit the same degree of positive emotion leading to physiological stress reduction, but specifically mid-range fractals with fractal dimension around $D = 1.4$. Human beings seem naturally attuned to a visual signal of fractal character and particular fractal dimension. The brain is constantly computing characteristics of our environment, evaluating features that are essential for our survival, so this resonance has deep meaning. Lacking a satisfactory explanation for why our body is built in this way, we have only clues as to the underlying mechanism. I list some of them below.

*First clue: from the structure of the mind.* The mammalian body, and especially the brain, is organized according to fractal morphology. The brain is a structured system of hierarchically-organized anatomical modules existing on distinct levels of scale. Measurements of magnetic resonance images (MRI) of the human brain confirm its essentially fractal anatomy (Kiselev *et al.*, 2003). Evidence from associative memory points to a parallel between thought processes and the brain's fractal physical structure (Mikiten *et al.*, 2000). Going further, Mikiten, Yu, and I conjectured that signal reception works like tuning a radio to a specific type of signal, which is consistent with the notion of resonance of our mind with fractals of a specific fractal dimension. Functional magnetic resonance imaging (fMRI) and magneto-encephalography (MEG) studies of the human brain reveal both spatial and temporal synchronizations among different regions of the active brain. Significantly, space and time measures in the brain separately show fractal patterning (Pincus, 2009).

*Second clue: from fractal antennas.* In a recent technological development, the discovery of fractal resonators in microelectronics by Nathan Cohen (Cohen, 2005) opens up the exciting possibilities of studying a parallel mechanism in electronic hardware. Antennas built using fractal geometry have been found to significantly outperform linear antennas. Indeed, a fractal antenna built on the design of Figure 5 proves to be extremely efficient in geographical locations with weak signal, where ordinary antennas cannot function properly. Advantages of fractal antennas include significant reduction in size without loss of receiving ability; and extremely wide bandwidth compared to linear antennas, which obviates the need for an additional tuning unit. That is, fractal antennas are able to capture different frequencies without either geometrical or electronic tuning. Conjecturing by analogy, fractal physiological structures that make up our body could somehow resonate with fractal structures in the external environment.

*Third clue: from dynamic fractals in human physiology.* So far in this discussion we have considered geometrical objects containing different scales. The same phenomenon exists in time, where fractals in the temporal dimension contain signals of different duration. The electrocardiogram (ECG) time-series of the human heart has fractal properties (West & Deering, 1995). The dynamics of the human heart contain many frequencies that describe the variability of the basic rate at 70 beats per minute, which in a healthy heart goes up and down from 50 to 110 in a temporal pattern with fractal components. In a remarkable observation, pathologies of the heart are associated with a departure from a fractal spectrum, when the electrocardiogram becomes more linear, or when the distinct temporal scales decouple. That signals the onset of a heart attack. The West-Goldberger hypothesis states: "*a decrease in healthy variability of a physiological system is manifest in a decreasing fractal dimension*" (West & Goldberger, 1987). These results on dynamic physiological processes suggest similar patterns occurring on spatial scales, which we already know.

*Fourth clue: from the Savannah hypothesis.* Several researchers, each starting from a different direction of reasoning, come to a similar conclusion about the influence of our presumed ancestral environment. The mid-range fractal dimension of a savannah landscape provides survival advantages such as effortless conveyance of basic structural information (Joye, 2007; Kellert *et al.*, 2008). Environments with higher fractal dimension, such as forest, can hide predators and thus present more danger, whereas environments with much lower fractal dimension are both too open and too exposed to offer protection and sources of food. If we are indeed tuned to this particular fractal environment because of our evolution, then we should respond with increased stress in environments with fractal dimension very different from a Savannah: those with considerably less or considerably more than the mid-range value around $D = 1.5$.

*Fifth clue: from eye motions.* Taylor and his associates propose an explanation for fractal resonance derived from measurements made on eye motions while scanning a picture. The eye executes a search procedure all over a visual in what is called "saccadic" motion consisting of many jumps of different length. The path itself is not regular, but follows regions of highest contrast (Yarbus, 1967). Other than picking out the regions of maximal contrast, the irregular motions correspond to a stochastic fractal called a "Lévy flight" (Taylor *et al.*, 2011). Taylor computed the fractal dimension of the Lévy flights of the eye while tracking fractal scenes of different fractal dimension. Interestingly, the fractal dimension of the eye path pattern did not change: it was fixed at $D = 1.5$. Therefore, it seems that the eye uses its own intrinsically fractal scanning procedure, which is unaffected by the fractal dimension of what is being scanned. It follows that cognitive resonance should occur for any line that has fractal dimension around 1.5.

*Sixth clue: from sharks foraging for food.* Animals looking for food tend to execute a stochastic search (random directions and path lengths) that resembles a Lévy flight, where a local region is searched thoroughly, then the animal moves some distance away and searches that new location. Not only the shark has been observed to forage in this way, but also the albatross. The straight lengths of the movements combine many short paths, several paths of intermediate size, and a few paths of longer length. This is the characteristic inverse-power scale distribution in fractals. Taylor conjectures that this efficient Lévy flight foraging search pattern applies just as well to the eye motions in seeking out information from a visual in the most efficient manner (Taylor *et al.*, 2011). The stochastic Lévy fractal eye motions when scanning a scene therefore come from an evolutionary adaptation to mathematics, and are not a characteristic peculiar to the eye's anatomy, thus supporting the fifth clue.

*Seventh clue: from artwork that reduces stress.* An enormous amount of art produced throughout human history needs to be evaluated for fractal properties, and, if it is indeed fractal, its fractal dimension should be measured. In a 1993 survey, Vitaly Komar and Alexander Melamid claimed that landscape paintings containing water, people, and animals were the most universally preferred by persons from all continents (Dutton, 2009). Note that the presence of water in a scene lowers the fractal dimension of contours to that of a "mid-range" fractal. The publication of this survey caused an uproar in the world of fine art, since realistic landscapes have long been considered "kitsch", and thus taboo. Yet interior designers and environmental psychologists know something, because dentist offices' waiting rooms contain precisely such visuals (along with photos of cute puppies): an application of biophilia to lower the stress of anxious patients.

While medical researchers increasingly appreciate the health benefits of fractal environments, there is diversity of opinion as to the optimal fractal dimension. Some researchers investigating this topic disagree with choosing the mid-range fractals as the ones preferred by the human perception system. Alexandra Forsythe and collaborators, while supporting the healing value of fractal surroundings, propose that the preferred fractal dimension is much higher, between 1.6 and 1.9 (Forsythe et al., 2010). As evidence, they present the fractal dimension of well-known paintings, such as Botticelli's "The Birth of Venus" $D = 1.86$, Monet's "Water Lilies" $D = 1.78$, and van Gogh's "Sunflowers" $D = 1.76$. Elsewhere, Ali Lavine computed Hokusai's "Great Wave off Kanagawa" to have $D = 1.73$ (Lavine, 2009). These numbers, if independently confirmed, would of course require reconciliation with the experimental data given by Taylor and others.

I offer my own two points of caution in way of explanation. First, in this paper we are most interested in paintings that are known to lower stress in the viewer. A work of art may be famous and well-liked but not necessarily have restorative properties. Indeed, it may appeal precisely because it induces excitement. Hokusai's wave is certainly fractal, but may not be good at damping environmental stress. From the distinction between stress-inducing versus nourishing kinds of excitement, we can tolerate a short exposure to a challenging and provocative artwork, but an environment with those characteristics is probably going to have adverse physiological effects on our organism because of chronic stress. Second, it is notoriously difficult to measure the fractal dimension of a picture using the box-counting method (Gonzato et al., 2000). If one is not careful, the result given by commonly-used software could be off by 50% or more when measuring genuine fractals. Worse still, one could actually get a value for the fractal dimension of a non-fractal visual, which is a nonsensical result. We need to be cautious about the reported numbers for fractal dimensions of artworks, and wait for more data.

## Conclusion

The work summarized here addresses how fractal visuals influence human beings during the performance of stressful mental work. Beneficial, restorative environments dampen the inevitable rise in physiological stress while performing a necessary task requiring concentration. The opposite, those environments that actually boost the stress levels of normal mental concentration, should be considered harmful to our health in the long term. Despite the voluminous literature on learning and workplace environments, the effect of fractal scenes on reducing stress has not yet assumed the central importance it deserves. Instead, we continue to see the same stress-raising environments reproduced in new offices, work environments, and schools of all types. Apologists for continuing such typologies insist on a largely mythical industrial efficiency, stylistic "honesty", inviolability of the principles of modernist design, etc.

We could, on the other hand, use recent scientific results such as the work reported here to drastically re-design learning and working environments. There exist sufficient preliminary results to do this. It is surprising from a scientific point of view, but expected considering the inertia of the design establishment, that direct research on how people are affected by the fractal qualities of their environment is still only of marginal interest. One would think that this ought to be a central topic for investigation, to which society should devote major effort and funding. Too much of what is taken for granted, but which is shown to be wrong by experiments, relies upon personal opinion. But when individuals are asked what they like, they invariably give back what they are taught as the prevailing opinion, thus perpetuating opinions that obscure facts. It is time for us to correct this deficit of information on the design of the built environment.

**Acknowledgment**: I am indebted to Neil Campbell and Christopher Stone who, while not necessarily agreeing with everything written here, provided helpful suggestions for revisions. Thanks to Richard P. Taylor for letting me use his figures and for his useful comments. Finally, Graham Cairns-Smith's marvelous book *Seven Clues to the Origin of Life* (1985) gave me the idea for the last section of this paper.

# References

- Nathan Cohen (2005) "Fractals' New Era in Military Antenna Design", *RF Design's Defense Electronics* (1 August).

- Denis Dutton (2009) *The Art Instinct* (Bloomsbury Press, New York).

- Ron Eglash (1999) *African Fractals: Modern Computing and Indigenous Design* (Rutgers University Press, New Brunswick, New Jersey).

- Alexandra Forsythe, M. Nadal, N. Sheehy, C. J. Cela-Conde & M. Sawey (2011) "Predicting beauty: Fractal dimension and visual complexity in art", *British Journal of Psychology*, Volume 102, pages 49–70.

- Ary L. Goldberger (1996) "Fractals and the Birth of Gothic", *Molecular Psychiatry*, Volume 1, pages 99-104.

- Guido Gonzato, Francesco Mulargia & Matteo Ciccotti (2000) "Measuring the fractal dimensions of ideal and actual objects", *Geophysical Journal International*, Volume 142, pages 108-116.

- Caroline M. Hagerhäll, Thorbjörn Laike, Richard P. Taylor, Marianne Küller, Rikard Küller & Theodore P. Martin (2008) "Investigations of human EEG response to viewing fractal patterns", *Perception*, Volume 37, pages 1488-1494.

- Judith Heerwagen & James A. Wise with the Herman Miller Knowledge Resource Group (2000) "Natural Aesthetics Affecting Cognitive Performance in the Workplace", known as "Project Savanna", Internal Report (February), Herman Miller Inc. Reported in "Evolutionary Psychology and Workplace Design", Herman Miller Inc, 2004.

- Katherine Jones-Smith & Harsh Mathur (2006) "Revisiting Pollock's drip paintings", *Nature*, Volume 444, pages E9-E10.

- Yannick Joye (2007) "Fractal Architecture Could be Good for You", *Nexus Network Journal*, Volume 9, No. 2, pages 311-320.

- Stephen R. Kellert, Judith Heerwagen & Martin Mador, editors (2008) *Biophilic Design: the Theory, Science and Practice of Bringing Buildings to Life* (John Wiley, New York).

- Valerij G. Kiselev, Klaus R. Hahn & Dorothee P. Auer (2003) "Is the brain cortex a fractal?", *NeuroImage*, Volume 20, pages 1765-1774.

- Ali Lavine (2009) "Chaos, Fractals, and Art", *MATH53 project*, Dartmouth University (3 December).

- Terry M. Mikiten, Nikos A. Salingaros & Hing-Sing Yu (2000) "Pavements as Embodiments of Meaning for a Fractal Mind", *Nexus Network Journal*, Volume 2 (2000), pages 61-72. Revised version is Chapter 7 of Nikos A. Salingaros, *A Theory of Architecture* (Umbau-Verlag, Solingen, Germany, 2006).

- David Pincus (2009) "Fractal Brains: Fractal Thoughts", *Psychology Today* (4 September).

- Robert H. Reiner (1995) "Stress Reduction's Common Thread", report of a study by Behavioral Associates, New York, appeared as a news item in the *JAMA — Journal of the American Medical Association*, 26 July.

- Nikos A. Salingaros (2003) "The Sensory Value of Ornament", *Communication & Cognition*, Volume 36, No. 3-4, pages 331-351. Revised version is Chapter 4 of Nikos A. Salingaros, *A Theory of Architecture* (Umbau-Verlag, Solingen, Germany, 2006).

- Nikos A. Salingaros (2012) "Beauty, Life, and the Geometry of the Environment", Chapter 2 of: Agnes Horvath & James B. Cuffe, Editors, *Reclaiming Beauty*, Volume I (Ficino Press, Cork, Ireland), pages 63-103. Edited version of an essay from the *Athens Dialogues E-Journal, Harvard University's Center for Hellenic Studies*, October 2010. http://www.math.utsa.edu/~yxk833/lifeandthegeometry.pdf

- Nikos A. Salingaros & Bruce J. West (1999) "A Universal Rule for the Distribution of Sizes", *Environment and Planning B*, Volume 26, pages 909-923. Edited version is Chapter 3 of Nikos A. Salingaros, *Principles of Urban Structure* (Techne Press, Amsterdam, Holland, 2005).

- Hans Selye (1974) *Stress Without Distress* (J. B. Lippincott Company, Philadelphia).

- Richard P. Taylor (2006) "Reduction Of Physiological Stress Using Fractal Art And Architecture", *Leonardo*, Volume 39, No. 3 (June), pages 245-251.

- Richard P. Taylor, A. P. Micolich & D. Jonas (2006) "Taylor *et al.* reply", *Nature*, Volume 444, pages E10-E11.

- Richard P. Taylor, Branka Spehar, Paul Van Donkelaar & Caroline M. Hagerhall (2011) "Perceptual and Physiological Responses to Jackson Pollock's Fractals", *Frontiers in Human Neuroscience*, Volume 5, Article 60, pages 1-13.

- Dorothy K. Washburn & Donald W. Crowe (1988) *Symmetries of Culture* (University of Washington Press, Seattle).

- Bruce J. West & Bill Deering (1995) *The Lure of Modern Science* (World Scientific, Singapore).

- Bruce J. West & Ary L. Goldberger (1987) "Physiology in Fractal Dimensions", *American Scientist*, Volume 75, pages 354-365.

- James A. Wise & Erika Rosenberg (1986) "The Effects of Interior Treatments on Performance Stress in Three Types of Mental Tasks", Technical Report, Space Human Factors Office, NASA-ARC, Sunnyvale, California.

- James A. Wise & Richard P. Taylor (2002) "Fractal Design Strategies for Enhancement of Knowledge Work Environments", Proceedings of the 46th Meeting of The Human Factors and Ergonomics Society, 2002, Baltimore, Maryland (October), HFES, California, pages 845-859.

- Alfred L. Yarbus (1967) *Eye Movements and Vision* (Plenum Press, New York).

# 27. Lecture Notes, Twelfth Week. Ornament and Human Intelligence

## Readings for the Twelfth Week:

- Alexander, *The Phenomenon of Life*, Chapter 11, "The Awakening of Space".

- Mehaffy & Salingaros, "Intelligence and the Information Environment", *Metropolis*, 25 February 2012.

- Salingaros, *A Theory of Architecture*, Chapter 4, "The Sensory Value of Ornament".

Ornament and function go together. There is no structure in nature that can be classified as pure ornament without function. In traditional architecture, which was more tied to nature, such a separation never existed. The breakdown of the human adaptation of architecture can be traced to the forced conceptual separation of ornament from function, a relatively recent occurrence in human history. It is only in 20th-century architectural discourse that people began to think of ornament as separate from function.

A key aim of this book is to judge form and structure according to a whole system comprising the physical setting together with the observer. Any influence the object or place has on the user is part of its function. But any ornament will certainly also impact the user, so the actual experience cannot separate any particular aspect as pure function. Our mechanistic split of what we somehow decide to be function isolated from ornament is true for simple machines, but is invalid for situations in which humans are involved.

In the process of design, the end product will acquire qualities of life when we go through an interactive sequence of steps. This approach is very far from the usual satisfaction of a minimal list of uses and abstract requirements. How do we know that what we are designing on paper or on a computer screen actually satisfies those uses when built? We don't. Actually, it is only through the re-use of solutions that have been found empirically to be successful that we can approach some measure of success in our designs.

Yet the fundamental lesson is that we cannot presume to know how to satisfy a purely functional need. A "simple" function without complexity does not give a good solution. Failure to take this evolved complexity into account has led to so many presumed functional solutions that immediately proved to be disastrous — unusable because they are inhuman. The search for geometrical coherence, through the rules we have discussed at great length, is what helps us here. Paradoxically to a person raised in the 20th-century mechanistic worldview, the search for coherence and wholeness leads us to a functional solution that is accurate and not illusory.

In this picture of how successful objects and places are built by paying attention to systemic coherence, ornament and function are inseparable. It doesn't make any sense to talk about one and not the other — just as in natural forms. Therefore, we need to learn how to design things that have the quality of life, that possess wholeness. And in doing so, function and ornament develop together, without our having to pay any particular attention to either category separately.

Examining some outstanding design solutions from the past might reveal some real surprises. What we thought to be a strictly functional solution could just as easily have arisen (and probably did) from considering the wholeness of the geometrical configuration. This holds true on every scale, from artifacts, to rooms, to buildings, to urban spaces. They work and give pleasure at the same time.

The coupling of environmental information with our own participation ties us to our environment. It is therefore no surprise that the informational qualities of the environment have serious consequences on our biological structure. Although still under investigation, it seems fairly certain that our cognitive abilities are shaped and affected by the type of information embedded in our environment.

A variety of laboratory experiments on animals show beyond any doubt that the young raised in more informationally-rich environments develop measurably higher brain capacity and intelligence. Animals raised in minimalist, information-devoid settings are lowest on the intelligence scale. These are structural physiological changes that affect intelligence in a permanent manner.

This effect was finally recognized in 1994, when the Carnegie Task Force issued a report warning that minimalist environments (among those lacking sensory experiences of all kinds) could permanently compromise children's intellectual development. And the type of information that triggers the tuning of our intelligence is precisely the ordered, coherent patterns we have described in this book. For human beings, the best evidence comes from classical music, not art or architecture. Children who study classical music tend to do much better at school in all subjects.

Our neuro-physiological system developed to handle the specific information presented by our ancestral natural environment. When humans began making things, our evolved framework for cognition automatically produced a specific class of objects that reflected a particular geometric coherence. This was the same natural coherence that formed our cognition mechanisms in the first place. Our mind therefore extends out informationally into the physical environment through what we make.

An interesting clue comes from our paleo-history. There is, at present, a serious debate on whether or not Neanderthal Man created art and ornament, with many researchers claiming not. This topic is of crucial importance because our own species, Homo Sapiens, did produce art and ornament as an essential component of our evolving intelligence and development. The Neanderthals, by contrast, show no progress in their technology or culture during their era of about 200,000 years. In the end, we probably killed them off. It is easy to conjecture that our increased intelligence — which gave us our unprecedented evolutionary advantage — is somehow tied intrinsically to our ornamental production.

During the last 50 years, scientists have discovered how we interact with the information field presented in our environment. For example, the eye scans a scene by following regions with high detail, differentiations, contrast, and curvature. Furthermore, the image is formed by moving along connected lines, called "scan paths". The eye-brain mechanism therefore recognizes and uses the high-$T$ regions of an image to obtain information (see Section 21). This finding validates the 15 fundamental properties (Section 19) and the three structural laws of architecture (Section 20).

Further research links the way we perceive our surroundings with the way this information is stored in our brain, and is then used to govern our actions and decisions. Our lives are in large part governed by these innate mechanisms of capture, integration, and response to external information. Our instinctive response to forms is hard-wired into our organism.

We come up against a contradiction between the design of buildings and our physiology, however, starting with the modernist period. It seems that their architects go out of their way to deny the visual and morphological features required by human cognition and physiology. Could this be an accident? I don't believe so. Contradiction and elimination of perceptual coherence is systematic, so it has to be the result of deliberate action.

I wish to develop the thesis that ornament is a primary manifestation of human intelligence. A false but widely-accepted assumption in architectural discourse for over a century states that ornament is simply imitative of nature, but that's not true. Ornament arises as a spontaneous creative act of the human brain. Someone could also create ornament that imitates nature only visually, but that is a separate matter.

The proof of the above thesis comes from individual neurons that have the specific function to recognize ornamental components. Everyone knows of the retinal cone cells that react to different color hues. What is less known is that those same receptor cells are responsible for our ability to see fine detail. Furthermore, the phenomenon of "color constancy" links color perception to the brain's advanced computational capacity. We automatically adjust actual color hues under different light conditions to perceive the "natural" color — only a brain with high intelligence can see colors.

Even less known outside scientific circles is the existence of a large number of cortical neurons (inside the brain, not in the eye) that are triggered only by ornamental elements. These include specific responses to crosses, stars, concentric circles, crosses with an outline, and other concentrically-organized symmetrical figures with some complexity. These patterns are therefore built into our cognitive neural structure. Since those neurons are there for a reason, we should be stimulating them.

Going back to the anatomy of our own brains, individual neurons that fire in response to higher patterns of complexity are situated in increasingly advanced (from the evolutionary viewpoint) regions of the brain. The relative number of pattern-sensitive neurons also increases as we progress from the more primitive to the more recently-evolved layers of the human brain. This finding correlates the perception of ordered visual complexity and ornament anatomically with the evolution of intelligence.

Now we need to describe what happens when all this wonderful apparatus for perceiving geometrical coherence in our environment, and generating it in artifacts and structures, is frustrated. Our body reacts with physiological and psychological distress. Minimalist and otherwise information-deprived environments lead to depression.

Colorless and featureless environments do not necessarily produce a numbing response, but can trigger distress with an active feeling of threat. The reason for this active effect is that minimalist environments trigger signals of our own pathology. There is a group of diseases that make us experience a normal, informationally-rich environment as if it were a minimalist environment, which creates alarm.

For example, macular degeneration and retinal detachment create anxiety because we lose our image of the environment. Or a cataract makes the eye's lens opaque. These are all diseases of the eye. Other pathologies occurring within the brain itself give similar signals of alarm. Separately, cerebral lesions from a stroke, and carbon monoxide poisoning cause "visual agnosia", where a person with perfectly-functioning eyes cannot "see" because their brain is no longer capable of recognizing forms and colors. Such "agnosic" patients cannot recognize structural coherence.

Another condition of brain damage that mimics a minimalist environment is "cerebral achromatopsia", when patients see only in shades of gray. This condition is far more severe than regular color blindness, where the number of perceived color hues is reduced by one. With cerebral achromatopsia, however, everything becomes gray. Organic objects such as people's faces and food become repellent because they express death. Those unfortunate patients live out their lives in a state of despair in a depressing world.

This material is taking architecture into a whole new direction, and people may not be ready for it; certainly those in the present educational system aren't. It is important nevertheless because it reveals that designed environments have significant effects (either positive or negative) on users. Obviously, this needs to be part of the curriculum so architecture students are forced to learn it. Perhaps an effective way to teach these lessons is to apply this method to build buildings that have positive effects on their users, then architects will learn from those built examples. Furthermore, within the context of form languages, it's possible to combine this method with the way we are constructing today so as to generate something interesting that will draw attention.

# 28. Intelligence and the Information Environment

### By Michael W. Mehaffy and Nikos A. Salingaros

*Metropolis, 25 February 2012. Reprinted by permission.*

Looked at in a certain way, the human environment is a kind of massive delivery system for critically useful information.

It gives us information about obvious concerns, like where we are, where we need to go, where we might find food, where to look out for dangers (speeding cars, unsafe drop-offs, etc.) and many other things. And more subtly but importantly, it tells us where we will most likely feel safe and well.

It now seems that when we find an environment beautiful, a form of integrated higher-level information telling us something important about the structure of the place, it is likely that it's doing something positive for us. A grove of delicious ripe fruit is likely to be much more beautiful than one of diseased trees and rotted fruit — and that's no coincidence. Our aesthetic discernments have evolved as sophisticated assessments of what is likely to be in our best interest as organisms.

Put simply, we have a natural hunger for beauty — because we have a natural hunger for the deeper, biologically relevant characteristics of places and things that we find beautiful. This works through information input and our neurophysiological system, which developed to process and interpret information and to discern its relevant and often hidden meaning beneath the obvious.

There is also evidence that we strongly prefer information that is grouped into patterns that we can mentally manage most easily — as the psychologist George A. Miller showed, we seem to prefer "chunks" of two and three, and, combinations of these, up to about seven or so. We also seem to have a natural affinity for the complex patterns that plants and other natural structures exhibit. This is one reason that we have an instinctive affinity for certain biological patterns, termed biophilia (see our 2011 essay "Frontiers of Design Science: Biophilia").

Research in environmental psychology reveals that we prefer information-rich environments, though we like them to be easily broken up into manageable higher-level informational "chunks": buildings and spaces that have coherent relationships, that have identifiable pathways and entrances, that are layered in room-like sequences, that offer enticement, that form complex circuits and spatial relationships. The most attractive streets for pedestrians have these kinds of intricate, information-rich structures.

And we prefer that the surfaces of buildings present us with rich information that we can "decompose" into manageable units that are still related among themselves and to the overall whole (they define a "system"). This means, among other things, that the structures at different scales do not have too abrupt a relationship to one another, but instead, have a coherent, proportional kind of relationship. Geometrical coherence, both on the same scale, and across different scales, seems to play a key role in what we perceive as beautiful and nourishing.

*Figure 1. Two buildings directly across from one another on Burnside Street in Portland, Oregon, presenting very different kinds and degrees of information to pedestrians: The building on the right offers information about time and aging, individual business activities, entrances, different room volumes inside, and much more. The building on the left has none of that information. Instead it has a series of panels devoid of information beyond color, and following a relentlessly repetitive pattern, but arranged in what the designers hope is an artistically pleasing way. We may or may not prefer the view on the left over the more "old fashioned" view on the right, based upon our cultivated artistic tastes, our preference for cleanliness, etc. But when it comes to the brain's hunger for stimulating information about its world, the view on the left offers only superficial and poorly nourishing information. Image: Michael Mehaffy.*

What about environmental art? Surely, as a cultural construct, art is a much more plastic phenomenon, shaped by creative expression rather than biological needs? Well, the answer is... yes and no. We can, indeed, distort the normal evolutionary relationships between people and their environments to create exciting, disturbing, provocative experiences of art — but such changes are not without consequence. In exchange for these short-term benefits, we may well create long-term negative consequences for human health and wellbeing. When we're talking about gallery experiences, this is probably a limited risk. But at the scale of ordinary human environments, experienced hour after hour, day after day, there is growing evidence that the effect could be disastrous.

One of the most fascinating and intriguing such impacts seems to be in the ability of the environment to stimulate the ability to learn. Incredibly, it seems, the environment can make you smarter — or dumber!

Some of the evidence for this surprising finding comes from animal studies. In an experiment conducted by R. Kihsinger et al. (2006), some trout were bred in minimalist tanks while others were raised in a more naturalistic setting — a tank that included a floor of pebbles. The brain size of those fish was then measured (specifically, the region of the brain that is responsible for intelligence), and both compared to that of wild trout. It turns out that brain size for the three groups was markedly different: significantly larger for those raised in a more naturalistic environment than for trout raised in minimalist tanks. Yet when compared to trout caught in the wild that are exposed to a far richer visual and otherwise experiential environment, the wild trout's brain was larger than even the laboratory trout raised in tanks lined with pebbles.

In related experiments by G. Kempermann et al. (1997), this time on mice, a significantly larger number of neurons were found in the region of the brain responsible for intelligence, in two similar groups, one raised in an architecturally enriched environment, and the other raised in featureless cages. In a separate study, A. Sale et al. (2004) found a vastly improved development of the visual system in the brains of mice raised in architecturally enhanced versus minimalist environments. Note that the portions of the brain responsible for visual acuity and intelligence are tightly interlinked.

These experiments vindicate a central finding by the father of modern neuropsychology, Donald O. Hebb, who claimed, in the late 1940s, that an environment enriched with ordered complexity enhanced intelligence in a permanent manner. Hebb concluded that rich experience of all types (and not only ordered visual complexity) is necessary for the full development of animal intelligence. A scientific breakthrough came in the 1960s when M. Rosenzweig and his research group established beyond any doubt that enrichment of the environment leads to structural changes in the brain of animals.

It seems that humans, and other animals before us, evolved what we now call "intelligence" as a tool to interpret the complexity — *incoming information* — of the natural environment. We eventually began to shape our own environment, and projected a similar complexity onto it — *outgoing information* — in the form of mural paintings, color, ornamentation, and fractal shapes. Since the beginning of our evolution into humans, characterized by our urge to build and to create art, we have been involved in a two-way mutual reinforcement of environmental complexity of a very particular kind.

Damaging any piece of this interchange mechanism damages the entire system. But what does this mean, in human terms?

Countless studies have established that the rearing environment dramatically impacts brain growth in children. In 1994 the Carnegie Task Force issued a report warning that children raised in experientially poor environments suffer permanent setbacks as compared to those raised in richer, more enhanced environments. This was in line with the Head Start program begun several decades earlier in the US.

Turning to philosophy and robotics gives us a new insight into what might be going on. In 1998, A. Clark and D. Chalmers proposed the "extended mind" concept, where the workings of our mind actually extend beyond the brain and into our surroundings. An interplay takes place between our thoughts and internal memories, and knowledge and information stored outside yet within ready reach. Mobile robots do, in fact, use their environment as their memory — they have no stored internal memory, and thus save enormous computational overhead. Rodney Brooks' Mars Explorer works in precisely this way. Its ability to navigate its environment comes from an "intelligence" that links internal processors with external information.

This implies that the environment is crucial to the development of our brain: our mind is an integral part of our environment, and if we wish it to engage our intelligence, the environment should embody the same degree of organized complexity as our neurological processes themselves. Two possible connective scenarios are thus strikingly contrasted. (1) In an information-sparse, minimalist environment, our mind stops at the skull's interior. (2) In a coherently complex environment, our mind can extend into and interact with the visual information stored outside. In the latter case, we are situated in a vastly richer information field that drives our brain's growth in order to process and interpret this information.

*Figure 2. Can Louis Sullivan make us smarter? Corner entrance to the Carson, Pirie, Scott & Company Store, Chicago, 1899. Image: Nikos Salingaros.*

Our brains' connections change — even in adults, but especially so in the forming child brain — in response to coherent complex inputs. Although data for the influence of architectural environments on humans is sketchy, it has been established that an activity certainly alters the brain's connectivity. Actively playing music or performing a sport, for example, reinforces the wiring of the neurons responsible for that physical activity. Parents the world over encourage their children to take music lessons, if they are in a position to do so, not to make them into professional musicians, but because the ordered informational complexity of classical music is believed to help students perform better in school.

*Figure 3. Three-way blending of complex information: the rhythm of Indian classical music, Bharatanatyam dance, and colorful folk art provide a rich learning environment for young persons. It's intriguing to wonder whether India's remarkably high production of future engineers, doctors, mathematicians, and scientists might have had a boost from this kind of rich cultural experience. Image: Alexia Salingaros.*

Granted, it's a leap from talking about mice and trout to suggesting that our everyday environment *requires* ordered complexity, and that this is not — as usually assumed — a simple matter of individual taste. If future experiments reveal influences on human beings, we expect to find that environmental factors do indeed shape our own intelligence. Most importantly, their effect on the developing intelligence of our children is bound to be even greater than on adults with fully-formed brains.

So what are the lessons for designers of the human environment? The information content of our creations has a profound effect upon human life, and potentially, human wellbeing. We may decide to create minimalist environments because somebody finds them ideologically exciting, arresting, or fitting expressions of industrial technology. That's essentially what the early Modernist architects did — and we're slowly beginning to recognize the profoundly damaging consequences of that fateful approach.

Or we may decide to impart other kinds of information — the dramatic expressions of new avant-garde art, the eye-catching advertising of products, or the packaging of exciting industrial forms — or perhaps some mesmerizing combination of these. But to the extent this information disrupts and displaces other kinds of information to which we are biologically attuned, the evidence suggests, it can do great harm.

So it seems that if we truly want the wellbeing of our users — if we see ourselves as honored design professionals, with a duty of care — then we must work to imbue our environments with the kind of information richness that human beings actually need. This is a different way of looking at design, but perhaps a vitally needed one.

# References

- Andy Clark & David J. Chalmers (1998) "The Extended Mind", *Analysis*, Volume 58, pages 7-19. Available from <http://consc.net/papers/extended.html>.

- Gerd Kempermann, H. Georg Kuhn & Fred H. Gage (1997) "More hippocampal neurons in adult mice living in an enriched environment", *Nature*, Volume 386, 3 April, pages 493-495.

- Rebecca L. Kihslinger & Gabrielle A. Nevitt (2006) "Early rearing environment impacts cerebellar growth in juvenile salmon", *The Journal of Experimental Biology*, Volume 209, pages 504-509.

- Michael Mehaffy & Nikos Salingaros (2011) "Frontiers of Design Science: Biophilia", *Metropolis*, November 29.

- Alessandro Sale, Elena Putignano, Laura Cancedda, Silvia Landi, Francesca Cirulli, Nicoletta Berardi & Lamberto Maffei (2004) "Enriched environment and acceleration of visual system development", *Neuropharmacology*, Volume 47, pages 649–660.

# 29. LECTURE NOTES, THIRTEENTH WEEK. ARCHITECTURE ITSELF AS A BIOLOGICAL SYSTEM

## Readings for the Thirteenth Week:

- Mehaffy & Salingaros, "Complex Adaptive Systems", *Metropolis*, 6 August 2012.
- Salingaros & Masden, "Architecture: Biological Form and Artificial Intelligence", *The Structurist*, No. 45/46 (2006), pages 54-61.

Architecture is part of the earth's living system whether we acknowledge it or not. Our construction activity can be complementary to life's processes, or it can contradict and damage them. The decision is up to the architect, the client, and society at large. It might be a good idea to stop imposing architecture as the will of one or a few individuals, and allow design to arise in a more biological manner. The question is: how can architecture itself be turned into an ecological system?

We can mimic the actual process whereby biological forms arise: they develop as specific groupings of systems, and evolve to solve specific problems. The resulting organic forms are intimately connected to the processes by which they grow. Note how different this idea is compared to the imposition of a form based solely on some design aesthetic.

Beginning from the many components of a building, it would be good to adapt them mutually to each other, as a key feature of the design process. How does one do this in practice? The method of decomposition and refactoring helps: it makes it possible to visualize subsystems, and to make sure they all cooperate with each other.

For example, designing a building involves at least five distinct system decompositions. These could be concerned with:

(*i*) Harmonizing the building's exterior with its environment and avoidance of geometrical conflict, which of course includes adaptation to climate, orientation to the local solar and weather patterns, etc.

(*ii*) Connecting the site to the circulation networks present in its environment.

(*iii*) Shaping public spaces, from a sidewalk to one or more open plazas.

(*iv*) Planning interior paths for comfortable connection and flow.

(*v*) Identifying the interior spaces in relationship to each other.

There could be other systems as well, based upon individual needs, conditions, and uses.

The living environment, be it natural or man-made, is a fabric of connections between systems with definite geometrical characteristics. Such an environment needs to evolve its own design to a large degree in order to be both practical and pleasant to use. It also has to be allowed to evolve after it is built. Adaptation need not stop on inauguration day. Note that traditional environments continued to evolve for centuries, with harmful growth kept in check by a commonly-accepted form language and the strict application of evolved pattern languages.

The key to successful design is adaptation. On the shortest timescale, this requires that individual users are able to alter the material structure of the building in some way so as to optimize the information exchange. Something as simple as the ability to open a window and close shutters or curtains achieves this objective. But notice how the deterministic approach of most of contemporary architecture has ended this freedom: windows are designed as hermetically sealed, an integral part of the wall so they don't open.

Adaptation of the design to human use, before the building is built, occurs only if the design process follows a number of steps coupled with feedback. There can never be a top-down imposition of a ready-made form appearing from within the architect's mind. Furthermore, adaptive design is the opposite of either generic or minimalist design. Those are mutually incompatible approaches to the built environment.

We are talking about architecture as if it's a system that possesses its own intentionality and the capacity to adapt. Not architecture as the expression and imposition of some human will, which has unfortunately become the norm in our post-industrial age. Exploring this idea brings us to a list of seven qualities that all living systems satisfy.

Living structure is known to manifest several natural properties such as:

1. organized-complexity (information storage);

2. metabolism (energy use);

3. replication (self-reproduction);

4. adaptation (the organism changes itself to better profit from its environment);

5. intervention (the organism changes its environment);

6. situatedness (embedded in the world through sensors);

7. connectivity (information processing).

In biological entities, all the above processes usually occur together, but theoretically, these are separate concepts.

We have spent much of this course in describing organized complexity, and how to measure it using various techniques. Biological structures and processes work through mechanisms that are both complex and organized. The same holds true for the products of traditional architectures. Information from structures that optimize human life and actions is condensed and encoded into the traditional built urban fabric. This encoding leads to ornament on the smaller scales, and to a network of connected urban paths and spaces on the larger scales.

Let's now examine the above biological mechanisms in more detail. Metabolism is the exchange of information and materials with the environment, and keeps an organism's organized complexity at the required level to maintain life. In the architectural analogy, buildings metabolize via weathering and repair. Notice how modernist architects tried to deny metabolism for buildings, by seeking an elusive non-weathering material. Even though the search was a failure, it was the original idea that denies architecture as a living process.

Replication is the process of creating copies of a structure. Generations of organisms have evolved to a certain coherent form, and an individual organism preserves that successful template by making copies of itself. Buildings also replicate, as a successful typology will be copied. Modernist buildings were remarkably prolific in replicating around the world, despite their documented serious flaws in adaptation to climate, energy, and human use.

However, an answer to this puzzle (i.e. replication despite the non-adaptation) can be found in the marked simplicity of modernist buildings as compared to traditional buildings. The former are more akin to viruses because they neither metabolize, nor adapt to their environment. This gives them a replicating advantage because they have less complexity to reproduce.

Biological organisms adapt to their environment in two distinct ways. First, sensory organs adapt to the immediate situation on the short term using feedback, which is necessary for the survival of the organism. Second, the genetic pool (but not any individual organism) adapts to changing conditions, or to profit from an advantageous change acting on the longer term. This is evolution.

We face a contradiction with modernist typologies that do not adapt — being instead an international style — yet are very successful at proliferating. It is still possible to understand this as an adaptation, not to the actual user, but to the client who builds speculatively. Typical modernist construction offers advantages to the steel, glass, and concrete industries, and to a number of engineering firms that now dominate the construction market. Those players make tremendous profits from the now standardized industrial building techniques. The present economic model based on cheap fossil energy drives the worldwide reproduction of non-adaptive buildings.

Moving to the other properties of living structure, intervention actively changes an organism's environment. The act of building is an intervention. Buildings that can influence their immediate environment through passive or active energy use act in this manner. There is, of course, a tremendous difference between passive temperature control and the use of fossil fuels to achieve the same result. And these two very distinct ways of energy intervention lead to radically different typologies for the buildings themselves.

All organisms are situated, because they are embedded in the natural environment. They possess sensory mechanisms that dictate and adjust the organism's behavior through feedback. Organisms are constantly sensing their surroundings. Buildings normally don't do that, yet with recent advances in technology, we now have the capacity to create intelligent buildings. I believe the architectural profession is handicapped by almost a century of non-adapted buildings, however, and is not prepared to use sensors towards adaptation. The only practical reason to sense the environment is to then respond to it via adaptation and intervention. New, experimental design is finally leading in this promising direction.

Life works through connected structures. All living tissue contributes to create a connected complex system, which is the organism. Furthermore, each organism is connected intimately to its environment. A living system connects chemically with its food, using metabolism to generate energy. Life also depends upon acquiring and actively using information from the environment: avoiding damage and threats, or seeking beneficial situations. Another informational system consists of internal sensors that tell the organism that all of its own components are working well. Yet another informational system is the genetic information that defines the organism's structure.

Why don't all buildings embody living structure? They could, but architects and society at large have been sidetracked by a bug in our cognitive system. Humans have the unique ability among other organisms to carry an abstract representation of the world in their minds. This ability allows us to learn from our environment and to store information for future use. It is also liable to corruption, however. People tend to manufacture a false and hence dangerous alternative reality, and then base their actions upon that non-living fantasy world, instead of the natural world. This leads to disconnection from the real world, and its symptoms can be seen in the non-adaptive architecture of the 20th and 21st centuries.

# 30. COMPLEX ADAPTIVE SYSTEMS

*By Michael W. Mehaffy and Nikos A. Salingaros*
*Metropolis, 6 August 2012. Reprinted by permission.*

Today the world of design is in a position to benefit enormously from advances in sciences, mathematics and particularly, geometry — probably not in a way that many designers realize.

As humans we are remarkably good at conceiving the world as a collection of objects, their geometric attributes, and the ways they can be taken apart and re-assembled to do spectacular things (either perform marvelous tasks for us, or provide an aesthetic spectacle, or both). This way of designing underlies much of our powerful technology — yet as modern science reminds us, it's incomplete. Critical systemic effects have to be integrated into the process of design, without which we are likely to trigger operational failures and even disasters.

Today we are experiencing just these kinds of failures in large-scale systems like ecology. As designers (of any kind) we must learn to manage environments not just as collections of objects, but also as connected fields with essential features of geometric organization, extending dynamically through time as well as space. This is a key lesson from the relatively recent understanding of the dynamics of "complex adaptive systems", and from applications in fields like biology and ecology.

At issue is not just avoiding failures. Though our designs can certainly be impressive, nature's "designs" routinely put us humans to shame. No aircraft can maneuver as nimbly as an eagle (or a fruit fly), and no supercomputer can do what an ordinary human brain does. The sophistication and power of these designs lies in their complex geometric structures, and more particularly, in the processes by which those structures are evolved and transformed within groupings or systems.

We can readily see that in the natural world, forms arise as adaptive evolutions that solve specific kinds of problems — an eye gathers information about predators and prey, a wing or leg allows rapid movement, and so on. Anatomical forms do not arise within one large undifferentiated collection; they develop as specific groupings of systems and sub-systems. These systems in turn relate to and comprise other, larger systems.

*Figure 1. The ecosystem of a coral reef requires continuous mutual adaptation of individuals and species, like Yolanda Reef in Ras Muhammad nature park, Sinai, Egypt. Photo: Mikhail Rogov, Wikimedia Commons.*

The structural dynamics of systems are consequences of interactions between parts and wholes. This is a new science built upon a previous generation of biologists recognizing the adaptive processes of form generation, and their characteristic geometries — what is now known as "morphogenesis". Pioneers like D'Arcy Thompson saw that living structures had characteristic groupings that were intimately connected to the processes by which they grew.

Crucially, these pioneers came to see that formal and aesthetic characteristics were not separate, but were systems-specific geometric attributes. Over evolutionary history, organisms had learned to identify such attributes, the better to respond effectively to their environments. Our own capacity to experience beauty is, from an evolutionary point of view, just such a biological recognition of what is most likely to promote our wellbeing.

*Figure 2. Soap bubbles form a complex pattern as a result of their mutual adaptation. It was not put in. Photo: Timothy Pilgrim, Wikimedia Commons.*

What does this mean for designers, in concrete terms? It means that all the parts have to be mutually adapted to each other to an adequate degree, through a process of some kind. So let's consider a general procedure for adaptive design, one that uses these new insights from systems theory.

First, we will need to decompose a design problem so that it actually represents fundamentally distinct yet overlapping subsystems. Second, we will employ several alternative decompositions of the system into more tractable subunits or components. As is known since the work of complexity theorist Herbert Simon, a hierarchical complex system has several inequivalent decompositions.

Connectivity dictates how to perform each of the problem decompositions based upon one different aspect of the entire system: the designer has to discover and give equal weight to connective components as well as to the structural components. Relations among objects are just as important as the objects themselves, and system decomposition in terms of relations makes that clear.

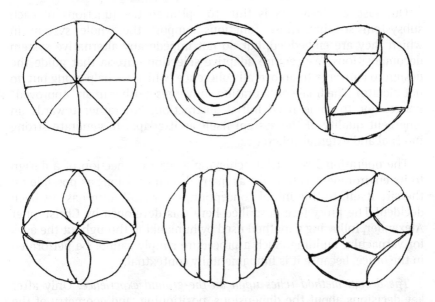

*Figure 3. Six distinct ways (among an infinite number of possibilities) of partitioning a disk to implement radial sectors, or concentric rings, or linear strips, etc. In an analogous manner, we can decompose a system according to distinct conceptualizations, for example to emphasize the distribution of interior spaces, or the path structure, or exterior urban spaces, etc. Drawing by Nikos Salingaros.*

For example, designing a building involves at least five distinct system decompositions. These could be concerned with: (*i*) harmonizing the building's exterior with its environment and avoidance of geometrical conflict, which of course includes adaptation to climate, orientation to the local solar and weather patterns, etc., (*ii*) connecting the site to the circulation present in its environment, (*iii*) shaping public spaces, from a sidewalk to one or more open plazas, (*iv*) planning interior paths, (*v*) identifying the interior spaces in relationship to each other. There could be other systems as well, based upon individual needs, conditions, and uses.

Each of these problems requires a system decomposition that defines a distinct type of subsystem of the entire design. And each has to be addressed separately, at least initially. Of course, eventually everything will have to be recombined, and a professional with experience will in practice handle all of the subsystems simultaneously. But since this method is unusual for today's designers, we offer this artificial separation to make the point of alternative decompositions.

Our task as designers is thus to optimize the functions of each subsystem so that those functions support the whole system in which they are embedded, but do not impede any alternative system decompositions. We require adaptive selection criteria that guide the design to converge to an overall coherence (which we help along but do not dictate). The final configuration converges neither to an "approved" image, nor to some fixed initial abstraction, but rather towards an emergent quality of the system itself as it adapts to generate strong internal and external coherence.

The operational secret for achieving a tight connection of a design to its environment is to make as many design decisions as possible on the site itself. In this initial conception, no overall form has yet been decided! The procedure described here was developed by Christopher Alexander, following a method used by humankind throughout the ages for vernacular building. Such a procedure simply cannot be performed in the office, because it is fundamentally contextual.

*The design method relies upon on-the-ground experience.* Only after key decisions about the dimensions, positioning, and geometry of the various subsystems have been taken in the actual setting using one's imagination aided by physical props, then, this information can be transferred to a scale model, sketch, and computer screen.

Adaptive design's principal aim is to facilitate the different components of a particular subsystem so they assemble themselves into a coherent subsystem. For example, the conditions and uses require specific internal paths, but there is freedom in connecting them into a network — this must be done in a way consistent with all the other system decompositions.

Here is where the real novelty lies: we let each distinct subsystem develop according to rules for adaptation, and our role as designers is merely that of facilitator. Namely, we are not going to dictate its design using any preconceived ideas or images (a shocking suggestion for contemporary practitioners), only search for the possibilities that satisfy the constraints of use, site, environment, etc. In this way, the components we have to work with will, in a real sense, "assemble themselves". This phenomenon is called *self-organization* — a very important topic that we discuss extensively in our 2011 essay *"Frontiers of Design Science: Self-Organization"*.

The result should still have a degree of roughness, for reasons that will become clear later. This procedure is repeated for each distinct subsystem to give us several subsystems that are more-or-less coherent within themselves.

In the end, we superimpose and combine all the different subsystems into a coherent whole. Crucially, the distinct subsystems will engage in a way that makes functional sense. Again, we don't impose our will, but simply facilitate an intimate union of all the subsystems. In the case of a building as discussed above, there will be at least five subsystems, and these will need to merge together.

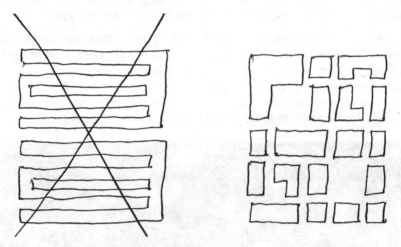

*Figure 4. Non-adaptive versus adaptive plans for a group of buildings. Left, the plan is only a formal geometrical idea; right, the plan reflects typical adaptations to several distinct systems of human needs, such as complex spatial volumes, movement, definition of usable urban space, connectivity on a human scale, etc. Drawing by Nikos Salingaros.*

The final design will be a structural compromise among all the alternative system decompositions, which compete with each other in design space. It is important to accept and handle this "conflictual" component of design, which arises from the need to accommodate several distinct systems, each one of which has its own optimum, but which could very easily degrade another subsystem's functionality. Thus, the intertwining of the distinct subsystems can only be achieved through each of the subsystems compromising to some extent. This is how the larger whole achieves an optimum configuration.

This description might sound exotic — but something like this goes on all the time in natural systems. It's the process by which the mitochondria adapt to the cell nucleus and vice versa, or the organisms within a reef ecology mutually adapt to one another. At our best, we do the same thing — or we let the natural processes around us do this for us. We "copy nature", or we go through an "optimization cycle", for example.

But as we noted earlier, too often, we humans tend to treat the products around us as separated things of very limited function that we can choose to isolate or recombine at our whim, with little consequence. This is, functionally speaking, a mistake. According to a key principle from systems theory, we can only treat systems as closed up to a point. Ultimately we have to see the ways in which all systems are partly open and inter-connected. Biological and ecological systems — of which we humans are ultimately an inseparable part — are open systems.

A key lesson for designers of all kinds follows: that product design can't really be separated from environmental design. We are all, in some sense, environmental designers, working in the human environment. Since every system is only partially closed, we have to find ways to work on these systems *as open systems* — that is, as parts of larger, optimizing wholes. Routine failure to do so has led to our ecological misfortunes.

*Figure 5. Human places are systems of room-like structures that span many scales — literal rooms indoors, and then more room-like outdoor spaces. These systems are made to adapt well to our activities and needs (especially our need for privacy) and to be adaptable by users — we can close doors and windows, draw curtains, etc. On the right, a composite example of a typical mixed-use London street. Photos by Michael Mehaffy.*

This means we must come to see (and work on) these systems of spaces where we live as a kind of *fabric of connections* between partially open sub-systems of spaces with geometric characteristics. As designers, our job is to weave together parts of this fabric into more life-supportive, *continuous* structures. We discuss the details of this structure elsewhere (in what is known as "place network theory"); but for now, we can think of this structure as a network of room-like structures, each with a membrane-like connection to the other spaces around it. (Think of rooms with doors and windows, gardens with gates and hedges, etc.)

An important aspect of adaptive evolution is afforded to users in such environments. They give us the capacity to control the degree of stimulation and variety, to explore intricate and varying layers of space, to locate rich geometrical structures that we users might find interesting and beautiful. We might elaborate on these structures as a way of clarifying them and making them more legible — or even more beautiful. It is the freedom to evolve our environment (in part), thereby vastly broadening its functionality, which is missing from the deterministic approach of most contemporary architecture.

As we alluded to earlier, research in environmental psychology reveals that such aesthetic characteristics are essential attributes of human wellbeing — and a crucial point is that they are not separate from this cellular, systemic structure of the human environment. The boundaries of different spaces become identifiable borders, and the geometrical centers become identifiable points around which local temporal symmetries might regularly appear. We might see regular patterns of repetition or alternation, or other characteristic patterns of human use and movement that arise from the particular geometry. It seems we are hard-wired to find geometries that generate these patterns aesthetically interesting, and often very beautiful. (Elsewhere, we have discussed the fascinating and promising topic of *biophilia* in more detail.)

*Figure 6. Two places in London, not far from one another, with opposite system characteristics. Left, a "place network" that is a well-articulated system of geometric spaces. Right, a place without a network — a jumble of poorly-articulated abstract parts, with little relation to human experience or need. Photos by Michael Mehaffy.*

This, then, is a key role of environmental designers: to facilitate such adaptive evolutions in both short and long (i.e. more permanent) time scales. Understanding and applying the geometric properties of human space, particularly its patterns of connections, is essential. We, as urban designers, or as architects — or really, as designers of *any* kind — have to take this problem seriously. The art of our work lies in the way we elaborate and elucidate these deeper realities of life.

215

Understanding geometric systems within environments gives us a remarkably coherent way of approaching the problems of the human environment. The question at stake is whether we can actually *design*, in the deepest spatial sense — that is, harness the *organizational* power of evolutionary systems, to generate richer, more connected, more adapted, more *alive* human environments.

Again, we must contrast this approach with today's dominant "business as usual" approach — a holdover from an earlier pre-modern industrial mode of design (indeed, of science). Instead of creating and transforming mutually adapted systems, disconnected objects are created and assembled, and then aesthetic "packaging" is layered onto them. Someone creates the "guts" of the car, and then somebody else places a sleekly "styled" body on top. Or we create filing-cabinet like buildings around prosaic "programs", and then we create razzle-dazzle aesthetic veneers, outside and perhaps inside — all package, no substance. Or we create filing-cabinet cities of superblocks and segregated zones, and then we "shrub them up" with various forms of landscaping and ecological gizmos. This last example often comes with a phony "sustainable" label.

And in the process, we leave a toxic planetary wreckage, the consequences of which, it is more than ever clear, we simply will not survive. This, too, is a necessary adaptation we must make — one that will challenge our orthodox thinking, about the very methods and aims of design.

## Reference

- Michael Mehaffy & Nikos Salingaros (2011) "Frontiers of Design Science: Self-Organization", *Metropolis*, 1 November.

# 31. ARCHITECTURE: BIOLOGICAL FORM AND ARTIFICIAL INTELLIGENCE

*By Nikos A. Salingaros and Kenneth G. Masden II*

*The Structurist, No. 45/46 (2006), pages 54-61. Reprinted by permission.*

This paper utilizes ideas from biological life to examine the architectural condition in which we live. We reveal how modern-day designs have come to operate in exclusion of any connection between the built environment and the primary animating properties of living structure, i.e. (*i*) organized-complexity, (*ii*) metabolism, (*iii*) replication, (*iv*) adaptation, (*v*) intervention, (*vi*) situatedness, and (*vii*) connectivity. Architecture today for the most part seems empty and lifeless, devoid of the requisite innate information necessary to engage sentient human beings in their everyday lives. Unintelligible in its form and application, architecture as a built form no longer carries with it the power to affect the lived experience. Drawing analogies from living structure and artificial intelligence, we find the promise of a new direction for architecture in the 21$^{st}$ century. Looking to modern robotic science and technology, a strong correlation can be made between biologically-driven functions of living structure and the adaptive processes that once gave form to architecture, and which now serve to steer the Mars Explorer.

## 1. Introduction

Architects today act in one important aspect very differently from most other human beings; and indeed, from other organisms that define the biosphere. In the business of their day, architects set forth ideas that shape the living experience for others, ideas that take form in the world around us. Surprisingly however, many contemporary architects and their work are no longer *situated* in the world they serve. During their training, an architect's internal representation of the real world is replaced by an abstract, formal set of images. Although this practice pre-dates our own time, it is now exacerbated by the increasing reliance of architects upon computer-based images, not only for design, but more importantly, as a preferred alternative to the physical world. Yet, these images do not fully represent reality, but rather reveal fictitious objects that don't really exist.

Increasingly, architects are distancing their work from the physical world with representations of a false, artificial reality. It is in this process of an internalized vision that contemporary expressions of architecture are rendered. And it is these expressions that now give form to the built environment as manifested in the mind's-eye of the architect. Understanding how our world, body, and mind work together to inform our soul of its existence exposes the problems inherent with such visions.

## 2. From the Natural to the Unnatural

Although architecture has embodied a variety of different designs and styles throughout the ages, the most successful buildings and urban environments have an essential commonality with living forms, i.e. material properties and an assembled nature. It is important, however, to distinguish between superficial resemblance, which can lead to dysfunctional and inhuman buildings, and an approach based upon a genuine understanding of life processes.

Historically, building design evolved through the natural occurrences and processes of the earth and the structural principles of the physical world. Imbued with a deep understanding of human needs and activities, traditional methods of design and construction revealed an honest (real) expression of the built environment. As human beings came to master their natural environment, they began to extend their designs beyond the physical limits imposed by form and materials. Seeking to advance their architectonic expressions, master-builders raised their great cathedrals from the earth, reaching higher and higher.

Unable to transcend human existence, yet still innately compelled by the need to overcome the limitations of the materiality of building, the study of architecture began to develop independently of its natural environment. Formalized within the condition of academic studies, architecture soon became the intellectualized property of the University. This set into motion a process that would ultimately render architecture as an artificial and abstract expression of man's disconnected philosophical and ideological ponderings.

Architects today continue to fool themselves into believing that philosophy or ideology can substitute for a cogent understanding of the natural processes of the earth, and the structural principles of the physical world. Even though all great architectural works of the past were derived from some aspect of nature, or perhaps in spite of this, a peculiar choice of philosophy is misused in contemporary architecture to supplant nature. By rejecting natural and human mechanisms, architecture has oriented itself away from essential principles of physical structure, toward an aestheticized and internalized expression of the built environment. This is not meant as a critique of any specific style. It is more of an observation about the processes involved in contemporary architectural thinking.

In an effort to better understand how architecture is fundamentally grounded in the natural world, we need to delve further into biology. Curiously enough, many of the twentieth century's pioneering architects have been strongly influenced by the same properties of living structure that we discuss here. Nevertheless, they only had a cursory understanding of the scientific basis of this body of knowledge. As a result, the built applications did not fully realize the intention. To make things worse, thoughtless imitation of such innovative prototypes reduced these ideas to superficial expressions, which ultimately gave way to one or more fashionable styles.

## 3. Properties of Living Structure

Living structure is known to satisfy several natural properties such as: organized-complexity (information storage); metabolism (energy use); replication (self-reproduction); adaptation (the organism changes itself to better profit from its environment); intervention (the organism changes its environment); situatedness (embedded in the world through sensors); and connectivity (information processing). In biological entities, all processes usually occur together, but theoretically, these are separate concepts.

### 3-i. Organized-complexity.

Following Christopher Alexander (Alexander, 2002-2004), we associate biological and architectural order with the organization of complexity, which represents the compression of information. An ordered structure has to be complex, yet it is also ordered because it has a large number of correlations that lead to an overall coherence. In architectural examples, correlations arise as visual symmetries and connections, which are easily perceived (Salingaros, 2006: Chapter 1). Life, whether biological, artificial, or architectural, results from the physical concentration of information. A noncomplex structure, on the other hand, requires little mathematical information to create, leading to simplistic structures without any internal differentiations. The world of rectangular building blocks that characterizes industrial architecture and urbanism is mathematically empty. Many architects perceive a superficial "ordering" in this empty world because of alignment and lack of distracting substructure. Seeking uniformity in this way, however, can be seen as a misreading of the actualities of order.

One particular insight of Stephen Wolfram is illuminating, because it surprisingly links uniformity with randomness. Wolfram points out that uniformity of structure is not simple, but is instead the result of intentionally directed processes:

*"But in nature uniformity often seems to be associated with quite complex microscopic behavior. Most often what happens is that on a small scale a system exhibits randomness, but on a larger scale this randomness averages out to leave apparent uniformity ..." (Wolfram, 2001: page 353).*

Here we have a perceptive statement of how uniformity arises from randomness (i.e., disorganization). The implications for design are significant, since uniformity is thereby linked not to simplicity or order, but to disorganization.

## 3-ii. Metabolism.

An animal or plant metabolizes in order to maintain its organized-complexity. The complex physical structure is there to permit metabolism, replication, and connectivity. Metabolism is a process by which existing sources of order are absorbed, and disorder is shed, so that the organism maintains its structural organization. In the case of a developing organism, such as an embryo or young animal, the entity metabolizes at the same time as it increases its organized-complexity until it reaches some optimal stable plateau. Towards the end of the organism's natural lifespan, metabolism fails to maintain its organized-complexity at the optimal plateau for different reasons, which signals the onset of aging. Metabolism maintains the single individual, whereas replication maintains the design (i.e., template of structural information) after the individual dies.

The act of weathering and repair, therefore, can make a building more alive. This might shed some light on Japanese building tradition, in which some holy shrines are entirely rebuilt in the exact manner every few decades. There develops a psychological bonding between human beings and a structure that shows fractal patterns with weathering (but not if it becomes ugly or falls apart). In this analogy, minimalist, non-weathering structures do not metabolize. We are thus questioning the drive towards sleek building surfaces and geometries that oppose natural processes, and suggest that older techniques that accommodated the inevitable weathering are in fact more adaptive.

## 3-iii. Replication.

Replication is often considered as the main characteristic of living structure. Organisms reproduce by making copies of themselves.

Nevertheless, it is possible to have a replicating structure that does not metabolize, as for example a virus (Salingaros, 2008). It is also possible to have an entity that metabolizes but cannot replicate; there are examples in animals such as mules — those exceptional typologies cannot propagate directly.

The simplest non-metabolizing templates (viruses) replicate more readily than animals with a higher complexity, because the latter's investment in metabolic and connective systems raises their organized-complexity (Salingaros, 2008). Among metabolizing organisms, again those with a lower degree of organized-complexity (e.g., bacteria) replicate much more readily than higher animals, and are thus more abundant.

## 3-iv. Adaptation.

There are several different types of adaptation: an organism adapts to its environment by responding on the short term, and also the genotype (i.e., its DNA) adapts in the long term by evolving so as to better profit from existing or changing environmental situations. Short-term adaptation depends on connectivity to the environment — being *situated*. Long-term adaptation follows a Darwinian selection process that culls portions of a population that are marginally worse adapted. Subsequently, survivors breed to define a new population having more of the positive adaptive trait.

We argue here for an architecture of adaptation, and criticize contemporary trends as being fundamentally non-adaptive. The reason that a non-adaptive architecture was able to develop is that the selection process among buildings and architectural styles is not as direct as selection among organisms (Salingaros, 2006). Selection in architecture is driven by forces external to the natural process of adaptation, i.e. fashion, opinion, and politics.

## 3-v. Intervention.

Another way that organisms can act (when they are capable of doing so) is to change their environment to the organism's advantage. This is in some ways the opposite of adaptation. Nevertheless, the interventive practices that have survived evolutionary (natural) selection always appear as combined adaptive/interventive applications. Animals build nests; beavers build dams; a squid ejects ink to help it escape from a predator; certain plants inject chemicals around them that prevent competing plants from growing; etc. Humans are champions at this: we applied our intelligence for clothing, shelter, hunting, and agriculture, which give us an unbeatable advantage over all other animals.

Traditional architecture and urbanism concisely represent both adaptation and intervention. However, since about the middle of the twentieth century human constructions have become primarily intervention, with little or no attention paid to adaptation.

## 3-vi. Situatedness.

A living organism is naturally embedded in the world, interacting directly with it via direct sensory mechanisms. External feedback from internal sensors dictates the organism's behavior: recognition and pursuit of a food source; recognition and reaction to an environmental threat; fight or flight when faced with an aggressor; etc. An organism is *situated* in its environment, and is constantly sensing the state of the environment. Although one of the properties of living structure, this property is best understood from research in robotics rather than biology (Brooks, 1999; 2002).

*Situatedness* depends upon the existence of sensory mechanisms that provide information about the world, and those, in turn, require a connective framework. The opposite of being *situated* is to exhibit behavior that is decided on the basis of abstract descriptions. We are not aware of any lower organisms that can do this — it logically appears to be a capability of animals with sufficient neural development for memory storage. An organism cannot form and act on an internal representation of the world unless it has sufficient capacity to store it as memory.

## 3-vii. Connectivity.

In biology, correlations arise as connective mechanisms. These include structural ones, such as plant stems, animal bones, arteries, and ligaments; and informational ones such as in hormonal fields, nerves, eyes, and photosensitive surfaces on leaves. All of these are prime examples of organized-complexity, and each instance employs a complex physical network to perform a connective task.

An embryo develops by repeatedly splitting cells, so that its growth is obviously bottom-up, guided by genetic instructions in the DNA. Nevertheless, Alexander argues that embryonic development is impossible without a global control that keeps the growth from getting out of hand (Alexander, 2002-2004). Whether this is due to a process of iteration in which each component helps to support and guide the development of other components, or to hormonal fields, what is important is that a global communication occurs. Each component (cell) of the embryo communicates chemically with the entire embryo existing at that time, so that each cell checks its position and future growth. In this way, embryonic cells develop either into muscle tissue or brain tissue, depending on their relative position at a particular time in the process.

A living system is one that acquires and actively uses information (Dyson, 2001). Information transfer takes many different forms in biology. Hormonal and nervous systems in animals are essential for interacting with the external world, and also for communicating internally within the organism. Stored genetic information encodes templates that permit the replication of individual cells, which replace worn-out cells in the body on a regular basis. For example, all except brain cells are routinely replaced in a mammal. Inherited information (across generations) is also stored in the brain, enabling all the instinctive behavior routines that permit animals to function. As we move up the evolutionary ladder, information and its processing plays an increasingly central role in life. The higher mammals are capable of learning, which is made possible by information storage mechanisms.

Human beings have evolved the ability to process information, both immediate (which is embedded in our environment) and stored (as mental images). Architects, in the process of distancing their work from actuality, have begun to rely more on stored information than immediate information (Salingaros, 2006). The ability to store an artificial representation can go awry when such an artificial image replaces the real world. This ultimately leads to a state of disconnection, where a human being connects with some senses and emotions, but not with others. Many contemporary architects, in their efforts to impose abstract architectural and urban solutions on the environment, do just that.

## 4. Architecture and Biological Processes

Using science and technology constructively and humanely we can begin to sense the intimate connection between living structure and architecture (Alexander, 2002-2004). We believe there is a direct analogy that can be drawn between metabolism in biological entities, and the process of maintaining complex structure (form) in non-biological ones. Buildings as non-natural artificial entities require varying degrees of repair by human beings after being built. Does the act of repair make the structure more alive? Does the process of repair in some way constitute a form of metabolism?

Considering human dominance of the world, and our physiological dependence on the physical structures we build around us, we can assume that there is an inherent necessity for buildings to replicate (even though they are inanimate entities). Often we see the replication of form in the built environment considered as a predicate of place, i.e. through indigenous localized forms. The replicating form is something that works within the limits of the material systems available in a certain region, and responds to local climatic conditions. So within a specific region very similar forms replicate and adapt to the programmatic differences and varying site conditions.

What are the forces that affect the survival of specific architectural templates? For example, building glass-walled high-rise buildings in both hot and cold climates is disastrous from an energy point of view. And yet, large rectangular buildings were universally adopted as an early twentieth-century design typology. This and other industrial examples are nonfunctional, but are copied from templates that have no relevance to human needs. There is a contradiction here with biological replication.

Non-adaptive forces in the built environment (dominant in a culture of architectural media-hegemony) give form to replicating structures around the world. Architectural and urban structures that simply replicate instead of growing out of very explicit local needs follow the architect's internal visual template that was developed generically, and not adaptively. This seems to be the crucial disconnection (Salingaros, 2008). In deepening the biological analogy, Freeman Dyson identifies metabolism with the emergence of proteins (analogous to physical structure), and replication with the emergence of nucleic acids (analogous to a reproducible design typology) (Dyson, 1999). We wish to identify connectivity with the emergence of complex sensory organs and communicative pathways in biological structure. Thus, connectivity is a much higher system function than either metabolism or replication, and makes possible adaptation, intervention, and *situatedness* in organisms. We are convinced that the architectural analogues of these properties are essential for a human built environment.

*Situatedness* is necessary for several of the other properties to occur. An architect who is not *situated* can respond neither to context, environment, nor the physicality of form. The architecture that comes out of this precondition turns out to lack connectivity and thus the ability to adapt.

## 5. Informational Processes, Robots, and Adaptation

Adaptation in living structure (forms) takes many different expressions at different scales. Internal adaptation balances temperature and chemical gradients leading to homeostasis and osmosis-regulation. This is essential to maintain the components of each organism in good working order. Next, we see adaptation to the physical environment, such as turning towards sunlight, reacting to temperature and threats, and adjusting thickness of fur for different seasons. Some reactions are immediate, whereas others adapt to longer-term environmental changes. Those adaptive mechanisms are essential for the survival of the individual organism. Finally, species adaptation occurs via natural selection. When an organism's physical mechanisms cannot cope with changing external conditions, some variants of a species die off; leaving those that might already have a slightly better adaptation. By evolving through survival, a species gradually changes its physical characteristics.

An architecture of adaptation must follow certain rules. The design process should consist of a large number of steps, so that feedback can influence the final product. This method is well known in adaptive software design, where the goal is left more loosely defined so that the designer can concentrate on the sequence of steps in its development (Highsmith, 2000). Every design decision must be guided by its affect on the whole as it exists at that instant. This means that a design must communicate with each of its components (usually in the mind of the designer). A design has to develop by paying attention to the whole (e. g. landscape, surrounding buildings, historical culture) at each stage (Alexander, 2002-2004). That is possible only if communicative systems exist that link the small scale to the large scale, and allow for feedback (Alexander, 2002-2005; Salingaros, 2006). As there is no "nervous" or "hormonal" system on a building site or drawing board, the human brain must convey these connections through its own decisions.

Adaptive design is the opposite of generic or formalistic design. Adopting an adaptive design method imbibes the built environment with life, and at the same time replaces the lifeless industrial forms that have replicated uncontrollably since the early modernist era. Only a global conception establishes a framework of communication among all its constituent parts. This is not a formalistic method that imposes a preconceived order; but instead a mechanism for connectivity. The connective and feedback network then enables the form to evolve by conceptualizing the whole, just as in an embryo, rather than by the accretion of isolated parts (Alexander, 2002-2005).

Understanding basic life processes eventually leads us to questions about higher life forms, such as what constitutes intelligence. Biologists do not have all the answers to how we interact with our environment. For further insight, we turn to robotics engineers and experts in artificial intelligence. Laboratory robots provide an analogy of the sophisticated systems for processing environmental information that distinguish intelligent animals from other life forms.

It was assumed in the past that intelligent action occurred in three steps: information input; comparison with a stored representation; followed by a decision for action. Robots that work in a different way proved this hypothesis wrong. Rodney Brooks created robots that have no internal representation of the world: they use their environment directly for all their decisions (Brooks, 1999). The external world already contains all the information needed to reach decisions. Enormous computational resources, better used elsewhere, are saved by not duplicating this information inside memory. Built along these principles, Brooks' Mars Explorer robot was very successful at navigating the planet's rough terrain (Brooks, 2002). We can learn a lesson from this. Life forms are probably using intelligence without internal representation to connect with, and navigate their environment. Brooks argues that it would be hugely inefficient to do otherwise (Brooks, 1999).

Robots that work with the alternative three-step process have also been built, but they get stuck on (and are severely limited by) their internal representation; they are incredibly slow to react, and cannot recognize novel forms. The reason is simple to see. Any internal representation of the world has to be abstract, formal, and highly simplified. In the robotics world, that means a universe made up only of monochromatic regular solids such as cubes, cylinders, and pyramids. Even so, robots built in this manner still get confused if an object in their abstract geometrical environment is not perfectly aligned, or if it casts a shadow (Brooks, 2002).

An organism or robot that bases its behavior on direct sensory contact with the world is *situated*. By contrast, a robot or organism whose behavior is based upon abstract descriptions (internally stored information) is not *situated*, and thus cannot be said to satisfy all of the components of living structure. We argue that contemporary architects are no longer *situated* in the world, and are thus fundamentally different in their perception of the built environment from other human beings. True, this is not an inheritable genetic trait, but is only the result of a form of psychological conditioning that often occurs in today's media-driven culture. Nevertheless, the architectural profession has ensured the continuation of this trait across generations, by conditioning students to interact with the world via abstract images instead of via their direct sensory perception.

We again turn to navigation for an analogy of *situatedness*. Driving a car requires continuous sensory input and an interpretation of the immediate environment. While an abstract road map may guide the overall journey, the countless intermediate decisions are based on being *situated* in the physical road network, responding to every variation of the environment. Taking this temporal example, we propose its spatial analogue as the appropriate model for an adaptive architecture, in which design is sensitive to forms, needs, and surroundings at every stage.

## 6. Architecture and Intelligence

This discussion touches upon the question of how discovered information is stored by an intelligent system that uses its physical environment as its primary representation. Such information is stored externally, by imprinting it on the environment. Human beings have many different options for how to do this. Representing information as structure can take many forms, including calligraphy, representational ornament, geometrical ornament, with the built object increasing in size up to architectural and urban spaces. In a fundamental sense, therefore, the traditional informationally-rich built environment can be interpreted as an information storage system, in and of itself. By contrast, the contemporary built environment and its architecture fails as an informational storage device. It is strictly an attempt at externalizing abstract mental images deficient in organized-complexity.

The type of information that is preserved in the traditional built environment is organized-complexity: precisely the type of information that defines living systems themselves. Thus, the traditional built environment consists of evolved and discovered solutions (schemata) that make our life easier and more meaningful.

Ollivier Dyens raises further questions about a stored internal representation, when that representation is entirely artificial. This is crucial to contemporary architecture, since increasingly, architects' world-views are formed by computer images. More than just formal systems, computer images substitute for a world that never existed. According to Dyens:

*"Digital imaging technology suggests models of life based on a completely different representational style, one that is founded not on reproduction but on production ... With digital images, there are no primary, original moments to which we can point and say: 'This image is an analogy of that*

*thing or that object'. On the contrary, digital images are, at once, worlds and models of worlds. Since digital images are not tied to exterior dynamics and do not extend toward exterior phenomena — such as concepts, referents, ideas, etc. — representation becomes an abyss, imploding into an endless collection of possible meanings." (Dyens, 2001: pages 87-88).*

An organism that exists in a symbolic abstracted domain is not totally alive, since there is nothing to ground it to the real world. It is more like a computer, executing an algorithm but not participating in the external world. This entity resides partially or entirely within its own model of an artificial world. One may go further and suggest that such an organism is not intelligent. As stated by Brooks:

*"It is hard to draw the line at what is intelligence, and what is environmental interaction. In a sense it does not really matter which is which, as all intelligent systems must be situated in some world or other if they are to be useful entities. The key idea from intelligence is: 'Intelligence is determined by the dynamics of interaction with the world'." (Brooks, 1999).*

In a direct analogy with the two types of robots mentioned above (those that work with and without an internal representation), architects have been imprinted with an artificial internal representation of the world that is irrelevant to physical reality. They judge the built environment by comparing it to this internal representation. By contrast, non-indoctrinated people (which includes everyone else) react directly with their environment, using their own senses and intuitions to make decisions about architecture. Based on the computational mechanism by which people respond to their environment, we have identified two distinct entities: psychologically-conditioned individuals (i.e. many of today's architects), and biologically-driven individuals (i.e. the majority of the rest of us).

## 7. Conclusion

Indigenous architecture represents human intelligence supported by memory (stored information) embedded in an external representation. Forms, spaces, textures and materials have evolved adaptively, in a way to maximally connect to the user. People build things that help them live and at the same time give back emotional satisfaction. Design decisions are based on direct perception and interaction with the form.

Formal architecture, by contrast, is more often than not an imposition of formal rules or external images, and buildings are judged by how closely they conform to some internal ideal stored in the architect's memory. While this method is fine for certain situations, that process is by definition not humanly adaptive. An internal representation is independent of reality; it is not checked and is thus prone to corruption, and can eventually replace the real world. Many an architect's judgment is driven by an artificial world picture that has nothing to do with human systems of perception. Architectural education has been geared towards the goal of generating this internal world picture (a representation of an artificial world) that is at odds with the physical world.

This analysis helps to explain the amazing disagreement between architects and everyday people about what constitutes a "good building". This difference of opinion is well known for domestic residences, where the tastes of architects are often diametrically opposite to those of everyone else. Another example is a recent debate about new buildings that maintain the spirit of Thomas Jefferson's original buildings on the campus of the University of Virginia. The faculty of its architecture school condemned the contextually conceived — i.e., adaptive, hence traditional-looking — buildings in the harshest possible terms. By contrast, everyone else, from students, to faculty, to the university trustees and visitors to the campus, loves them. What is probably happening is that everyone else is responding viscerally with those forms (by connecting to them in an immediate sense), whereas the reactions of architecture faculty come from comparing them to a stored internal representation of an artificial world.

Just as biological systems and natural processes give form to all living structures, so too these formative devices once rendered architecture and the built environment replete with life. Animated within the processes of everyday existence, architecture served humankind as an adaptive necessity, and as a conveyor of information — one which worked to attach and engage human beings with their everyday environments. With the onslaught of industrialization, which sponsored an extended physical condition, the natural relationship between human beings and their environment has been severely compromised. We argue for an architecture of adaptation, one structured within the limits of natural processes and imbibed with informational content, such as needed to facilitate a more immediate (contextual) determination of architectural form.

# References

- Christopher Alexander, *The Nature of Order: Books One to Four* (Berkeley, California: Center for Environmental Structure, 2002-2005).

- Rodney A. Brooks, *Cambrian Intelligence* (Cambridge, Massachusetts: MIT Press, 1999).

- Rodney A. Brooks, *Flesh and Machines* (New York: Pantheon Books, 2002).

- Ollivier Dyens, *Metal and Flesh* (Cambridge, Massachusetts: MIT Press, 2001), pages 87-88.

- Freeman Dyson, *Origins of Life*, Revised Edition (Cambridge: Cambridge University Press, 1999).

- Freeman Dyson, "Is Life Analog or Digital?", *Edge* (2001). Available from <http://www.edge.org/3rd_culture/dyson_ad/dyson_ad_index.html>. Edited version published as "Can Life Go On Forever?", Chapter 5 of *A Many-Colored Glass* (Charlottesville: University of Virginia Press, 2007), pages 83-101.

- Nikos A. Salingaros, *A Theory of Architecture* (Solingen, Germany: Umbau-Verlag, 2006), Chapter 1.

- Nikos A. Salingaros, *Anti-Architecture and Deconstruction*, Third Edition (Solingen, Germany: Umbau-Verlag, 2008).

- James A. Highsmith, *Adaptive Software Development* (New York: Dorset House Publishing, 2000).

- Stephen Wolfram, *A New Kind of Science* (Champaign, Illinois: Wolfram Media Inc., 2001), page 353.

# 32. Lecture Notes, Fourteenth Week. Natural and Unnatural Form Languages

## Readings for the Fourteenth Week:

- Alexander, *The Phenomenon of Life*, "Conclusion".
- The 1982 Alexander-Eisenman Debate, *Katarxis N° 3, September 2004*.
- Alexander, "Some Sober Reflections on the Nature of Architecture in Our Time", *Katarxis N° 3, September 2004*.

The concept of living structure, and its support coming from direct experience and from science, offers a basis for doing and understanding architecture. This platform is a sensible way of approaching design and building, because it is beholden neither to ideology, nor to individual agendas. Moreover, it should be contrasted to the irrationality of other schemes that currently appear in and seem to drive architectural discourse.

If we seek meaning in the built environment, then we cannot continue to use interpretative schemata that lack intellectual coherence. Something as important as architecture cannot be founded upon arbitrary bases. Well, it could, and in my opinion actually has been for several decades, but the result is, not surprisingly, unsatisfactory and far from ideal. We would prefer an architecture that is consistent with human feeling, and in which design decisions are based on observation and empirical verification. The bottom line is that buildings have to provide good, healthy environments for human beings, and to inflict the least possible damage to the Earth's ecology.

This book presented a body of work that provides a universal basis for judging whether architecture is sound or not. The criteria used to justify inclusion of a structure in the class of "good" buildings are divorced here from opinion, changing fashions, power interests, etc. They appeal to the human population as a whole, which is interested in a healthy environment. Indeed, the strength of the tools we studied lies in that they are felt to be useful by people from different cultures and backgrounds.

The strongest proof of the validity of the model we covered comes from its intimate relation to the physical world. Such a link is not commonly discussed among architects, who tend to live in an artificial universe of their own making: a world of images divorced from reality. Some architects have found innovation by contrasting with nature, which seems to be a formula for design innovation ever since early modernism, and those architects have become quite successful commercially in doing so. Nevertheless, humanity in the past has never done well to deny or to go against nature, because eventually that practice leads to collapse in one way or another.

Our model also provides a much-needed working link to the great artistic and architectural achievements of the past. Such concerns are explicitly forbidden in a discipline driven only by incessant innovation. One rule in that game is to never look back. Students are made to study architecture as history, but are not allowed to learn practical tools from it nor apply the lessons to their design projects. "See and admire, but don't think of re-using anything!" It is astonishing that people are ready and eager to jettison their cultural heritage in order to follow the latest fashion.

Coming to the end of this book, we can now judge those structures that are allied with our own life, and distinguish them from those that either ignore or violate biological processes. We can choose to erect buildings by giving them any qualities we wish them to embody. But at least now we have a basis for judgment that is accessible to analysis. Both Christopher Alexander and I believe in building things that enhance living structure, but we cannot influence others — they must decide for themselves what properties to incorporate into their designs.

To showcase how different our concept of architecture is from other practitioners', we have the famous 1982 debate between Alexander and Peter Eisenman. This was a historically crucial moment for architecture, because it marked the first public presentation of Alexander's "The Nature of Order", at the Harvard Graduate School of Design. It was also the turning point that was to bring postmodernist and deconstructivist architecture to international prominence. Postmodernism was taking off at precisely this time, and deconstructivism followed, becoming famous with the Museum of Modern Art exhibit in 1988.

This debate is as relevant today as when it took place, since the issues it raised continue to dominate contemporary architecture and architectural discourse. Among several surprises, what is astonishing is how Eisenman initially tries to convince Alexander that they are talking about the same thing, when in fact, their thoughts about design are diametrically opposed. Alexander is right to be suspicious, despite the similar vocabularies being used.

The debate reveals many things for those readers ready to draw conclusions from subsequent events. First, Eisenman and several other architects had embraced a method of design based on images, using the shock of the new and a disregard of the science that Alexander used for his own design method. Second, it's clear that the architects who went on to become "stars" in the period following this debate, Eisenman among them, appropriated anything that sounded good in order to justify their often dysfunctional designs.

Third, the debate also reveals the weak points of Alexander: he trusted science and objective truth to overcome deliberate confusion and marketing hype. But the world does not work that way. As we know from the advertising industry, what sells best is not necessarily what's best for you. Eisenman, on the other hand, perfectly understood the system and was already using the French deconstructivist philosophers to boost acceptance of his own designs. He was building up his momentum for a rise to the top in a system that works like consumer marketing rather than science.

After several probing verbal exchanges, Alexander eventually uncovers the fundamental disagreement he has with Eisenman, and which he suspected from the very beginning. When this is revealed, it comes as quite a shock. Alexander is genuinely alarmed, as if he never imagined any architect (especially someone already famous like Eisenman) to hold such deliberately alienating views. And as a reaction to discovering this purposeful transgression of form and order, Alexander gets very angry.

Incidentally, the building that sets off the dispute is Rafael Moneo's Town Hall at Logroño, Spain. Moneo, Eisenman agrees, wants to produce disharmony and incongruity, which Alexander finds appalling. Yet Eisenman defends this approach to architecture as being perfectly valid. Which viewpoint won? Subsequent events tell us. Eisenman became an established Starchitect, teaching at Yale University and winning major commissions worldwide. Moneo himself went on to head the Harvard Graduate School of Design (where this debate was taking place) during 1985 to 1990. He then won the Pritzker prize in 1993, and was subsequently commissioned in 1996 to build the Los Angeles cathedral (a building I have criticized in a 2012 review). The architectural power brokers decided the direction of architecture: Alexander was left behind and pushed out of the system.

Eisenman explains how he creates forms that make him feel high in his own mind, instead of considering the mundane needs of the user. Thus it comes as no surprise that he wants to express a stressed conception of life through his buildings' twisted and unbalanced form. This honest admission of following a design philosophy that makes buildings uncomfortable points to vastly different values from Alexander's scientific rationality. And saying so openly (in the early 1980s) gave an example for young architects to follow, which is what they did. Critics associated an attraction of the mind to architectural form with intellectual and material progress, whereas feelings and connections to the earth are interpreted as common and a thing of the past.

A theory of architecture is useful to humankind as a whole, only if the theory resonates with the deep feelings and direct experience of ordinary people. An alleged theory cannot look down on the public and talk only to some small elite. It cannot treat the common person as ignorant, and presume to claim there is no truth about anything in architecture. There is indeed, and the truth exposes the absurdity of much contemporary architectural discourse trying to hide under a relativist bluff. Perhaps this is why Alexander and his understanding of architecture were marginalized by a fanatical relativism, prompting a much later comment by Eisenman: "I think Chris unfortunately fell off the radar screen some time ago".

If values in architecture have been arbitrary, or at least idiosyncratic for several decades, as Alexander suggests, how could this situation have lasted for so long, and why does it still go on? It seems that a culture of images serves capital-induced development, and especially speculative building. And so we are faced not simply with silly or absurd form languages assuming central prominence, but with a powerful and entrenched system that favored this event. The system consists of the construction industry now entirely dependent on industrial materials and production methods, the licensing process that has been adjusted to permit only approved images, the banking sector that finances speculative construction, the insurance industry that approves only a certain type of construction, etc. And this system is fed by the architecture schools.

The system makes an enormous amount of money for the developer, but does not have to generate either good architecture, or a healthy environment for the user. Remember that for several decades now, the client is no longer the user: the client is the developer. Architects therefore do what the developer wants, which is to sell the building as an image. This is totally distinct from a building as a living and working environment for people. Those architects who are the most effective salespersons for developers are consequently rewarded above all others, with prizes, commissions, and influence.

Therefore, we find ourselves facing two very different conceptions of what architecture is and ought to be. On the one hand, the present-day system promotes a culture of images, and its built-in inertia makes sure that very little else can be built. A student cannot even learn the techniques to design anything outside the current system. On the other hand, the approach and material of this book makes it possible to understand how architecture actually works to adapt itself to human use and sensibilities. How the built environment influences people, their health, and their activities. And that understanding helps us to sustain life on earth.

# 33. CONTRASTING CONCEPTS OF HARMONY IN ARCHITECTURE

*The 1982 Debate between Christopher Alexander and Peter Eisenman*

*Prepared for the web by Nikos A. Salingaros from published sources. Katarxis N° 3, September 2004. Reprinted by permission.*

**Peter Eisenman**: I met Christopher Alexander for the first time just two minutes ago, but I feel I have known him for a long time. I suddenly sense that we have been placed in a circus-like atmosphere, where the adversarial relationship which we might have — which already exists — might be blown out of proportion. I do not know who the Christian is and who the lion, but I always get nervous in a situation like this. I guess it is disingenuous on my part to think that with Chris Alexander here something other than a performance would be possible.

Back in 1959, I was working in Cambridge, U.S.A., for Ben Thompson and The Architects Collaborative [*Walter Gropius's firm*]. I believe Chris Alexander was at Harvard. I then went to Cambridge, England, again not knowing that he had already been there. He had studied mathematics at Cambridge and turned to architecture. I was there for no particular reason, except that Michael McKinnell told me that I was uninformed and that I should go to England to become more intelligent.

**Christopher Alexander**: I'm very glad you volunteered that information. It clears things up.

**Audience**: (Laughter)

**PE**: In any case, Sandy [*Colin St. John*] Wilson, who was then a colleague of mine on the faculty at Cambridge and is now professor at the School of Architecture at Cambridge, gave me a manuscript that he said I should read. It was Alexander's Ph.D. thesis, which was to become the text of Chris's first book, "*Notes on the Synthesis of Form*". The text so infuriated me, that I was moved to do a Ph.D. thesis myself. It was called "*The Formal Basis of Modern Architecture*" and was an attempt to dialectically refute the arguments made in his book. He got his book published; my thesis was so primitive that I never even thought of publishing it.

In any case, I thought that today we could deal with some of my problems with his book. But then I listened to the tape of his lecture last night, and again I find myself in a very similar situation. Christopher Alexander, who is not quite as frightening as I thought — he seems a very nice man — again presents an argument which I find the need to contest. Since I have never met him prior to this occasion, it cannot be personal; it must have something to do with his ideas.

Chris, you said we need to change our cosmology, that it is a cosmology that grew out of physics and the sciences in the past and is, in a sense, 300 years old. I probably agree with every word of that. You said that only certain kinds of order can be understood, given that cosmology. You said the order of a Coke machine is available to us because of our causal, mechanistic view of the world. And then you brought up that the order of a Mozart symphony is not available to us. Don't you think that the activity of the French "Structuralists" is an attempt to find out the order of things as opposed to the order of mechanisms, the ontology of things as opposed to the epistemology of things, i.e., their internal structure? This kind of philosophical inquiry has been part of current French thought for the last 20 years. Don't you think that it is something like what you're talking about?

**CA**: I don't know the people you are talking about.

**PE**: I am talking about people like Roland Barthes, Michel Foucault, Jacques Derrida.

**CA**: What do they say?

**PE**: They say that there are structures, in things like a Mozart symphony or a piece of literature, and that we can get beyond the function of a symphony or the function of a piece of literature to provide a story of knowledge, that we can get beyond those functions to talk about the innate structure or order of these things. And that this order has little to do with the hierarchical, mechanistic, and deterministic order of the past 300 years. Rather it is based on an alternative to Western values as determined by metaphysics. This order suggests not so much an opposition as an alternative view, which suggests that structures are not dialectical in nature but, rather, that they are made up of differences.

I was very much in sympathy with the things you were saying in your lecture. In fact, I would like to think that for the past 10 or 15 years of my life I have been engaged in the same kind of work. My post-functionalist essay in *Oppositions 6* proposed another aspect of architecture outside of function.

**CA**: I am not sure I know what you are driving at. See if this is right? One of the people on our faculty, I think, would probably espouse your point of view in some way. His attitude reflects a whole school of thought that has developed — crudely called Post-Modernism or whatever. Anyway, there is a school of thought, a serious group of theorists who have begun to talk about architecture in a quite new way in the last 10 years. And this faculty member says to me, from time to time, something like this: "Essentially, Chris, they're saying exactly the same thing you are. Why are you riding your horse as though you are some lone messenger when, in fact, everybody is talking about the same thing."

But what these Post Modernists and Structuralists are saying is not the same thing as what I said last night at all. Of course, I think there are people who are very serious and want to move the many with the privileged view of architecture that they have in their heads. But words are very, very cheap. And one can participate in intellectual discussions, right, left, and center, and you can go this way or you can go that way. Now then, I look at the buildings which purport to come from a point of view similar to the one I've expressed, and the main thing I recognize is, that whatever the words are — the intellectual argument behind that stuff — the actual buildings are totally different. Diametrically opposed. Dealing with entirely different matters.

Actually, I don't even know what that work is dealing with, but I do know that it is not dealing with feelings. And in that sense those buildings are very similar to the alienated series of constructions that preceded them since 1930. All I see is: number one, new and very fanciful language; and two, vague references to the history of architecture but transformed into cunning feats and quaint mannerisms. So, the games of the Structuralists, and the games of the Post Modernists are in my mind nothing but intellectualisms which have little to do with the core of architecture. This depends, as it always has, on feeling.

**PE**: Let us just back off for a minute. I wish we had some pictures here. I don't want to polarize this between the heavy, Eastern intellectual and the California joy boy. You cannot ask people, as you did last night, to believe you because you have done 25 years of intellectual work — which I have followed very carefully and which is very intellectual — and then say "I am California magic". So I want to get away from these kinds of caricatures because we are not going to get anywhere with them. That is number one.

Number two: for you to plead ignorance of ideas that are in current use, does not make me an intellectual and you not, or vice versa; it means that you are interested in your cosmology, and I am interested in mine. So that is a wash. I did not come here to play "do you know" and get anxious about things. I am very interested in the whole self. In the Jungian cosmology, you may be a feeling type and I may be a thinking type. And I will never be able to have the kind of feeling that you have, and vice versa. We all live with the tyranny of the opposite. So I don't want to get into that game, because you win all the time. So why not start over.

**CA**: Let's have a go. That was a very good first round.

**PE**: I want to get out of the ring and try again. I came in on the wrong side. I certainly became the lion and you the Christian, and I have always wanted to be a Christian.

**CA**: I appreciate the very charming way you are bringing this into a slightly nicer state. Actually, with regard to what you said a moment ago, the business of the feeling type and the thinking type does need to be talked about. I know something about Jung's classifications. That we have different make-ups is probably an undeniable fact. But, somehow, the substantive core of the matter, to me, is the essence of what the debate about architecture must lead to. If you say: "Well, look, you're a feeling type, and I'm a thinking type, so let's not discuss that because we are always going to be on different sides", then it removes from this discussion what I feel to be the absolute heart and soul of the matter when it comes to buildings. Now I don't want to deny at all what you are saying about personalities. But I really cannot conceive of a properly formed attitude towards buildings, as an artist or a builder, or in any way, if it doesn't ultimately confront the fact that buildings work in the realm of feeling. So when you say, "Look you're that type, and I'm this type, and let's agree not to talk with one another about that fact", what's the implication? Is the implication that you think that feeling is not related to buildings? Perhaps you could answer that.

**PE**: Of course, if you are a feeling type, you *would* think that feelings are the essence of the matter; and I cannot help thinking, as a thinking type, that ideas are the essence of the matter. It is not something that I can walk away from. We all have a shadow, and my shadow is feeling. I accept that you are that way. I am asking you to accept me the way I am rather than dismissing what I say as not being at the heart of the matter. For you, feeling is the heart of the matter, because it is the only way you can configure the world. I cannot configure the way you do because then I would not be me, and you would not want me to do that.

**CA**: I'm not so sure about that.

**PE**: It is not I who is into tyranny. Let's see if we can discuss substantive issues. All I am saying is: do not put people down who cannot get at ideas through feeling. At least 50% of the people here cannot.

**CA**: You're saying to me, on the level of personal decency and person-to-person respect, let each of us recognize that we have our different attitudes towards the world, and let's not mix them up with the central, substantive matter at hand. That's what you're inviting me to do.

**PE**: That's what I was hoping.

**CA**: I will suspend that, if you can deal with that. I fully understand that what you're saying concerns you, and I'm quite comfortable with the person-to-person respect, given our different attitudes and so forth. The trouble is that we also happen to be dealing with a matter that I believe intellectually is the central issue. Intellectually, not from the point of view of feeling. It's very, very difficult for me to stay away from this issue because, if I don't talk about it with you to some extent, I will actually never know what you're really talking about. So, if you will permit me, I'd like to go into this matter and see where we come to. You see, there is a debate going on here, and there is also a disagreement — I believe of substance. I'm not even sure whether we work in the same way. That's why I would like to check out a couple of examples, buildings. Now, I will pick a building, let's take Chartres for example. We probably don't disagree that it's a great building.

**PE**: Well, we do actually, I think it is a boring building. Chartres, for me, is one of the least interesting cathedrals. In fact, I have gone to Chartres a number of times to eat in the restaurant across the street — had a 1934 red Mersault wine, which was exquisite — I never went into the cathedral. The cathedral was done *en passant*. Once you've seen one Gothic cathedral, you have seen them all.

**CA**: Well, pick a building you like. Pick another.

**PE**: Let's pick something that we can agree on — Palladio's Palazzo Chiericati. For me, one of the things that qualifies it in an incredible way, is precisely because it is more intellectual and less emotional. It makes me feel high in my mind, not in my gut. Things that make me feel high in my gut are very suspicious, because that is my psychological problem. So I keep it in the mind, because I'm happier with that.

You see, the Mies and Chiericati thing was far greater than Moore and Chiericati, because Moore is just a *pasticheur*. We agree on that. But Mies and Chiericati is a very interesting example, and I find much of what is in Palladio — that is the contamination of wholeness — also in Mies. I also find alternation, as opposed to simple repetition. And you said things which are very close to my heart. I am very interested in the arguments you presented in your lecture. You said something about the significance of spaces between elements being repeated. Not only the element itself being repeated, but the space between. I'm very interested in the space between. That is where we come together.

Now the space between is not part of classical unity, wholeness, completeness; it is another typology.

It is not a typology of sameness or wholeness; it's a typology of differences. It is a typology which transgresses wholeness and contaminates it. If you say A/B A/B, that is an alternation of wholes outside of the classical canon, which tries to take A and B and bring them into symmetry — as in B/A/B/A/B. In other words, there are three B's with one in the center, and two A's as minor chords. When you have A/B/A/B/ you have alternating pairs with no center, closure or hierarchy. A/B/A/B/A is complete. A/B/A/B is not. What is interesting about serial structures is the spaces between, not the elements themselves, but the differences between the two. You were talking about that last night when you gave an example of something that was not dealing with wholeness at all in the classical sense. Maybe we would benefit from talking more about this. Or not?

**CA**: I don't fully follow what you're saying. It never occurred to me that someone could so explicitly reject the core experience of something like Chartres. It's very interesting to have this conversation. If this weren't a public situation, I'd be tempted to get into this on a psychiatric level. I'm actually quite serious about this. What I'm saying is that I understand how one could be very panicked by these kinds of feelings. Actually, it's been my impression that a large part of the history of modern architecture has been a kind of panicked withdrawal from these kinds of feelings, which have governed the formation of buildings over the last 2000 years or so.

Why that panicked withdrawal occurred, I'm still trying to find out. It's not clear to me. But I've never heard somebody say, until a few moments ago, someone say explicitly: *"Yes, I find that stuff freaky. I don't like to deal with feelings. I like to deal with ideas."* Then, of course, what follows is very clear. You would like the Palladio building; you would not be particularly happy with Chartres, and so forth. And Mies ...

**PE**: The panicked withdrawal of the alienated self was dealt with in Modernism — which was concerned with the alienation of the self from the collective.

**CA**: However painful it is, we are doing pretty well right now. We're not being rude to each other, and things are moving along really nicely. It does seem to me, since we have locked into this particular discussion, that we ought to stay with it.

I want to tell a story that I told this morning. About two or three years ago, I was asked by the faculty at Berkeley to show some pictures of things I had been working on, and ended up locking horns with some people who were challenging my work. I recognized that their comments were coming from a place similar to that which you were just talking about, because the things that I make come from a very vulnerable spot. What happened was, one of the people who has been most vociferous in this field, a few days later, whispering privately in a corner said: "You know, I really shouldn't have said those things to you, but I've been making plans like this myself for some time but dare not show them to anybody". And this is, I have found, in dealing with various men in the profession over the last 10, 20, years, quite frequently you have this theme, where there's actually real fear about simple, ordinary, vulnerable stuff.

I will give you another example, a slightly absurd example. A group of students under my direction was designing houses for about a dozen people, each student doing one house. In order to speed things up (we only had a few weeks to do this project), I said: "We are going to concentrate on the layout and cooperation of these buildings, so the building system is not going to be under discussion."

So I gave them the building system, and it happened to include pitched roofs, fairly steep pitched roofs. The following week, after people had looked at the notes I handed out about the building system, somebody raised his hand and said: "Look, you know everything is going along fine, but could we discuss the roofs?" So I said: "Yes, what would you like to discuss about the roofs?" And the person said: "Could we make the roofs a little different?" I had told them to make just ordinary pitched roofs. I asked, "What's the issue about the roofs?" And the person responded: "Well, I don't know, it's just kind of funny." Then that conversation died down a bit. Five minutes later, somebody else popped up his hand and said: "Look, I feel fine about the building system, except the roofs. Could we discuss the roofs?" I said: "What's the matter with the roofs?" He said, "Well, I have been talking to my wife about the roofs, and she likes the roofs" — and then he sniggered. I said: "What's so funny or odd about that?" And he said: "Well, I don't know, I ... "

Well, to cut a long story short, it became clear that ... [*Alexander goes to the blackboard and draws different types of roofs*]. Now, all of you who are educated in the modernist canon know that as an architect, a respectable architect of the 1980s, it is quite okay to do this, you can do this, you can do this, you can do this, but please [*he points to a pitched roof design*] do not do this.

So, the question is, why not? Why does this taboo exist? What is this funny business about having to prove you are a modem architect and having to do something other than a pitched roof? The simplest explanation is that you have to do these others to prove your membership in the fraternity of modern architecture. You have to do something more far out, otherwise people will think you are a simpleton. But I do not think that is the whole story. I think the more crucial explanation — very strongly related to what I was talking about last night — is that the pitched roof contains a very, very primitive power of feeling. Not a low pitched, tract house roof, but a beautifully shaped, fully pitched roof. That kind of roof has a very primitive essence as a shape, which reaches into a very vulnerable part of you. But the version that is okay among the architectural fraternity is the one which does not have the feeling: the weird angle, the butterfly, the asymmetrically steep shed, etc. — all the shapes which look interesting but which lack feeling altogether. The roof issue is a simple example. But I do believe the history of architecture in the last few decades has been one of specifically and repeatedly trying to avoid any primitive feeling whatsoever. Why this has taken place, I don't know.

**PE**: This is a wonderful coincidence, because I too am concerned with the subject of roofs. Let me answer it in a very deep way. I would argue that the pitched roof is — as Gaston Bachelard points out — one of the essential characteristics of "houseness". It was the extension of the vertebrate structure which sheltered and enclosed man. Michel Foucault has said that when man began to study man in the 19th century, there was a displacement of man from the center. The representation of the fact that man was no longer the center of the world, no longer the arbiter, and, therefore, no longer controlling artifacts, was reflected in a change from the vertebrate-center type of structure to the center-as-void. That distance, which you call alienation or lack of feeling, may have been merely a natural product of this new cosmology.

The non-vertebrate structure is an attempt to express that change in the cosmology. It is not merely a stylistic issue, or one that goes against feeling, or the alienation that man feels. When man began to study himself, he began to lose his position in the center. The loss of center is expressed by that alienation. Whether understood by modern architecture or not, what Modernism was attempting to explain by its form was that alienation. Now that technology has gone rampant, maybe we need to rethink the cosmology. Can we go back to a cosmology of anthropocentrism? I am not convinced that it is appropriate.

**CA**: Let me just inject one thing. This is a pretty interesting subject. I just want to make one thing clear. I am not suggesting that it would be good idea to romantically go back and pick up the pitched roof, and say: "Well, it did a certain job for several hundred years, why don't we keep it, or use it again?" I am talking about a totally different language than that.

I think I am going to have to give a rather more elaborate explanation Up until about 1600, most of the world views that existed in different cultures did see man and the universe as more or less intertwined and inseparable ... either through the medium of what they called God or in some other way. But all that was understood. The particular intellectual game that led us to discover all the wonders of science forced us to abandon temporarily that idea. In other words, in order to do physics, to do biology, we were actually taught to pretend that things were like little machines because only then could you tinker with them and find out what makes them tick. That's all fine. It was a tremendous endeavor, and it paid off.

But it may have been factually wrong. That is, the constitution of the universe may be such that the human self and the substance that things made out of, the spatial matter or whatever you call it, are much more inextricably related than we realized. Now, I am not talking about some kind of aboriginal primitivism. I am saying that it may actually be a matter of fact that those things are more related than we realize. And that we have been trained to play a trick on ourselves for the last 300 years in order to discover certain things. Now, if that's true — there are plenty of people in the world who are beginning to say it is, by the way, certainly in physics and other related subjects — then my own contribution to that line of thought has to do with these structures of sameness that I have been talking about.

In other words, the order I was sketching out last night is ultimately, fundamentally an order produced by centers or wholes which are reinforcing each other and creating each other. Now, if all of that is so, then the pitched roof would simply come about as a consequence of all that — not as an antecedent. It would turn out that, in circumstances where one is putting a roof on a building, in the absence of other very strong forces that are forcing you to do something different, that is the most natural and simple roof to do. And, therefore, that kind of order would tend to reappear — of course, in a completely different, modern technological style — simply because that is the nature of order, not because of a romantic harkening back to past years. You probably understand this.

**PE**: What we have not been able to get at yet is that it is possible to project a totally different cosmology that deals with the feelings of the self. Alternative views of the world might suggest that it is not wholeness that will evoke our truest feelings and that it is precisely the wholeness of the anthropocentric world that it might be the presence of absence, that is, the nonwhole, the fragment which might produce a condition that would more closely approximate our innate feelings today.

Let me be more specific. Last night, you gave two examples of structural relationships that evoke feelings of wholeness — of an arcade around a court, which was too large, and of a window frame which is also too large. Le Corbusier once defined architecture as having to do with a window which is either too large or too small, but never the right size. Once it was the right size it was no longer functioning. When it is the right size, that building is merely a building. The only way in the presence of architecture that is that feeling, that need for something other, when the window was either too large or too small.

I was reminded of this when I went to Spain this summer to see the town hall at Logrono by Rafael Moneo. He made an arcade where the columns were too thin. It was profoundly disturbing to me when I first saw photographs of the building. The columns seemed too thin for an arcade around the court of a public space. And then, when I went to see the building, I realized what he was doing. He was taking away from something that was too large, achieving an effect that expresses the separation and fragility that man feels today in relationship to the technological scale of life, to machines, and the car-dominated environment we live in. I had a feeling with that attenuated colonnade of precisely what I think you are talking about. Now, I am curious if you can admit, in your idea of wholeness, the idea of separation — wholeness for you might be separation for me. The idea that the too-small might also satisfy a feeling as well as the too-large. Because if it is only the too-large that you will admit, then we have a real problem.

**CA**: I didn't say too large, by the way, I just said large. Quite a different matter.

**PE**: You said a boundary larger than the entity it surrounds. I think you said too large.

**CA**: I said large in relation to the entity. Not too large.

**PE**: Large, meaning larger than it needs be?

**CA**: No, I didn't mean that.

**PE**: Well, could it be smaller than it needs be?

**CA**: Unfortunately, I don't know the building you just described. Your description sounds horrendous to me. Of course, without actually seeing it, I can't tell. But if your words convey anything like what the thing is actually like, then it sounds to me that this is exactly this kind of prickly, weird place, that for some reason some group of people have chosen to go to nowadays. Now, why are they going there? Don't ask me.

**PE**: I guess what I am saying is that I believe that there is an alternate cosmology to the one which you suggest. The cosmology of the last 300 years has changed and there is now the potential for expressing those feelings that you speak of in other ways than through largeness — your boundaries — and the alternating repetition of architectural elements. You had 12 or 15 points. Precisely because I believe that the old cosmology is no longer an effective basis on which to build, I begin to want to invert your conditions — to search for their negative — to say that for every positive condition you suggest, if you could propose a negative you might more closely approximate the cosmology of today. In other words, if I could find the negative of your 12 points, we would come closer to approximating a cosmology that would deal with both of us than does the one you are proposing.

**CA** : Can we just go back to the arcade for a moment? The reason Moneo's arcade sounded prickly and strange was, when I make an arcade I have a very simple purpose, and that is to try to make it feel absolutely comfortable — physically, emotionally, practically, and absolutely. This is pretty hard to do. Much, much harder to do than most of the present generation of architects will admit to. Let's just talk about the simple matter of making an arcade. I find in my own practical work that in order to find out what's really comfortable, it is necessary to mock up the design at full scale. This is what I normally do. So I will take pieces of lumber, scrap material, and I'll start mocking up. How big are the columns? What is the space between them? At what height is the ceiling above? How wide is the thing? When you actually get all those elements correct, at a certain point you begin to feel that they are in harmony.

Of course, harmony is a product not only of yourself, but of the surroundings. In other words, what is harmonious in one place will not be in another. So, it is very, very much a question of what application creates harmony in that place. It is a simple objective matter. At least my experience tells me, that when a group of different people set out to try and find out what is harmonious, what feels most comfortable in such and such a situation, their opinions about it will tend to converge, if they are mocking up full-scale, real stuff. Of course, if they're making sketches or throwing out ideas, they won't agree. But if you start making the real thing, one tends to reach agreement. My only concern is to produce that kind of harmony. The things that I was talking about last night — I was doing empirical observation about — as a matter of fact, it turns out that these certain structures need to be in there to produce that harmony.

The thing that strikes me about your friend's building — if I understood you correctly — is that somehow in some intentional way it is not harmonious. That is, Moneo intentionally wants to produce an effect of disharmony. Maybe even of incongruity.

**PE**: That is correct.

**CA**: I find that incomprehensible. I find it very irresponsible. I find it nutty. I feel sorry for the man. I also feel incredibly angry because he is screwing up the world.

**Audience**: (Applause)

**PE**: Precisely the reaction that you elicited from the group. That is, they feel comfortable clapping. The need to clap worries me because it means that mass psychology is taking over.

**Someone from the audience**: Why should architects feel comfortable with a cosmology you are not even sure exists?

**PE**: Let's say if I went out in certain places in the United States and asked people about the music they would feel comfortable with, a lot of people would come up with Mantovani. And I'm not convinced that that is something I should have to live with all my life, just because the majority of people feel comfortable with it. I want to go back to the notion of needing to feel comfortable. Why does Chris need to feel comfortable, and I do not? Why does he feel the need for harmony, and I do not? Why does he see incongruity as irresponsible, and why does he get angry? I do not get angry when he feels the need for harmony. I just feel I have a different view of it.

**Someone from the audience**: He is not screwing up the world.

**PE**: I would like to suggest that if I were not here agitating nobody would know what Chris's idea of harmony is, and you all would not realize how much you agree with him ... Walter Benjamin talks about "the destructive character", which, he says, is reliability itself, because it is always constant. If you repress the destructive nature, it is going to come out in some way. If you are only searching for harmony, the disharmonies and incongruencies which define harmony and make it understandable will never be seen. A world of total harmony is no harmony at all. Because I exist, you can go along and understand your need for harmony, but do not say that I am being irresponsible or make a moral judgment that I am screwing up the world, because I would not want to have to defend myself as a moral imperative for you.

**CA**: Good God!

**PE**: Nor should you feel angry. I think you should just feel this harmony is something that the majority of the people need and want. But equally there must be people out there like myself who feel the need for incongruity, disharmony, etc.

**CA**: If you were an unimportant person, I would feel quite comfortable letting you go your own way. But the fact is that people who believe as you do are really fucking up the whole profession of architecture right now by propagating these beliefs. Excuse me, I'm sorry, but I feel very, very strongly about this. It's all very well to say: "Look, harmony here, disharmony there, harmony here — it's all fine". But the fact is that we as architects are entrusted with the creation of that harmony in the world. And if a group of very powerful people, yourself and others ...

**PE**: How does someone become so powerful if he is screwing up the world? I mean somebody is going to see through that ...

**CA**: Yes, I think they will quite soon.

**PE**: I would hope, Chris, that we are here to present arguments. These people here are not people who have rings in their noses, at least as far as I can see, and they can judge for themselves whether I am screwing up the world or not. If they choose to think I am screwing up the world, they certainly would not come here. These are open forums. For you to determine arbitrarily that I am screwing up the world seems self-righteous and arrogant. I have not had much of a chance to do so and neither have you. Precisely because I am uncomfortable with those situations which you describe as comfortable, I find myself having to live in New York. I do not live in San Francisco, even though I think it is a nice place. There is not enough grist there for me, not enough sand in the oyster. And my head starts — it may be my own psychological problem — but thank God, there is a loony bin called New York where eight million people who feel the way I do are allowed to be!

**CA**: Actually, New York is not created by that kind of madness. New York is certainly a very exciting place. When you compare it to Denmark or Sweden, I fully understand what you are saying. And I sympathize with you. Your observation seems to me a very reasonable one, objectively speaking. But that is quite a different matter. It's quite different from the original question: why should I feel so strongly, why should I get angry, because you are preaching disharmony? I was trying to explain to you why I get angry about it.

**PE**: I am not preaching disharmony. I am suggesting that disharmony might be part of the cosmology that we exist in. I am not saying right or wrong. My children live with an unconscious fear that they may not live out their natural lives. I am not saying that fear is good. I am trying to find a way to deal with that anxiety. An architecture that puts its head in the sand and goes back to neoclassicism, and Schinkel, Lutyens, and Ledoux, does not seem to be a way of dealing with the present anxiety. Most of what my colleagues are doing today does not seem to be the way to go. Equally, I do not believe that the way to go, as you suggest, is to put up structures to make people feel comfortable, to preclude that anxiety. What is a person to do if he cannot react against anxiety or see it pictured in his life? After all, that is what all those evil *Struwwel Peter* characters are for in German fairy tales.

**CA**: Don't you think there is enough anxiety at present? Do you really think we need to manufacture more anxiety in the form of buildings?

**PE**: Let me see if I can get it to you another way. Tolstoy wrote about the man who had so many modern conveniences in Russia that when he was adjusting the chair and the furniture, etc., that he was so comfortable and so nice and so pleasant that he didn't know — he lost all control of his physical and mental reality. There was nothing. What I'm suggesting is that if we make people so comfortable in these nice little structures of yours, that we might lull them into thinking that everything's all right, Jack, which it isn't. And so the role of art or architecture might be just to remind people that everything wasn't all right. And I'm not convinced, by the way, that it is all right.

**CA**: I can't, as a maker of things, I just can't understand it. I do not have a concept of things in which I can even talk about making something in the frame of mind you are describing. I mean, to take a simple example, when I make a table I say to myself: "All right, I'm going to make a table, and I'm going to try to make a good table". And of course, then from there on I go to the ultimate resources I have and what I know, how well I can make it. But for me to then introduce some kind of little edge, which starts trying to be a literary comment, and then somehow the table is supposed to be at the same time a good table, but it also is supposed to be I don't know what; a comment on nuclear warfare, making a little joke, doing various other things ... I'm practically naive; it doesn't make sense to me.

*(\*Note: This debate took place at the Graduate School of Design, Harvard University, on November 17, 1982. Most of the text was published in Lotus International **40** (1983), pages 60-68. A slightly different but more complete transcript was published in Studio Works **7** (Harvard University Graduate School of Design), Princeton Architectural Press (2000), pages 50-57. The present version taken from Katarxis 3 combines portions from both sources.)*

**Peter Eisenman** *is an architect based in New York City who is responsible for many well-known iconic buildings representing the deconstructivist style. He rose to Starchitect prominence with the Deconstructivist Architecture show at the Museum of Modern Art in 1998, organized by Philip Johnson and Mark Wigley. A writer as well, he has contributed essays on deconstruction, including a co-authored book with Jacques Derrida. He teaches architecture at Yale University.*

# 34. Some Sober Reflections on The Nature of Architecture in Our Time

*By Christopher Alexander*

*Katarxis No. 3, September 2004. Reprinted by permission.*

The following commentary is based upon a letter I wrote in response to William Saunders of the Harvard Graduate School of Design. Saunders wrote a review of Book I of *The Nature of Order* that I felt completely failed to grasp the ideas behind it. Indeed he did not even discuss those ideas, positively or negatively. Therefore, I felt some treatment of those ideas should be given in response, as well as some observations about the state of the profession, and reasons for the resistance to such ideas.

## An Objective Criterion of Architectural Value

*The Phenomenon of Life* — Book I of *The Nature of Order* — describes an entirely new, scientific, criterion of architectural value. It is based on twenty-seven years of carefully recorded observation.

The basic proposal made in the book is that degree of life is an objective and observable characteristic of buildings and other artifacts, that it depends on the presence or absence of an identifiable structure which may be called "living structure": and that *it is the presence or absence of this structure which distinguishes valuable buildings from less valuable, good architecture from bad.*

I want to make the observation that this is real science that produces real results, not academic work that only apes the forms of scientific investigation with manner, wording, and presentation. This is real science, in which empirical questions are being investigated, and, in spite of their inherent difficulty, the investigations are beginning to show sharable, empirical, results, which might, within a decade or two, begin to have profound effect on our society. And it is work which has massive implications for all the most basic questions of architectural design and planning.

I have written this book because of my wish to help set architecture on a firm foundation: and because of my conviction that these questions lie, inescapably, at the core of the work all of us architects do every day.

It is presented with arguments regarding the scientific difficulty of dealing with this topic. It is presented with hundreds of examples. It is presented with a background mathematical theory, which has been applied to architectural examples from buildings through history.

It is written in simple language, with careful evolution of ideas, from foundations and first principles, to concrete results, experimental technique, comparison with other comparable methods used in architecture.

If there is indeed a scientific criterion, which might be used to distinguish living structure from non-living structure, and well enough formulated so it could be applied to architecture, this would be momentous for the architectural profession — and for society in general — since it would potentially show the beginnings of a way forward from our present widely recognized difficulty of building good environments.

A very uncomfortable fact for many architects today is visible in *The Phenomenon of Life*, namely: that the criteria for living structure, if applied to current stylish architectural productions of our era, will in very many cases arrive at negative evaluations. Such a view, for the first time throwing objective doubt on the high priesthood of architecture, would be consistent with opinions held by many ordinary people who do not like the image-fed high architecture presently supported. The possibility exists, therefore, that if this book were to be taken seriously, either by architects, or by society at large, then the bubble of late 20th-century architecture, and its effort to scam the public, might, suddenly, be on the verge of being pricked.

## The Lack of a Shared Canon of Value

Possibly the most dangerous weakness in the architectural profession today is the failure of the profession to have a legitimate, shared, canon of value, one which resides in the deep feelings of ordinary people, and which resonates with their experience... or to grasp publicly experienced judgments of value as issues of fact, or to respect the values which "ordinary" members of the public have. Instead, the profession has erred, in the past, by looking down on the public, by holding up a highly idiosyncratic and specialized view of value, carried by "the few", viewing the common man as ignorant, and treating architects as people who believe they have the right and authority and political power, to keep on ignoring public opinion about architectural values, and pushing their own special brand of postmodern image architecture, that is largely out of touch with every man and every woman.

It must be that the postmodern, disemboweled majority of the architectural profession, have given up hope that there is truth about anything in architecture, in favor of the notion that there are merely attitudes, opinions and disguises, and that each person's disguise or point of view is equally valuable. This unhealthy position, inevitable under the impetus of Cartesian thought, is what dug the grave for architecture during the last fifty years. Yet those who espouse it are wrapped in the necessity of this belief, because it is a necessary belief to bolster and rescue the absurdity of their positions. So any line of thought which actually suggests that feeling, quality, are objective, must be anathema — because to admit the objectivity of these matters, would lay bare the poverty of their conceptions, and expose the whole profession and its activities, in the 20thcentury up to today, as a hollow sham.

What, then, is the actual content of Book 1, *The Phenomenon of Life*? The thesis is straightforward. It says that the positivistic separation of fact from value, and the notion that only facts can be objective while judgments of value can only be personal matters of opinion, is flawed, *and that there is a scheme of things, in which judgments of value may be examined empirically*: and that when so examined, the feelings of ordinary people, about value, when made in a certain special way, provide a plenum of judgment which is stable, and reliable, from person to person, and — by the way — conspicuously different in content from the notions of value which are prevalent among leading architects today.

There is a second part of this thesis: namely, that the value which is identified by these empirical methods, is generated by an identifiable, repeated structure that may be identified mathematically, and seen, repeatedly, in all naturally occurring structure, and especially in those structures which are commonly held to have life. By comparison with this class of structures, the structures put forward by architects of recent decades, are often lacking in life, and rather belong to a class of structures which must be considered dead.

The key issue, of course, is that both the original thesis itself, and the secondary observation, just mentioned, are supported by a wealth of empirical evidence, according to experiments which can be reported, and checked easily. The experimental procedures involved are unusual, but there are, nevertheless, sharable, and repeatable experiments. It should be said at once that the experiments are not opinion surveys, but rather experiments which use subjective judgments of a very special controlled sort, to obtain measures of life in things, events, and situations.

Thus the whole scheme of things, in which value takes on a new form, and in which judgments of value about buildings, can be checked and discussed in reasonable language, has experimental standing, and would have — if found reliable — enormous impact on the present and future conduct of architecture.

This thesis, momentous if true, and especially momentous for architecture, is clearly stated, and clearly argued in this first book of *The Nature of Order*.

## The Concept of Wholeness

Scientifically speaking, what is the origin of living structure? Where does it come from? And how may it be defined, to be accessible to discussion, experiment, debate.

The core of it resides in the idea of wholeness. In the last two decades, physicists and other scientists and philosophers of science have begun to discover that a wholeness-based view of the world is, essential to proper understanding of the purely physical universe. A view of wholeness as an existing, guiding structure is essential in quantum physics; essential in biology; essential in ecology; in one form or another, essential in almost every branch of modern science. Yet even in these rather precise fields, it has been difficult to forge a scientifically precise concept of wholeness. The idea places demands on science which stretch the very notions of scientific inquiry, since they require a view in which value, and the notion of the whole, and the inclusion of the observer in the description of what is observed, seem to be at odds with scientific method; yet must be included in order to reach results.

For scientists, it has therefore become necessary to find new methods of inquiry and observation, in which the whole, the self, feeling, and value, play a role within the very act of observation — yet — if it is to be part of science — these inclusions must leave science objective, unbroken, and reliable.

The conception, experimental techniques, and even the way to modify our essentially Cartesian view, so that it can admit self, "I", and feeling — are extraordinarily difficult. Yet they are necessary for the progress of science.

They are necessary, too, for the progress of architecture. This subject is of the greatest importance to architects and to architecture as a discipline — since every time we build a building, it is the degree of participation in the greater wholeness of the world around it, which will determine its success, harmony, and degree of life.

Why is this so important for architecture? The harmony of a given road or building with its landscape can only be understood, and made profound, if we have a picture of the wholeness that is being harmoniously adapted. The adaptation of the light and movement in a building lobby can only be understood if, once again, we have a picture of the structure of the whole which is supporting the adaptation. A window in a wall — its well-placed, well sized, well designed, according to its harmony within the whole — and to do it well, we need to understand the whole. I remember Peter Eisenman telling me that he was not interested in harmony! Because the world is so tormented, he wants to express the torment.

Well, bully for Mr. Eisenman! Not so bully for the unfortunates who have to inhabit his buildings.

Yet, important as it is, for some odd reason architects have been among the last to wake up to the world-wide intellectual and cultural movement in the sciences which seeks understanding of the concept of wholeness and the whole — and have been, and still are, extraordinarily hostile to this conception.

I well remember how my faculty colleagues at Berkeley reacted with intense hostility, when twenty-five years ago I first began speaking about wholeness as a necessary basis for architecture at faculty meetings. The very word "wholeness" incensed some of them and made them furious, maddened, as though it was a personal attack on them. And, sadly, it did not stop at that. In 1989 our chair, Howard Friedman, dared to propose that wholeness should, as a subject of study, be included in the Berkeley architectural curriculum. At the next faculty meeting, he was subjected to a vitriolic personal assault made against him by one of our faculty. As a result of the intensity of this verbal assault, the faculty meeting broke up. But before the faculty had even left the room, within the next few minutes Howard had a fatal heart attack. He was taken to hospital and died shortly afterwards.

Such a tragic event will not make the subject of wholeness and value go away. It merely indicates how much antagonism the concept can generate, possibly because it threatens to go deep into the fabric of present day practice and assumptions.

This kind of deep challenge is very painful for architects and architecture professors, and many of them react with astonishing hostility. Instead of giving sober reflection to the intensely difficult scientific and architectural problems, they choose merely to try and destroy the *author* instead of the *arguments* (which they do not present, or perhaps do not even understand). Perhaps they hope that this strategy will make the topic disappear altogether.

But the topic remains momentous.

## A Vision of Architecture as a Discipline Which Heals the World

The essence of the situation is an entirely different way of looking at architecture, in which every action, small or middle-sized or large, is governed by one all-embracing rule: *"Whatever is done must always be done in such a way as to provide maximum possible healing of the whole: the land, the people, the existing structure of the city."*

This rule is then to be applied when a window is placed in a wall; it is applied when a building is placed on a street; it is applied when a neighborhood is constructed or reconstructed in a city. In every case, what is paramount is the healing of the whole, the living wholeness of the earth, in that quarter, and the love and dedication which sustains it and preserves it and extends it.

This is entirely — totally — different from the present conception in which each thing done lives largely for itself: in which development, stylishness, and profit, are the guiding motives.

It is a new conception in which a new triad (Wholeness — Healing — Structure-preserving transformations) governs and replaces the old triad (Style — Profit — Advertising and Marketing advantages obtained through design), which governs all classical postmodern architecture of the mainstream today.

These are two different worlds: and no matter how much talk there may be, today, about ecology it is the second of these triads which ruled the architecture of the second half of the 20thcentury, in the 2% of the world where architect-designed buildings play a role.

The Earth, the city, the metropolis, may be shaped instead by a process focused on life, and on the healing of the Earth's surface, in metropolitan areas, and in nature, to work towards a living structure. In that case, the geometry, the design, the construction processes, will all be different — and what we now think of as architecture, will be given up in favor of a new vision, which is aimed primarily at the good of the Earth, and at its people, and the places, and animals, and stones of earth.

# Great Changes Coming in the Discipline of Architecture: The Idea of Healing

Mechanistic philosophy and the present arbitrary views of value that hold sway in architecture today are intimately connected.

First, the developer's ideal of profit, and the profit-oriented approach to architecture, building, and planning, inevitably work against wholeness, and against the healing of the earth. That is because the goals of value that can be stated within concepts of mechanism, are inherently unable to increase wholeness, or to heal systems.

Second, the very idea of healing, presupposes that we know what it means to heal, what health is, what, therefore, wholeness is. Still more vital, when thinking and speaking in the framework of a mental world governed by mechanism, any thought of value becomes an arbitrary, value impressed on the logic of the machine, external to it, and arbitrary therefore, in every respect that can be entertained or thought within the mechanistic world.

So, our values in architecture during the last fifty years, have been arbitrary, because they have been invented arbitrarily. They are protected by professionals only because they serve the goal of capital-induced development — the postmodern architect's bread and butter. So the values which have been created — the post modern images — like all other passing styles and images — work for capital, for profit, for development, but against wholeness, against health, against the well-being of the earth.

That is the literary and artistic heritage now being taught in schools of architecture, and now propagated through architects' buildings that serve the process of capital induced development.

This heritage does not serve wholeness. It does not serve the whole. It does not help to heal the world, or to rebuild Earth as a place where bees, people, breezes, stones, and lizards can run free... nor the starlings, spiders, urban foxes, water, businesses, restaurants, and taxicabs that populate the city.

I have spent my life, trying to find a sharable, rational, scientific model which brings this topic of life, wholeness, and harmony, into the open — especially as it touches the geometry of buildings, so that it allows us to share discussion and observation of its effects.

It is in our power to take an alternative path, one in which every single act of building, design, ornament, economic improvement — is always done in such a way as to be part of the healing of the Earth. This is possible even in the high-density metropolis, since there, too, we are capable of making nature.

But we cannot achieve this, or even move in this direction, without a respect for wholeness, made clear as a concept, and formulated so that it transcends all our current pretensions, concepts, and short-term ideals.

The future lies with profound understanding of wholeness as a concept, and as a basis for practice. Turning away from it is more than just short-sighted. It would be a tragedy for architects to inflict further damage on the troubled Earth.

Going the other way, in search of a viable, scientific view of life, which can become a basis for our architectural practice, is more moral than what we do now, more just, more beautiful. It goes more to the service of life. And all those who practice such a revised form of architecture, will probably feel more wholesome in themselves.

When the life of the environment plays such a fundamental role in the well-being of the Earth, and when science itself is struggling to understand the nature of wholeness in the majority of new scientific fields, it would be a great pity if a philistine attack on necessarily preliminary efforts to make progress in this direction, were to keep architecture as the last of the philosophical dinosaurs from the mechanistic age.

## The Implications of Wholeness-Based Architecture on Our Prevailing Architectural Values

The theory is so rich in detail, that we may draw extraordinary consequences from it. These are presented in volumes 2, 3 and 4. These consequences from theory have implications for the processes which a successful architecture must use, to reach buildings which have life.

They have implications which dictate some, and eliminate other, relationships between design and construction, as a necessary part of architecture.

It has implications for the involvement of people, in the design of buildings, and for the detailed ways in which this involvement is likely to be successful, or unsuccessful.

It has implications for the flow of money. It has implications for the handling of architectural detail, and for the successful integration of structural engineering, into the framework of design.

It has enormous implications, too, for the unholy alliance between architects and developers: an unholy alliance, possibly the darkest secret in the history of modern architecture, and one which has made architects little more than salesmen, writing advertisements several hundred feet high, claiming to be art, yet actually designed mainly as sign language to stimulate the flow of money into the developer's pocket.

It affects virtually every part of the profession we now know as architecture, and it indicates necessity for change, in almost all of them.

There is no question, that under the impact of this theory, architecture will be deeply changed: and it will be changed, for the better.

## A Note on Science

It may be worth concluding with a short statement about what science is, and what it is not. I make this observation as a Cambridge-educated physicist and mathematician, and later an architect and researcher who earned the first-ever AIA gold medal for research in architecture.

You are doing science when you figure out how something works. That is especially true if you figure out how something works, that people have not figured out before. You don't need to dress it up, you just need to work it out.

All the rest is dressing. Pompous language, format of summary and text and findings, footnotes, erudite references, carefully marshaled precedents ... all those are the means of science, the appearance of science, not science itself. Too often the appearance is presented to make something seem like science: but it is rare that someone actually figures out how something works.

The material in *The Phenomenon of Life*, and the material in *A Pattern Language* 25 years earlier, are both science. In both cases, partial workable answers have been given to questions about the way the structure of the environment affects people. In both cases we did, to a first approximation, genuinely figure how this works. It would have been possible, in both cases, to dress it up the actual discoveries in fancy dress: but it would not have changed the actual discoveries very much.

For example, it would have been possible to dress the 253 patterns in *A Pattern Language*, as anthropology — thus giving them the dressing of science, references, language and so on. It might have helped create an illusion of "hard" science. But it would not have changed the fact that we did genuinely work out, in part, how the environment supports human life in society. Of course not all 253 patterns are equally profound: but in nearly all of them something has been figured out about how the world works, and we knew more about it after the work was done than we did before. And because it is published in an available form, we know it for always — or until someone else goes further, and finds out more exactly, or more deeply, how those things work.

In *The Phenomenon of Life* other, deeper, discoveries are presented. They would not be made more significant by anthropological dressing, or psychological dressing. They stand by themselves, and the reader can see that, easily, by studying the text. There will be time for scientific fancy dress later, when the hard work of going into more detail, and doing more careful experiments, really begins. But the really hard work has been done.

*The Phenomenon of Life* defines criteria for life in buildings, and replicable tests for deciding how much living structure exists in different buildings. Of course the appearance of a real test of value in architecture may give the sweats to the profession; but if the profession is worth its salt, and they fear the concept, they can disprove the argument rather than failing to see the point. This is an invitation for adult debate.

# References

- Christopher Alexander, *The Nature of Order, Book 1: The Phenomenon of Life*, Center for Environmental Structure Publishing, Berkeley, 2002.

- Christopher Alexander, *The Nature of Order, Book 2: The Process of Creating Life*, Center for Environmental Structure Publishing, Berkeley, 2003.

- Christopher Alexander, *The Nature of Order, Book 3: A Vision of a Living World*, Center for Environmental Structure Publishing, Berkeley, 2004.

- Christopher Alexander, *The Nature of Order, Book 4: The Luminous Ground*, Center for Environmental Structure Publishing, Berkeley, 2004.

- William S. Saunders, "From Taste to Judgment", *Harvard Design Magazine*, Winter-Spring, 1999, number 7.

- William S. Saunders, "A Pattern Language: reviewed", *Harvard Design Magazine*, Winter-Spring, 2002, number 16.

# 35. Conclusion

At the conclusion of this course, the students told me that they had learned a great many things that are crucial to an understanding of architecture, but which are hardly ever taught in other architecture courses. To be precise, students had previously been told about the importance of various factors to the success of a design — site, surrounding architecture, regional adaptation, ornament (or rather excluding it), the relationship among distinct structural scales, proportions, trees and green areas — but were never taught exactly how to manage them. Now, those factors were taken into account by learning why they arise out of our own biology and natural processes.

An overall useful concept was connectivity: between open spaces, between structures, between different scales of a structure, between user and building, and so on. It is a basic tool for coherent design. Yet, connectivity is usually considered coincidental — an accidental effect of your design — or as secondary to structure and form. Students understood connectivity in a new way through our discussion of system complexity, where each part depends upon and adapts to every other part so that the system can work coherently as a whole.

As far as ornamentation, it now appeared to be much more important than just something pretty to look at. Ornamentation is linked to patterns on all scales — ultimately going back to the intense connectivity characteristic of good architecture (that is, good for our health). And ornament is tied to Biophilia, which for some students was the most striking and ultimately useful concept they learned in this course. They were especially disturbed that Biophilia usually goes unnoticed in a lot of designs that pay attention to totally different concerns. Since Biophilia makes such a big difference in the quality of life, it has to be integrated into designs.

All in all, students expressed a newly-found power to judge a building using objective criteria, no longer having to rely on vague notions of what is "correct". It is now possible to use a set of universal principles and criteria, such as Alexander's Fifteen Properties, to judge a building's attractiveness independently of any group's opinion. Students recalled occasions in the past when they had to acquiesce to an instructor's appraisal of a project, even when they felt that it was wrong, simply because of the power of authority. But such opinions were never explained; they just had to be accepted by the subservient party, which was terribly frustrating. The student learned nothing from such interactions.

Particularly telling was the admission that, before taking this course, they would have been seduced by Peter Eisenman's arguments in his debate with Christopher Alexander, but now saw things in a different light. They had developed a new appreciation of human feeling as the basis of adaptive architecture, and this is what Alexander emphasized. At the same time, they understood the evolution of architectural styles and the theories behind building design much better. They got a deeper glimpse into the process of innovation that respects factors essential to life.

The students were excited by the prospects of practicing architecture as an empirical, scientific process. Taking concepts from biology and applying them to their own work, as for example: the design purpose of individual parts, the evolution of organismic form, innovation through adaptation, selection through feedback, etc. This new way of thinking establishes a clear difference between abstract art as a personal statement by the artist, and architecture for human use. Students said that they would previously get really excited by innovative forms, including ones that looked "organic", but now know that the image is not important, and instead look for the adaptive process leading to the structure. "Good" architecture is both beautiful and functional, and makes a person psychologically and physically well.

# PART TWO
# COURSE ORGANIZATION
# AND PROJECTS

*"Musical details which I had previously considered to be ornamental were given the appearance of organic elements... "* — *Glenn Gould on Sviatoslav Richter's interpretation of Schubert.*

# 36. Discovering Theory from Measurements

In this course, students were introduced to actually measuring architectural *qualities* for the first time. While architecture's technical part consists of physical measurements, considering design qualities as inherently measurable is a novel step. The simple measurements and estimates performed as part of our two projects turned out to contain the seeds of a new theory of architecture. In this way, the students were introduced not only to mathematical modeling of design, but also to the very process of model formation, something that was new for them. I believe this hands-on insight into how human beings understand the world through science is an invaluable lesson for young architects, who will determine our future built environment.

The remaining sections of this book present the material used to carry out our two course projects, thus permitting an instructor or student to follow the quantitative analysis. This material is original, since it was developed for the first time in this course. I hope that others can profit from the experience and insight that my class acquired.

From the very beginning of the course, we discussed model formation side-by-side with our theoretical readings. The process of developing a quantitative theory of architecture was tied essentially to the material describing the findings of other researchers who have undertaken to do precisely this. Students saw for themselves how some of this research was done. Therefore, they did not fall into the catastrophic relativist trap of thinking that our readings were just another opinion, by yet another group of thinkers: and thus according to the usual faulty logic, as no more or no less valid than anyone else's thinking about architecture. In the end, relativism accomplishes the opposite of what it sets out to do: it validates the ideas that are supported by the most powerful group, and not the ideas that correspond more closely to reality.

The analytical process of discovering and deriving a theory in general goes as follows. A simple quantitative/statistical model is introduced for measuring complex phenomena, in this case elements of design complexity itself. Then we look for patterns and correlations among variables that at first seem independent. For example, our first project derived a correlation between the complexity of a Form Language as measured by the Kolmogorov-Chaitin Complexity and that language's regional adaptation (the method is described in Sections 37 and 38, below).

This correlation is a useful and potentially important concept in architectural theory, and it was possible to derive it here in a regular class! We used the online mathematical software engine *Wolfram Alpha* to plot the word count of each student's form language versus its regional adaptation estimated on a scale from 0 to 10. Each student entered one data point such as, for example, (*word count, regional adaptation*) = (336, 7). All the data points were plotted together using the function "Linear Fit". The result was that the points distributed themselves clustered around a straight line, which indicates a linear dependence of regionalism on complexity.

The result was not perfect, with observed deviations from a straight line. A useful additional lesson for the students, coming from the scientific method and thus novel to most of them, is that variations from a perfect result indicate that other, unknown factors are contributing. For this reason, we further elaborated the model for design complexity so as to separate organized from disorganized complexity. This was the purpose of our second project, which makes this distinction on a formal basis. A better, two-parameter model for design complexity uses several of Alexander's "Fifteen Fundamental Properties" in estimating two independent components of design complexity (*architectural temperature, architectural harmony*) = (*T, H*) (see Section 21 for a description).

The first innovative result of our course was to successfully link regionalism to complexity. This was one of the aims of the first class project. For the second, extended model, it was necessary to introduce parallel measures and estimates of regionalism that could be compared directly to our measures of organized versus disorganized design complexity. The second set of estimates of adaptivity and regionalism was considerably more detailed than the simple ranking on a scale of 0 to 10 used in the first project.

Regionalism in the architectural discipline thus far represents a concern with materials and a philosophical approach to locality. There is much discussion that brings in various historical factors and thinking about what regionalism means. Quantitative models that measure elements of design are not yet part of the typical regionalist discourse (nor of any other aspect of architectural theory, for that matter). Taking a bold innovative step, we introduced a model here that estimates regionalism in a two-parameter space, which represents (*geographical adaptation, human adaptation*) = (*x, y*) with points ranging from (0, 0) to (10, 10). I believe that this simple measure captures the essence of regionalism in a rather striking manner.

These measures and estimates for architectural regionalism were compared to the distinct set of measures and estimates of design complexity as described below (Section 39), using the pair of values (*architectural temperature, architectural harmony*) = (*T, H*) of the form language. These values also range from (0, 0) to (10, 10). A correlation was found between regionalism and organized complexity, thus extending and independently reinforcing the model from the first project. The data from these correlations will be used to write a research paper presenting our results.

Perhaps the overriding lesson for the student was that a quantitative approach to analyzing design and its adaptation is indeed possible, and it can be done in class using very simple tools of estimation. This potential reverses the usual way of teaching architectural theory. We now possess proof and justifications that draw on arguments from within architecture and science. In the educational rubric firmly in place since the middle of the 20th Century, a student does not question design canon, even though he or she might disagree with it on an intuitive level. While arguing and discussion are encouraged in architecture theory seminars, the debate feeds from sources in a way that no conclusion can ever be reached. Ultimately, the established viewpoint remains the unquestioned standard for guiding and evaluating a student's design. Nor is the student presented with actual tools that can be used to evaluate someone else's theoretical claims, or disprove them altogether. The quantitative approach to architectural theory developed in this class hopefully prepares the student to profit from a more independent way of thinking about architecture.

# 37. First Class Project: Documenting a Form Language and Estimating Its Complexity

Each student will choose and document one particular form language, will then design an example of a building using that form language, and will present it in class. Please use the "Form Language Checklist" as a guide (given below in Section 38). We will draw numbered lots to give the order of choice for each student, with no duplication, so that every student gets to cover a different form language. In that way, the class can be exposed to and learn from many different form languages. An in-depth study and analysis of your form language prepares you to use it as a design tool by understanding how a design arises from the combinatoric "linguistic" structure of forms. This method is not the same as merely copying superficial images from someone else's work.

Please use the same headings in the form language checklist (Section 38) and just fill out the details for your own form language as succinctly as possible. The entries include lists of materials, forms, sizes, etc. For some entries, a simple yes or no indicates whether something (a structural element, or property of that element) is present or not. It will be necessary to estimate both actual sizes of components, and relative ratios of sizes among different components. In listing the connections, an unusual element of interest (at least for today's design thinking) is to look for and document an intermediate piece that connects two other components. In many contemporary buildings, this intermediate connection is missing for stylistic reasons, so to perform this exercise, students will have to change the way they look at structures.

I want students to use the understanding obtained from their chosen form language to create a very simple design of a building. The function of the building and overall brief is up to them to choose. The aim here is to realize what it means to become proficient in "speaking" that form language (going only as far as the first few design steps). Students will present their form language and its characteristics, and their building roughly designed using it, in class. In addition, please compute the Kolmogorov-Chaitin complexity of your form language by using the word count of your completed checklist. The more "wordy" your checklist, the more complex is the form language. Also roughly estimate the regional adaptation of your form language on a scale of 0 to 10 (higher for better adaptation). This is the simplest possible estimate of regional adaptivity of your building, which represents the opposite of any abstract, formal, or "universal" design method. An "International Style" building will necessarily rank very low. The class will then plot these values for (*word count*, *regional adaptation*) together in a scatter plot to look for any correlation.

What is remarkable is that we are able to measure the complexity of a form language at all, and by a simple means such as the word count by a word processor. Yet this is what the results showed when we put everyone's data together and plotted it. The mathematical background for this model was covered in class (Section 9). We now have the beginnings of a new investigation of complexity in architecture. We will go further and correlate this complexity with adaptability and regionalism, in our second project.

Here are some guidelines for students to help in choosing their Form Language for this project.

1. I know that you are all eager to document a famous building, either from the 20th Century, or by some contemporary starchitect. But all of those are accessible only through photographs. Consider rather that the most useful evaluation of a form language (for your education) comes from any building that you can physically enter and study. So, think of choosing an accessible building of any age.

2. Architecture students are enthralled by the signature work of famous name architects, yet the majority of humanity lives and works in modest buildings. Consider studying a local building — house, office, bank, commercial building, government building — that is not particularly distinctive, but is typical of our living and working environment. Your analysis will be important.

3. One aim of this course is to validate historical form languages for use today. With this in mind, why not choose a local building that comes from an older architectural tradition? That will offer a wonderful opportunity for you to document its form language (usually a far richer language), and to analyze how you would adapt that form language to build a similar building today.

4. Some of you are working already part-time in an architecture office. The best candidate for your form language might be a building project that you have access to through your employer. Choose one that is either finished or almost ready, so you don't work only from drawings and renderings. That's important because you will need to judge the overall spaces and components on site.

# 38. FORM LANGUAGE CHECKLIST

NAME OF FORM LANGUAGE: location, era, name of architect, particular building?

DOCUMENTATION: is there a written description or set of working rules for this form language? (Instructions, not a philosophical or ideological justification).

MATERIALS: titanium, steel, glass, brick, concrete, wood, stone, adobe, thatch, etc.

COMPONENTS: walls, floors, roofs, beams, windows, doors, and their dimensions.

CONNECTIONS: cornices, joins, and moldings, meeting points of wall+wall, wall+floor, wall+window, door+wall, wall+ceiling, façade+roof, size of connection compared to what it joins.

OVERHANGS AND CANTILEVERS: type of supports, placed on top or bottom?

ARCHES: yes/no, type, spacing, height, dimensions.

COLUMNS: yes/no, type, size, width, alignment, inter-columnar spacing, fluting?

COLUMN CONNECTIONS: column+floor = base, column+top = capital, relative size.

RECTANGULAR OR OTHER GEOMETRY: rectangular, diagonal, or curved.

CHARACTERISTIC FORMAL SHAPES: overall geometry of components, their relative alignment, and their variety.

SUBDIVISIONS OF FORMS: yes/no, for walls, for windows, their relative dimensions.

GRAMMAR AND SYNTAX: what components relate to each other (symmetry), or should not relate to each other (asymmetry). Any hidden rules?

ENTRANCE: relative size to other components, method of definition, change of level?

PORCHES AND BALCONIES: yes/no, depth, roof connections, front grill or solid?

FLOOR PLAN: subdivision of space, order and hierarchy of rooms, circulation.

EXISTENCE OF SCALES: well-defined and usually repeating structure on 1mm, 3mm, 1cm, 3cm or 1in, 10cm, 1m or 1yard, 3m, 10m, and other scales.

COLOR: yes/no, which ones? Intensity? Do different colors harmonize?

LARGER SYMMETRIES: formal symmetries on scale of 10m down to about 1m.

SMALLER SYMMETRIES: sub-symmetries from 1m down to fine detail.

DECORATIVE ELEMENTS: non-functional large elements used only for style.

ORNAMENT: yes/no, type and design, scales on which it appears, extent.

SURFACES: materials and textures presented to user, "friendly" or not?

# 39. Architectural Regionalism Correlates With Design Complexity

Every student chose one particular form language (corresponding to a specific building) to document, and then measured its "complexity" by using the word count of their form language's description according to the completed "Form Language Checklist" (Section 38, above).

At the same time, each student was asked to estimate their building's regional adaptation on a scale from 0 to 10, with 0 being the least adaptive to locality, building culture, and specific user needs tied to local culture. Students were guided in this estimation by our class discussion of what regionalism means in the context of using local materials, employing traditional typologies, low-cost methods of energy use and optimization, historical continuity of design typologies and the use of traditional ornamentation, etc. Students could jump ahead and read the more detailed criteria for regionalism from the document "Quantitative Measures for Regionalism and Complexity" (Section 41, below), and those helped in estimating a single number for regional adaptation.

Each student presented an ordered pair of numbers (*word count, regional adaptation*) for their project and I plotted all of them together. Here is an incomplete graph of our class data:

Plot of the least-squares fit:

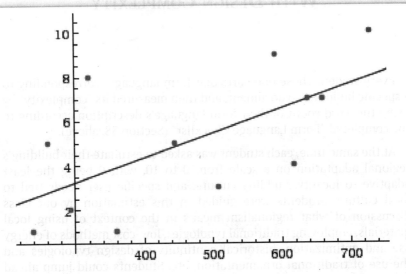

*Project 1. Regional Adaptation (vertical axis) versus Complexity of a Form Language as measured by the word count of its verbal description (horizontal axis).*

While this plot doesn't really prove a linear relationship, it does indicate that the regional adaptation correlates with the complexity of a form language. This result is all the more striking because the students' projects varied as to the analysis of the chosen buildings, and even with the specific writing style of each student. Obviously, a measure of form language complexity that depends on the word count is also dependent upon the verbosity of each individual student! Despite the evident inaccuracies of the method, these results open a very promising topic for more detailed investigation. Realizing this, our class immediately moved on to the second project (see Sections 40 and 41, below), which tries to compute the regional adaptivity of a building using far more precise criteria than the single number of the original model.

By turning to Alexander's fifteen fundamental properties, our original estimate of design complexity is also vastly improved in the second project. The complexity measure that I developed to estimate the "degree of life" in a building eliminates possible sources of error. As formulated in this model, the fifteen properties give a more accurate two-dimensional estimate of design complexity. This is far superior to the single-number Kolmogorov-Chaitin complexity measure of a form language.

It is fair to say that after seeing the above graph as it was produced in class, some students experienced a drastic change in their architectural preferences. This was a surprise. During our discussion evaluating each building in the context of all the results brought together, several students said that their choice of building "turned out not to be a good example after all". Pressed to explain this, they stated that they were originally attracted to their building because of the usual architectural design criteria, but our analysis showed them that more important qualities facilitating human use and simple economics were lacking. As a result, they would never use that form language to build a building nowadays, but would adopt a far more adaptive form language. And that now, they understood how to judge whether a form language was adaptive or not.

# 40. Second Class Project: Evaluation and Classification of Form Languages

In the first project, each student was assigned a particular form language to document. In this second assignment, that form language will be analyzed to determine its suitability for application to building today. A report should be prepared consisting of about 2-3 pages of text, with an unlimited number of figures. Every student will present their report to the class in electronic form, and a written (printed) version will be submitted to me for my files and for grading. Please address the following description in writing up your assessment.

Students in the class will undertake a classification of their different form languages according to their regional/global and natural/unnatural characteristics. Use the "Quantitative Measures for Regionalism and Complexity" outline (given below in Section 41) to measure two independent components for regionalism from geographical and human adaptations. Estimate the architectural regionalism values $(x, y)$ for your form language.

The regional measures $(x, y)$ of a form language are another innovation altogether. Cutting through the stylistic prejudices of the past several decades, we ask crucial questions about a building's true adaptability. These measures provide a first approximation to actually *measuring* adaptability, and consequently lead us to a better understanding of sustainability questions. Not to put too fine a point on it, this represents a new way of thinking about regionalism and sustainability: a quantitative approach that sidesteps the old stylistic straitjacket imposed on the discipline. And this modest beginning opens the way for a better quantitative model and further development.

Next, compute the architectural temperature $T$ and architectural harmony $H$, to obtain another ordered pair of values $(T, H)$ that measure complexity for your form language (use the model's description from Section 21). We will plot these points together in one graph for the entire class, and look for correlations among all the different variables. Finally, all students will evaluate their own form language for general use today, and present their analysis in class.

The complexity measure represented by the values of $(T, H)$ is much more sophisticated than the earlier measure of complexity via the Kolmogorov-Chaitin word count. Without getting into details, the

Kolmogorov-Chaitin complexity distinguishes simple from complex languages, but it cannot distinguish between ordered and disordered forms of complexity. Those have opposite effects on the user that is confronted with buildings having organized versus disorganized complexity. A more refined application of the Fifteen Fundamental Properties in terms of the (T, H) approximation separates the two types of complexity. In this way, we can *measure* what is intuitively obvious in a complex design: that is, whether it is also coherent or not.

# 41. QUANTITATIVE MEASURES FOR REGIONALISM AND COMPLEXITY

## Regional Measures of a Form Language: Geographical and Human Adaptations From (0, 0) to (10, 10)

Please estimate, on a scale of three options from 0 to 2, the following qualities inherent in your form language. Give a score of 0 for each quality in the left-hand-side descriptor, and a score of 2 for each quality on the right-hand-side. If you cannot decide on either descriptor because you feel that the quality lies somewhere in-between, give a score of 1. Clearly, these coupled architectural qualities represent pairs of opposites.

The first group of measures adapt to geography, here called $x$-values:

$x_1$: global typology → regional typology;

$x_2$: use of imported materials → use of local materials;

$x_3$: independent of local climate → adapted to local climate;

$x_4$: not energy efficient → concerned with energy efficiency;

$x_5$: relies upon global industry for energy efficiency → uses low-tech energy solutions.

The second group of measures adapt to human beings, here called $y$-values:

$y_1$: concerned with global style → tries to reinforce historical traditions connected with local culture;

$y_2$: adapted to abstract formal rules → adapted to human physiology;

$y_3$: spaces and surfaces defined by philosophical concerns → spaces and surfaces adapted to human psychology;

$y_4$: children's needs are not an obvious concern → adapted specifically to children;

$y_5$: based upon the intellectual choices of an elite → geared towards giving emotional pleasure to all people.

Compute a total score by adding up all the variables for both groups separately. The score is recorded as an ordered pair $(x, y)$ = (*geographical adaptation, human adaptation*) and will range from values of (0, 0) to

(10, 10). Different buildings can be compared by plotting their $(x, y)$ values on a two-dimensional graph.

For an overall measure of regional adaptability, we define a percentage measure as the product $R = xy$. Since $x$ and $y$ take values from 0 to 10, $R$ will be a number from 0 to 100. This numerical measure is defined here for the first time. If we wish to label it, $R$ is a combined measure of the regional and human adaptability of the form language. This number provides a convenient percentage estimate that can be used to compare with the value for "*Architectural Life L*" as defined in the next paragraph. Whereas $R$ arises out of the usual concerns for regional adaptation, $L$ is strictly due to geometrical factors of the form language. Therefore, this comparison is very instructive in establishing a correlation between the geometry of design and the adaptability of a building.

## Compute the perceived degree of Life of the Form Language: Architectural Temperature and Harmony From (0, 0) to (10, 10)

The tools to do this are described in our *Ninth Week Lecture Notes* (Section 21), which review the model explained in our textbook: Salingaros, *A Theory of Architecture*, Chapter 5, "Life and Complexity in Architecture From a Thermodynamic Analogy". Compute the architectural temperature $T$ and architectural harmony $H$ for your form language, to obtain another ordered pair of values $(T, H)$ that range from (0, 0) to (10, 10). Even before undertaking a comparison to the regional adaptation, you can compute the perceived "degree of life" of your building as a percentage value from the product $L = TH$. Compare this value to all the different buildings studied in class. Do you feel that this percentage measure $TH$ corresponds to the degree of visceral connection you would physically experience with this building?

## Correlation Among the Variables

Can you find a correlation among all these different variables? There are two main correlations to investigate. First, we look for internal correlations between the measures of architectural regionalism $(x, y)$. Are the geographical $x$-values correlated to the human $y$-values? Second, is the measure of architectural regionalism $(x, y)$ correlated to the measure of the architectural life $(T, H)$ and if so, why? Namely, does the degree of geographical and human adaptation correlate with the rather abstract complexity measure as determined by the architectural temperature and architectural harmony?

Plot of the least-squares fit:

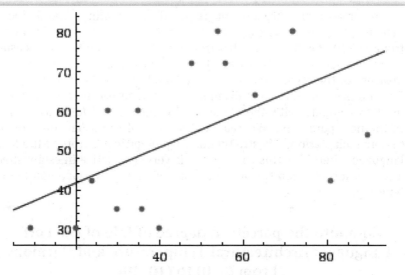

*Project 2. Regional Adaptation as measured by the product xy (vertical axis) versus Architectural Life of a Form Language as measured by the product TH (horizontal axis).*

## Classification of Form Languages

The class will discuss all the form languages together and plot the computed values to position each form language on a master graph. In this way, we gain an understanding of the entire set of form languages based on their adaptive use as measured by architectural regionalism and architectural life. This interpretation of architecture has nothing to do with fashions, design ideologies, politics, etc. that have determined architects' evaluation of very different form languages.

Plot all the buildings from the entire class on one plot, showing the Regional Adaptation measure *R* (vertical axis) versus the Architectural Life measure *L* (horizontal axis). How do these values correlate? This plot is meant to provide a more accurate understanding of regionalism versus geometrical complexity than our first model (Section 39). Is there a similar linear dependence of regional adaptation versus complexity that we found in the much simpler model of the first project in this class? Based on these results, do you think it possible to create a regionally adaptive building by using a form language with a low value of architectural life *L*? Can we consider a sustainable architecture for the future — which will necessarily have high regional adaptation

$R$ — without incorporating design elements that also give it high architectural life $L$?

## Evaluation of the Fitness of a Form Language

Based on this analysis, do you judge your form language more or less fit for building in contemporary society? Again, the form language is validated because it has been used successfully by many people over a long period of time. Or is it an unproven experimental form language? It could be the latter, especially when used over and over to create a "look", but every time failing to provide a genuinely comfortable living and working environment. It is now possible, with the tools of this course, to make a judgment largely free of prejudice. This is especially so if a form language looks "old-fashioned", ruled out of current practice by ideology for the past several decades. In the usual contexts where only "contemporary" form languages are allowed, we would lose all of this extremely useful information.

## Recommended Changes to a Form Language

Are there any modifications that you suggest to your form language that would make it more fit for building in contemporary society? A form language is not rigidly set in time, and any improvement is welcome as long as it leads to better adaptation for the user and the natural environment. Undertake the "genetic evolution" of your form language by making some changes. Then check its fitness by re-computing the measures for architectural regionalism $(x, y)$ and for architectural life $(T, H)$. If these fall as a result of the changes made to the form language, then something is not right! Natural selection would allow only changes that raise both these values.

## Overriding Factors

Are there other factors that have guaranteed the success of your form language, as seen in the number of built examples, and which are independent of the analysis undertaken here? Discuss how those factors can override the model of fitness computed as outlined above. Namely, are there unnatural selection rules in place that in fact contribute to the success of your form language despite it violating the regional, adaptive, and human factors? This in itself is a form of evolution: it's just not acting according to natural criteria. Ideology, vested interests, and bureaucratic inertia could all be driving the use of a particular non-adaptive form language.

# Investigating this crucial topic further

The central question of architecture is — and has been for over one century — the appropriate form language to use in building for contemporary society. In this course, we have developed analytical methods for evaluating form languages studying both their evolution through time, and through deliberate changes made by an architect. Hopefully, this rubric will help young architects to achieve adaptation and individual expression together in their own designs. The end of our course is only the beginning of an architect's quest for design solutions. The student is directed to the discussion of form languages in Chapter 16: "Form Language and Style" of Christopher Alexander's Book 2 of *The Nature of Order: The Process of Creating Life* (Center for Environmental Structure, Berkeley, California, 2002), pages 431-460.

# 42. Notes For Students on the Framework of This Course

## Course structure & responsibilities

This class is meant to be something of a hybrid between lecture, seminar, and a bit of studio. The seminar aspect will focus on reading and discussion. For the studio aspect there will be one project that allows you to apply the concepts and approaches discussed with regard to the theoretical basis of architecture. These concepts will be presented and discussed by the class. Both of the projects are intended to broaden your understanding of the design process by combining thinking with doing, theory with practice. In pursuing your individual projects, it will be necessary for you to use your critical and analytical powers to a greater degree than is normal for architecture students.

## Weekly reports on reading assignments

Complete all readings to gain a thorough comprehension. The material that we cover is quite difficult, and considerable effort has to be made to understand it. You will need time to comprehend it fully, so don't expect to absorb the concepts just by skimming through it. A much deeper understanding is required than architecture students are used to, so be prepared to put in extra time. I will expect every student to summarize and analyze each week's knowledge content obtained from assigned readings and in-class discussion of the readings in a printed report with 2 pages of text maximum. Figures and illustrations may help, and those can be additional pages of unlimited number. Many reports will have to summarize several different reading assignments, so please synthesize and be brief. There will be 14 reports, each one counting for 4% of the grade.

## Some guidelines for preparing the weekly reports

1. You must convince me that you have thoroughly read the material. Please do not discuss material from another week's reading, unless that is directly relevant here.

2. Avoid quoting the author of the readings. Simply saying something does not validate it; if one of our authors said it does not prove you

understand it, or even that it is right. Instead, you should explain whether you think it's true based on the evidence presented.

3. What is the author's argument?

4. Upon what evidence is the author relying to validate the idea presented?

5. Does the author's conception relate to the essential qualities of the architectural discipline?

6. What are the criteria for judgment and criticism, and do you agree with them?

## In-class discussion

You are required to attend class and are expected to participate in the discussions. I will be noting who is actively involved in constructive dialogue. This will count for a percentage of your grade (4%).

## Study groups

It is strongly recommended that study groups of 2-5 students get together to discuss the assignments and readings, and to prepare for the projects. It has been found that working within a study group builds confidence and deepens understanding, and that all members of the group do better in the course. Be careful, however, to prepare individual submissions for your weekly reports and projects, with no duplication or overlap among those of the different study group members.

## Projects

There will be two projects throughout the semester, lasting approximately three weeks each that cover and expand on issues raised in class. These projects will together count for 40% of your grade.

The first project, starting at the beginning of the class, will assign a specific form language to each student. We will conduct a lottery in class by distributing numbered pieces of paper, then students can choose their preferred form language based upon their number, beginning from 1. Students will document their form language, and will use it to design a building of their choice. Both form language and a rough rendering of the building will be presented in class by each student. This is a small design exercise focused on utilizing the concepts discussed in class.

The second project will be an analysis project. After the main body of theoretical material has been digested, we can judge a form language according to its regional adaptability, and also by its degree of natural qualities. Each student's form language (from the first project) will be classified in a general classification, and the class will collectively prepare a chart that locates each student's form language on it. This result will be discussed in class.

# 43. COURSE SYLLABUS

This list is included here for any instructor who wishes to follow more or less the same structure for the course as I did. The readings refer to chapters from our two textbooks: Christopher Alexander's *The Nature of Order, Book 1: The Phenomenon of Life*; and Salingaros' *A Theory of Architecture*. All other material is included in the present book.

## Week 1.

The structure of a scientific theory. Requirements for a mode of thought to be a theory for architecture. Discourses and modes of thought that are not theories.

**Readings**: Alexander, Prologue & Chapter 1. Salingaros, "Architectural Theory", extracts from AAAD (also available in Chinese, French, Italian, and Russian). Edward O. Wilson, "Integrated Science and the Coming Century of the Environment".

## Week 2.

Form Languages. Vocabulary of forms and tectonics, and their combinatorial properties. Richness of a form language, and measures of its complexity.

**Readings**: Alexander, Chapter 2. Alexander, sampler from "A Pattern Language". Salingaros, Chapter 11.

## Week 3.

Different examples of Form Languages. Classical, historical, regional, etc. Industrial-era form languages. Form languages of famous architects. Three Laws of Structural Order.

**Readings**: Salingaros, Chapter 1 (also available in Spanish). Salingaros, "Kolmogorov-Chaitin Complexity". Salingaros & Masden, "Against Ecophobia".

*Begin first project: Each student will choose and document one particular form language, will then design an example using that form language, and will present it in class. Please use the "Form Language Checklist" as a guide. We will draw lots to determine a ranking of choice for each student, so that each student studies a different form language.*

# Week 4.

Comparison among different form languages. Degree of complexity as a measure of their adaptivity. Regionalism as adaptation to locality. Regional versus global: a practical dimension for classifying form languages. Philosophical justifications for form languages.

**Readings**: Alexander, Chapter 7. Léon Krier, "Building Civil Cities". Salingaros & Masden, "Politics, Philosophy, Critical Theory".

*Continue first project: Students will present their form language and their building designed using it, in class. Compute the Kolmogorov-Chaitin complexity of your form language by using the word count of your completed checklist. Also estimate the regional adaptation on a scale of 0 to 10 (higher for better adaptation). The class will then plot these values together in a scatter plot to look for any correlation.*

# Week 5.

Adaptivity of a form language to human life. Human physiology and psychology. A direct and useful test: Alexander's 'Mirror of the Self'. Evidence-based design.

**Readings**: Alexander, Chapters 8 & 9. Mehaffy & Salingaros, "Evidence-Based Design".

# Week 6.

Biophilia: our evolved kinship to the structure of biological forms. The nourishment human beings experience from natural forms. Hospital design and healing environments.

**Readings**: Alexander, Chapter 10. Mehaffy & Salingaros, "Biophilia". Salingaros & Masden, extract from "Neuroscience, the Natural Environment, and Building Design".

# Week 7.

Geometrical basis for natural forms. Alexander's 15 Fundamental Properties, and how they lead to the phenomenon of life.

**Readings**: Alexander, Chapter 5.

# Week 8.

Scientific background for the Fifteen Fundamental Properties. Fractals and hierarchical scaling. The logarithmic constant as average scaling ratio.

**Readings:** Alexander, Chapter 6. Salingaros, Chapters 2 & 3.

# Week 9.

Organized complexity. A model to estimate life in architecture. Computation of architectural temperature and architectural harmony. Experiments that correlate the theoretical predictions with perceived degree of life in buildings.

**Readings:** Alexander, Appendix 6. Salingaros, Chapter 5.

# Week 10.

Adaptive recursion as a means of achieving geometrical coherence. The field of centers and wholeness. Complex adaptive systems as transformations.

**Readings:** Alexander, Chapters 3 & 4 and Appendix 3. Mehaffy & Salingaros, "The Transformation of Wholes".

*Begin second project: Students will evaluate their form language according to measures of adaptability and complexity, and present their analysis in class. First, estimate a language's natural/unnatural and regional/global characteristics. Then, compute the architectural temperature T and architectural harmony H, to obtain another ordered pair of values (T, H) for each form language. Please use the "Quantitative Measures for Regionalism and Complexity" description.*

# Week 11.

Recursion and fractals. Different scales in a design, and how they are connected to each other. How fractals reduce stress.

**Readings:** Mehaffy & Salingaros, "Scaling and Fractals". Salingaros, Chapters 6 & 7. Salingaros, "Fractal Art and Architecture Reduce Physiological Stress".

*Continue second project: The class will plot the points obtained in the Regionalism and Complexity analysis in one graph for the entire class, and look for correlations. We will undertake a classification of different form languages according to their values for Regionalism and Complexity. We will then discuss the suitability of each form language for general use today, and what modifications can be made to optimize its applicability.*

## Week 12.

Theory of Ornament. Ornament and human intelligence. A model of stress in minimalist environments based on the analogy with human pathologies.

**Readings**: Alexander, Chapter 11. Mehaffy and Salingaros, "Intelligence and the Information Environment". Salingaros, Chapter 4.

## Week 13.

Architecture itself as a biological system. Organizational lessons from biology and robotics we can apply to design.

**Readings**: Mehaffy & Salingaros, "Complex Adaptive Systems". Salingaros & Masden, "Architecture: Biological Form and Artificial Intelligence".

## Week 14.

Classification of Form Languages: natural languages and unnatural languages. Different conceptions of what architecture is, and what direction it should evolve towards.

**Readings**: Alexander, Conclusion. The 1982 Alexander-Eisenman Debate. Alexander, "Some Sober Reflections on the Nature of Architecture in Our Time".

# 44. Postscript

## A Letter From Zaheer Allam

Dear Prof. Salingaros,

Thank you once again for allowing me to peruse your lecture notes on Architecture Theory. After a careful read through, I have some thoughts on the subject which I would like to share with you.

Some of the precepts highlighted through the lectures are truly enlightening. I particularly loved the insights you provided on the way modernism was born to the detriment of culture and its subsequent evolution without consideration to purpose. This emphasizes the need for a new, intelligent type of architecture; one focused on purpose and practicality as opposed to catering solely to the aesthetic values of its architects and designers. You also managed to bring to life the importance of a quintessential architectural necessity: that of being connected to our surroundings as we are connected to our world; hence, the "sense of belonging". This primeval psychological need is all too often neglected in our design principles and practice.

Your voice is an impressive echo throughout the papers and your ideals could not have been more eloquently expressed. I wish that there were more visionaries like you who are involved in research and thus give ground to critical thinking as opposed to blind over-emphasis on aesthetic design. This would have given rise to a more humanistic approach to designing, hence creating a symbiosis between people and the material world.

I also believe that this current obsession for aesthetics has its foundations in the present architectural curriculum. Not enough emphasis or progressive incentive is given towards architectural research, thereby highlighting aesthetics as the sole aspiration to fame and success. This tends to create an obsessive focus on design at the detriment of the basic ground ethics involved in the process.

I hope your philosophies on these issues are shared by others, be they academicians or professionals, so that a constructive change process can be set into motion: that of a move from a modern "architecture" into an era of utilitarian design.

I await with anticipation further enlightenment from your formidable mind.

Thanks & regards,

*Zaheer*

**Zaheer Allam** *is a young architect based in Mauritius. He was educated in Malaysia and the USA, and is involved in Green design and cultural and environmental sustainability.*

# INDEX

Glide Symmetry 47
Goldberger, Ary 108, 171, 175, 185
Golden Mean 132
Good shape 126-127
Gothic 108, 168, 171, 240
Gould, Glenn 263
Gradients 126, 128, 225

# H

Hagia Sophia 139
Hand-Painted Tiles 128
Hanson, Brian 12
Harvard Graduate School of Design
    232-233, 249-250
Healing 65, 83, 85, 93, 94, 98, 100,
    102, 107-109, 117, 129, 170, 181-
    182, 186, 255, 256, 265
Hebb, Donald O. 198
Heerwagen, Judith 96, 101, 120, 176
Herman Miller Furniture Company
    176
Hierarchical Complexity 31, 111, 210
Hierarchical Scaling 121, 127, 131-
    133, 160, 170, 183
High-tech 63, 95, 112
Hong Kong Foster Bank 139
Hospital Design and Healing 83, 86,
    94, 99, 108, 119
Hospital Look 96
Human Intelligence 97, 118, 120,
    192-194, 198-201, 226-228
Humanistic Basis 79, 118
Human Physiology 106-108, 115,
    119-120, 173, 184, 194, 276

# I

Imperfections 83, 128
Implied (Latent) Center 126-128, 143
Incentive of Science 59
Increased Intelligence 120, 193
Increase in Brain Size 97, 120
Increasing Complexity 97, 109, 144,
    150, 220

Industrial Look 44, 95-96, 118
Industrial Materials 24, 43-44, 95-96,
    111, 117-118, 234
Informational Collapse 52, 128, 151,
    155
Informationally-Minimal 53
Informationally-Poor Structures 76
Information Environment 75, 97, 101,
    107-109, 140, 157-159, 162-163,
    171, 185-186, 192-202, 205-207,
    219, 222-229
Information Exchange 107, 157, 162-
    163, 204-205
Information Field 75-76, 101, 107,
    117, 193, 199, 222
Intellectual Submission 77-78
Intelligence 117-120
Intelligent System 227-228
International Style 66, 73, 78, 206,
    268
Intervention 205-206, 217-219, 221-
    222, 224
Ise Shrine Complex 24

# J

Jackson, Richard 86
Jobs, Steve 88, 91
Joye, Yannick 95, 108, 119-120, 171,
    175, 183, 185

# K

Katarxis 12, 249
Kellert, Stephen 101, 110, 114, 175
Kidney 149
Klotz, Clemens 90
Kolmogorov-Chaitin Complexity 46,
    49, 51-55, 264, 267, 272, 274-275
Komar, Vitaly 186
Konarak Temple 139
Krier, Léon 26, 68-74
Kunstler, Jim 70

*"In my view, the second person who began to explore the deep connection between science and architecture was Nikos Salingaros... He had been working with me helping me edit material in The Nature of Order, for years, and at some point — in the mid-nineties I think — began writing papers looking at architectural problems in a scientific way. Then by the second half of the nineties he began making important contributions to the building of this bridge, and to scientific explorations in architecture which constituted a bridge." — Christopher Alexander*